MARY'S STORY

The Beauty of the Lonely Heart

THE UNTOLD REVELATION IN HER OWN WORDS

Nancy Rhodes

ARS METAPHYSICA

an imprint of Sunbury Press, Inc.
Mechanicsburg, PA USA

ARS METAPHYSICA
an imprint of Sunbury Press, Inc.
Mechanicsburg, PA USA

Copyright © 2023 by Nancy Rhodes.
Cover Copyright © 2023 by Sunbury Press, Inc.

Sunbury Press supports copyright. Copyright fuels creativity, encourages diverse voices, promotes free speech, and creates a vibrant culture. Thank you for buying an authorized edition of this book and for complying with copyright laws. Except for the quotation of short passages for the purpose of criticism and review, no part of this publication may be reproduced, scanned, or distributed in any form without permission. You are supporting writers and allowing Sunbury Press to continue to publish books for every reader. For information contact Sunbury Press, Inc., Subsidiary Rights Dept., PO Box 548, Boiling Springs, PA 17007 USA or legal@sunburypress.com.

For information about special discounts for bulk purchases, please contact Sunbury Press Orders Dept. at (855) 338-8359 or orders@sunburypress.com.

To request one of our authors for speaking engagements or book signings, please contact Sunbury Press Publicity Dept. at publicity@sunburypress.com.

FIRST ARS METAPHYSICA EDITION: September 2023

Set in Adobe Garamond | Interior design by Crystal Devine | Cover by Gabriel Edelstein | Edited by Taylor Berger-Knorr.

Publisher's Cataloging-in-Publication Data
Names: Rhodes, Nancy, author.
Title: Mary's story – the beauty of the lonely heart : the untold revelation in her own words / Nancy Rhodes.
Description: First trade paperback edition. | Mechanicsburg, PA : Ars Metaphysica, 2023.
Summary: The life of Mary, Mother of Jesus, is detailed based on revelations received by the author after visiting her home in Turkey.
Identifiers: ISBN : 979-8-88819-077-7 (paperback) | ISBN : 979-8-88819-078-4 (ePub).
Subjects: RELIGION / Christian Theology / Mariology | BODY, MIND & SPIRIT / Ancient Mysteries & Controversial Knowledge | BIOGRAPHY & AUTOBIOGRAPHY / Religious | BODY, MIND & SPIRIT / Channeling & Mediumship.

Product of the United States of America
0 1 1 2 3 5 8 13 21 34 55

For the love of book!

To my mother, Alice Rhodes Adler, who embraced *Mary's Story* with her whole heart. Her wisdom at age 98, sustains and inspires me every day of my life.

PREFACE

∼

I am with you always,

Now and forevermore.

Beloved ones, I hold you gently and surround you with tenderness

And a love so deep.

As you draw closer to me and feel this love truly in your heart,

You will pass it on to others,

For that is the purpose of my book:

To tell the truth of love.

—MARY

ACKNOWLEDGMENTS

There are many people who have graced my path on this journey of *Mary's Story* and who have so generously given their guidance, insights, and expertise.

Roger Jeff Cunningham, professor of Psychology, was present in Ephesus, Turkey, when I had the spiritual experience, and his devotion and faithfulness ever since have kept the spirit alive for the unfolding of this book. His work as Scribe, as Mary referred to him, made it possible for my communications with her to be diligently recorded, word for word, for well over a decade, and in fact, continue to this day. His trust, encouragement and belief are paramount to the realization of *Mary's Story*.

Barbara Eubanks, opera singer and my cherished friend, was the first reader whose encouragement and insights meant everything in the world. Her tears as she read the manuscript sustained us and continues to do so. And gratefulness to my second reader, the wise Dr. Timothy Smith, dear friend who has traveled on this journey offering deep insights. And to Jodi Serota, metaphysical educator and artist, founder of the META Center, whose sound healing workshops opened up new vistas of intuitive creativity.

My thanks to my Pastor, Dr. James A. Forbes, Jr. who embraced the story with wisdom and understanding; and gratitude to Reverend Charles Ryu, who befriended me and embraced the book while I was writing at Stony Point Retreat Center; and thanks to the late Walter Wink, Theologian and author, whose sincere interest in the book as well as his knowledge of the ancient world and religions were invaluable.

Many thanks to the actress Martha Kearns, who led us to Maggie Crawford, formerly Editorial Director, Mass Market of Warner Books, Inc. who guided us early on with professional and compassionate advice.

Extraordinary thanks to the proofreading eye of Joya Carlton who miraculously showed up at my office, proofread the early drafts, and disappeared soon after, only to be recently re-discovered and is now a well-respected Vegan Chef!

Sincerest special thanks to Bruce Stevenson, a magnificent opera tenor, who not only brought his experience as a professional proofreader of books but brought his heart and soul to the project with his emotional connection to *Mary's Story*. My thanks to Tom and Jaynie Coleman who lent their home surrounded by trees and a mountain stream for respite and solace as well as proofreading a final draft.

Thanks to Edith Beaujon whose Group of Interfaith Ministers gave me opportunities to discuss ideas from *Mary's Story*, and who also introduced me to Bill Coty who filmed portions of my reading from the manuscript. Many special thanks to Allen Flagg, who led Dream Workshops and the New Physics Discussion Groups which I attended at FIONS (Friends of the Institute of Noetic Science), who made possible one of the first readings I gave; and to Marion Darby, beloved neighbor at Manhattan Plaza whose heart and spirit were divinely moved by *Mary's Story*.

My thanks to Raymond Forsythe, treasured friend, and former Encompass Board Chairman whose expertise will help bring *Mary's Storyy* into the world. And Professor Tara Hyun Kyung Chung, author, and professor at Union Theological Seminary whose course I attended, *Mysticism and Revolutionary Change: Spirituality for Authentic Transformation* was a great source of inspiration and helped me place *Mary's Story* in this context. She generously arranged the opportunity for me to speak about *Mary's Story* in Korea.

My deep gratitude to Ronald Rand, author, actor, Fullbright Specialist, and cherished friend, who believed in and supported my work in every way and led me to Lawrence Knorr and Sunbury Press.

And to all the readers, friends and arts colleagues who read sections of the manuscript and encouraged this uncharted journey, my deepest thanks.

FOREWORD

It was December 1989 and I had just finished directing a production of *West Side Story* for the State Theatre of Turkey in Istanbul. Roger, my life partner, flew over for the opening and we had made plans to visit Ephesus and Pamukkale. Two summers before, a friend and I had traveled through parts of Turkey, stopping for a short visit in Ephesus. There was one site we had tried to see but could not find. So, when Roger came over, I decided to show him Ephesus, but also find the one place I had missed—Mary's house, the home of the mother of Jesus who had fled to Turkey after his crucifixion.

I remember it was a particularly mild December, and our Turkish guide and driver drove us several miles along a modern road leading from the Magnesian Gate, so called because it marked the beginning of the road to Magnesia on the Maeander, and up a winding hill directly to Mary's House, or Meryemana, as it is known in Turkey. According to an ancient tradition this was the house occupied by the Virgin Mary during the last years of her life. It is believed she was placed in the care of St. John, who brought her to Ephesus sometime between AD 37-48.

My initial interest in this site was as a tourist. I had seen everything else at Ephesus, but this was the one place I had missed. The car pulled up, and Roger and I got out to look around. There was a lovely view. As we approached the house, we noticed only a few tourists, and one caretaker. The house was a small, stone dwelling with only a few windows. As we went inside, I remember thinking how could someone live in such a small, cold place? I looked around the single room and noticed an altar against one wall. After a time, I left and walked outside. A soft breeze was whistling through the trees, and as I walked down an incline toward a water fountain, I remember noticing the tree branches rustling. I stood for a moment looking up into the trees, listening to the wind. Then I took a drink, turned around, and proceeded to head back to the waiting car.

Suddenly, I found myself walking over to Roger and telling him I was going back in the house. He nodded and went on to wait for me in the car. This time, as I went into the house, it was completely empty--no tourists, not even the caretaker. I sat down on one of the benches for a moment, planning to take just one more look and then leave. Without warning, I was overcome with emotion. In my mind, like a vivid recall of old memories, I saw a series of photographic scenes flash before me, portraying what appeared to be Mary's life.

I had the overpowering desire to weep. It took all my willpower not to throw myself to the floor and weep uncontrollably. I held in my emotion on some level, fearing someone would enter the house and see me in this state. Then, a voice spoke to me clearly, distinctly, "*Tell my story.*" And again, the voice spoke. "*Tell my story.*" It was Mary. The emotional images continued, film-like scenes and situations of which I felt I was a part, and again, overcome with emotion which I could not explain, I had the peculiar feeling that I had known Mary, that I was somehow involved in the scenes I was witnessing in my mind.

Somehow, I pulled myself together and got up from the bench. I don't know precisely how long I stayed inside the house, but it couldn't have been longer than thirty minutes. As I walked out to the car, I remember noticing the look on the Turkish Driver's face. I could tell he knew something had happened inside the house. I must have been pale and looked disoriented; I could barely speak. I did not tell Roger about what happened until hours later.

Now, perhaps, someone may be thinking, well, of course, when you visit a religious site, all sorts of emotional things happen. But in my case, I had no special religious training about Mary and even though I was raised as a Christian in the Lutheran Church, I only thought about her life at Christmas and at Easter. I considered myself a spiritual seeker, more than religious in the traditional sense.

The experience I'd had inside Mary's house was so real that I could not shrug it off. I had been asked to tell her story. But how? When I returned to New York I browsed through the religious sections of various bookstores, looking for a book about Mary's life. I never found anything except books about Mary sightings and mythological interpretations, a few books written for young mothers describing Mary's attributes.

At last, I implored Roger, what am I to do about this? He replied, "You meditate, don't you? Why don't you try to bring Mary into your meditations and see what happens?" And so, little by little, over a year's time, I felt a growing connection and on January 22, 1992, I began to tell her story, while in a deep meditative state, and Roger wrote out what I said.

I can't explain why I had this unusual experience. It remains a mystery to me. In the story, however, Mary says that she called me back to her house,

> "... the loneliness of your heart was so great that in the presence of my home, your heart opened like a waterfall and filled every inch of my house, for I understood your need and all those like you. I asked you that day to tell my story, and so you shall. When I called you to my house, I approached you simply through your heart, releasing and receiving the eternal love between us. Your mind was flooded with memories and I spoke to you clearly, asking you to tell my story. I gave you the story as a gift; I placed it in your hands. It is told through your heart, connected to mine, and it is an illumination that I am now asking you to give freely and fully to all those who will receive it."

Mary touched my heart and awakened me to the greatest and deepest source of love. In receiving her story, experiencing her emotions, and following the journey of her life, I found healing within my own heart, in the love-filled arms of Mary, my Mother, the Mother of us all.

I offer this story just as it came to me, the greatest gift of my life, and I hope with all my heart that it will be so for you, dear reader.

—Nancy Rhodes

Mary's House, located on Mt. Koressos (Mount Nightingale), near the ancient city, Ephesus, Turkey.

Inside Mary's House.

CHAPTER 1

Now we shall begin. I am Mary, Mother of Jesus. I am in a mood of celebration to be here with you.

My story really begins in the beginning of time in a world of magnificent light. Light was everywhere and there was no darkness—only brilliant, pure light. All the colors of the rainbow exist within the light, and those colors burst forth to create all the beautiful aspects of the world. The world is made of color and light. Light and pure light, nothing else, only this. Every tree, every thought, every movement comes from light and color seen through light. It is very simple, very pure, and absolutely complete.

When I was a little girl, I used to play in the tall grasses of the meadow by myself. I could hear the world talking. I would play and dance in the meadow and chase after the colors that I saw floating all around me. I thought to tell my mother about these things that I saw, about these colors, but something inside me told me not to mention it. I learned very early to keep my counsel—to see things, to play with them, to even talk with them . . . but to keep it to myself.

I was a quiet child. I did not have many friends or children to play with because we were far away from the other members of the tribe. There seemed to be some reason for this, which I did not hear about when I was small. I grew up talking to all the big things around me. I talked to the wind, the grass, the water. I talked to the animals. I talked to the trees, to the leaves, to the sky, and always I saw things in terms of color and light.

Some days I spent indoors with my mother, who had much work to do. She wove cloth, made clothes, baked bread, built fires, and did many chores. She always sang when she worked and hummed and made beautiful sounds, so as a child, I was filled with melodies and songs. I heard the fire crackle and the sound of my mother grinding wheat into flour for bread. There was always singing with the members of the tribe, and although I never sang so much myself, I always listened to everyone else. I was the kind of person people didn't notice. I was there and yet I wasn't there. I was always in my own world, very happy and content.

One day a butterfly flew around me in a circle. It was a big butterfly, yellow, velvety, with black spots on it. This butterfly flew around and around and around and sat upon my hand, and then it spoke to me. Actually, it whispered "Mary, Mary," said the butterfly, "you see all the colors, you see the light. Mary, Mary, you can fly with us, too." And then it flew up off my hand and disappeared.

Now I thought I would tell someone about this, but everyone seemed too busy and there was much to do. So I kept this to myself, as I really did not want to disturb the family with any of this.

Sometimes my mother scolded me. She felt I was daydreaming too much and thought I should play with other children; so I was sent away to live with my aunt who had nine children. I was sent there to live so I would become more social. I was very sad to leave my meadow and all the nature I had come to know so well.

I now lived with a big family—lots of noise, talking, laughing, shouting, running, working. They teased me because I did not know how to play their games and because I didn't know how to talk to any of them. They seemed to know more things than I did. Sometimes the older boys would pull my hair, call me funny names, hide things from me, or spill the milk—and then say I did it. Many times I was punished for things I did not do. It wasn't because they were really cruel; it was just that I was the newcomer, the outsider. I was a bit unusual, I must admit, and I did talk a bit different because we lived in another part of the countryside. I had a slower way of talking from my cousins and they found that to be amusing. I was lonely for my mother and her singing. Many times I would cry as I went to sleep at night. Once my uncle came home, very afraid, and was talking about soldiers and people who might hurt our tribe. He said that we all needed to be prepared to flee on very short notice. There always seemed to be people who didn't like us. All of these things made me miss my home very much.

CHAPTER
2

In many ways, it was a joyful time to be with so large a family because before this I really was quite lonely. I remember one day my uncle came and took me for a long walk with just the two of us. I remember everyone looking and whispering when we left together. He took my hand and we started to go through the field toward trees in the distance. There was an olive grove, and it was too far away for me to go by myself. My older cousins would go there, but I was not allowed, so I knew this was a special trip, my uncle taking me to the olive grove. I felt very grown-up and special that he would take me on this walk. He didn't say anything to me for a long time; he just pointed out certain flowers and certain leaves. He pointed in the direction where my parents lived; yet as we walked, I felt there was something on his mind that he wanted to talk to me about. I knew that he would get to it when he was ready.

As we drew closer to the olive grove, I sensed that my uncle was more relaxed and prepared to talk to me about what was on his mind. The olive grove had a circle of trees and was very cozy. There were some benches and a small table, and my uncle asked me to sit down. He drew out some bread that my aunt had fixed, and he laid it on the table and sliced a small piece of cheese. He picked some of the olives off the tree and made a special kind of meal for us there. He said a prayer—and we began to eat.

Finally, he said, "Mary, we have been very happy to have you in our home. I have been watching and observing how much you have been learning." He told me that he noticed I was very good with chores outside the house, especially with planting and gathering eggs and other tasks having to do with the animals. He complimented me on how well I helped my aunt, but he said he was worried about my difference from the other children. He felt that I didn't really seem to play their games and join in with their activities enough. He was very concerned that I wasn't really very happy and that I might be too homesick for my mother and father. These words made me uncomfortable. I had a piece of bread crust in my hand. I began to twist it and look down because I didn't know what my uncle wanted me to say exactly. I felt that he could see right through me. Biting my lip, I began to cry. My uncle was very sorry and he patted my hand; then he patted my head, and my tears went away. I looked up at my uncle and said to him, "Yes, I believe I am homesick." He said, "Then, Mary, we shall make a journey back to your home." As soon as he said that I was very relieved.

I knew that my uncle wanted to ask me another question as he hesitated and offered me some more olives to eat, and then he said to me, "Mary, when you are outside, I've noticed that you seem to be talking to someone—and there is no one there. I have never said anything about this to you, Mary, but I have observed it and so have your cousins—and your aunt, too—and well, Mary, I am rather concerned about this. Who is it that you are talking to?"

I was very surprised when he asked me this because I have always talked to the trees, to the skies and to the animals, to the angels and to the small creatures I saw running through the leaves; but I was just beginning to realize that not everyone saw them. I had not thought about it until my uncle asked me; yet as soon as he did, I realized that this was probably why my cousins had been laughing behind my back. It had gotten very hot under the olive trees while I was sitting there. I felt very hot all over my body because my uncle was staring at me so strongly and I didn't know what to say. I just didn't know what to say.

My uncle touched my hand and said, "Mary, come now, child, you are safe with me. You can tell me who you were talking to." I took a great big deep breath, and I looked up into my uncle's face and I said, "Well, Uncle, there are so many things I see—I see all sorts of people in the leaves and the trees. The rocks talk to me and different blades of grass. I hear words from the sky, and one time a butterfly spoke to me. I have always heard these things and we just always talk—ever since I was a little girl. They are very nice and friendly, and they do such interesting things. I'm so happy to know that they are here, all around me all of the time. Sometimes they tell me their names, and sometimes they sing and do dances; then, sometimes they just go to sleep, and I don't see them at all. They are my friends."

My uncle got up from the bench and walked to one of the farthest trees in the olive grove. He picked some more olives, and then he came back and sat down again and said, "Well, Mary, what you tell me is very interesting, and I believe what you tell me. The only question I have is . . . why can't I see them? Can you tell me that, Mary?"

I put my head down and shook my head, and then my uncle said, "I think that is all for today, Mary. Let's not be concerned any further. I think you'll feel better now that you know you will be going home to visit your father and mother, so don't cry; it will be all right."

We gathered up our things and began to walk back toward home. We didn't say much. I was very quiet, even though I saw many of my friends as we walked along; when they called out to me, I pretended that I didn't see them. My uncle put his hand on my shoulder, and I knew he was trying to reassure me. Still, I realized that he didn't understand. This is when I first really began to know how different I was from other people.

Many people have wondered why I, Mary, Mother of Jesus, have appeared to poor, uneducated peasant girls, village girls. You see, I really understand so much about the lonely heart and much of my story is about the beauty of the lonely heart—about the poor, about the uneducated, about the very simple— I understand these people, because I see their beauty. I know what is inside their hearts that no one else can see. When I was older, angels came to speak to me quite often. It was the natural progression for me because I always spoke to higher entities, whether it was the trees, the earth, or the sky; but in many ways longing to be normal left my heart lonely. I have such great love in my heart for everything because I hear the words of each blade of grass, I know what the butterfly says, I know what the bark of the tree says, I know what every ant, every fish, every rock says. I could hear their words, their songs, their thoughts, and perhaps I was closer to people whose hearts were lonely because they were quieter, and somehow, I drew closer to them.

CHAPTER 3

By this time, I was living once more with my parents. I had left my uncle's family and was again spending most of my time doing household chores, but mostly working outside as that was my favorite work. I helped my mother bake bread twice a week in an area of our house that opened onto the courtyard. Bread was the staple of our diet, along with olives, fruits, and some meat, although we did not eat as much meat as others did.

My family chose not to eat so much meat, preferring cheeses, fruit, and bread. I remember my mother's face as she baked bread, for it was heavy work and quite hot; her cheeks would become inflamed and very red as she placed the bread in the hot oven. She always did that part and would not let me, since she was afraid that I would burn myself. I always watched and admired her strength. When we sat down at the table to break bread, I remembered in my prayers to be as thankful for my mother's labor as well as for the flour and wheat from which the bread was made.

My task was to mix the flour together, to stir it, and to test to see if the dough was ready to be kneaded. I found this task to be quite pleasant, since I enjoyed the smell of the dough and the feel of it. I became quite proficient at timing the dough, knowing when it was ready, and shaping it into loaves.

The flour was ground in the village. There was a mill where people could take their grain and have it ground, so that we did not have to do this part of the labor ourselves. This was not always the case, however;

when I was very young, my mother had to do this task as well. The mill was a great relief for my mother.

I remember the smell of the bread and the excitement of seeing the loaves as they came out of the ovens. I always felt that it was a magical thing because I tried to picture in my mind what really happened with the dough that I had so carefully kneaded and shaped. I wondered what happened inside that oven to make the bread change and become delicious-tasting, crispy brown, with such a delectable odor.

One day, I was sitting near the door with the bread my mother had earlier taken out of the oven when a Roman soldier approached. He had been traveling for many days and looked quite tired and very dusty. I was frightened when I looked up and saw him in the doorway because I knew he was not from our village or our tribe. From the way he was dressed, I somehow understood he was a soldier.

My mother had gone to pick some fruit quite far away from the house, and I was alone. He stood in the doorway and said he was hungry and asked if I could feed him. He was so tall and so large that he completely filled the doorway, and I began to feel trapped. There was something in his manner that frightened me. I said, "Please have a seat outside and I will bring you bread and something to drink." He answered, "It is very hot out there and I want to come inside." I didn't know what to say. He took a step in through the door, and I backed up against the table. He walked in further and said to me, "My, what pretty hair you have." I was trembling because I had never had a stranger come forward like this and I was hoping my mother would hurry back. I said, "My mother will be here any minute, and I would like for you to wait outside until I prepare the food." He kept coming toward me, and he grabbed me around the waist and said, "It's been a long time since I've seen such a pretty face as yours." Now my heart was pounding. His arms and hands were so large, and he squeezed my arm very tightly. His face was sunburned and there was dust and dirt in his hair. I thought to myself, when will my father return? Where is my mother? Someone please, please help me. He was pushing me toward the corner of the room, and I began to tremble and shake. I was shaking as if I were in a terrible snowstorm. I tried to cry out, but he put his hand over my mouth, and he pushed me down. I was like a mouse, squashed. I couldn't move—he was so huge, and I was so afraid. I bit his hand and he slapped me. I tried to kick, but it was impossible. Then I fainted. When I awoke, he was gone.

My mother had seen friends in the orchard and had stayed longer than usual. When I awoke, still no one had returned. I got up, feeling disoriented. I felt very dizzy and sick to my stomach. I began to cry. I ran outside. As the light hit me, I became very ill and fainted again. I don't know how long I lay there, but something in the grass began to speak to me.

They were calling to me, "Mary, Mary you must get up. Wake up now. It is all right. Don't be afraid. It's all right. You'll be taken care of." The voices led me to a tree; I collapsed leaning against the trunk. Then, I began to dream, to hallucinate. It was as if I could see through everything; as I looked at the trees in front of me, I could see through to the blades of grass in the field beyond. I saw all kinds of creatures peering at me from the leaves. I looked up at the sky. I just lay there, overwhelmed and not understanding what was happening to me. I felt that I was seeing all of the invisible things suddenly become visible. All of the forces of the universe, instead of just being nameless forces like wind and gravity, were actually people or creatures. They actually had faces and forms. I had seen many things before this, but this was the first time that everything was transformed.

After what seemed like a very long time, I heard my mother's voice in the distance, calling my name. Two of her friends were with her, and they were laughing and having some fun together. She didn't see me lying by the tree, but she was calling out to say they were on their way.

When they found me by the tree, my mother knew immediately that something was terribly wrong. She dropped her basket of fruit and knelt by me. She asked, "Mary, my child, what is wrong?" I could hardly speak, but as I focused on my mother's voice, I began to come back to the normal way of seeing.

My mother's friends ran to the house to get some water because I was fainting again. The next thing I remember was cold water being put on my forehead, face, neck, and wrists. My mother was upset, and the two women seemed to look very confused. My mother asked again, "Mary, dear child, are you all right? Please, please speak to me. Can you hear me?" I remember just barely hearing her voice, and somehow I nodded my head. They gave me some goat's milk, propped me against the tree, and continued to put cold water on me.

Finally, they lifted me up, and we began to walk back to the house. They took me inside, my mother laid me down and continued to ask me what had happened to me while she was in the orchard. I just shook my head. My mother heaved a big sigh and covered me with a blanket. She told me to sleep and that we would talk about it after I had some rest.

Time passed, and as I was sleeping, I heard voices in the background. My mother and father were talking, and the tone of their voices was very serious. I was too exhausted to really hear what they were saying.

The next day I woke up very early, before my parents. It was cold and I was shivering once again. I looked up from my bed and saw a figure, a beautiful person, in a kind of mist. By this time I wasn't even trying to understand because I had been seeing so many inexplicable things. This person sparkled and smiled while saying, "It is all right, Mary," before he disappeared. In that moment I felt healed. There was an energy in the air that seemed to transform me.

I rose up out of my bed and went to the basket where we kept our bread and sliced thick slabs of it, putting butter and honey on it until I ate an entire loaf. I watched the light change as dawn neared. After receiving that message, I had no memory of what had happened to me, but I would always remember that beautiful person who smiled.

CHAPTER
4

There came the day when it was discovered that I was going to have a child. I was very young, fourteen or fifteen, maybe going toward sixteen, but I understood the processes of life and when I realized that something was different, I became very concerned. Days passed after my realization and I did not tell my mother as I wanted to understand what was happening. There was a stream that led into a larger body of water quite a distance from where we lived. I decided to go there to think about my situation. I told my mother I wanted to visit a friend of mine in another village and that we might go to the lake. I took some bread and some cheese and some fruit in a satchel, and left early in the morning to begin my walk.

It was early spring and very beautiful and as always I could see and hear the creatures of the forests, and trees, and grasses. As I walked, I felt a presence beside me. I felt the presence around me, almost as if it were letting me know it was protecting me. I continued to walk and I saw all the beauty of nature everywhere I looked. Because I could see all of the creatures of nature that make up the larger picture of nature, it was always a dazzling sight to behold. As I walked, I felt completely engulfed in this dazzling, spectacle of the light-filled entities that make up the entire universe, as you know it on your planet. I knew in the midst of all this, that I was destined to perform an important function. Possibly I felt this so strongly at that moment because I felt a part of the totality of nature. I felt neither larger nor smaller than anything else around me.

I was all of, and part of, everything. I wanted to go directly to the water. I had no strong reason to visit my friend; I only needed an excuse to tell my mother why I was making such a long walk.

Eventually, I came to the water's edge. It was about mid-afternoon, perhaps a bit earlier. I sat and took my sandals off, placing my feet in the cool water. It felt so good on my toes. I saw fish, and some birds, and I felt the presence that had been around me during the trip, now sitting beside me. It began to speak. Its voice was soft and soothing, and I began to feel almost sleepy, almost floating. And the voice said, "Mary, we are pleased with you. You are a pure creature, for you are light and free. Because of your purity, you can see the light in all things. We love you, Mary, we love you greatly. We wish for you to assist in bringing this light and purity to many others."

And then, the voice faded, and I only heard the sound of the water lapping against the bank of the lake. Then I lay down and just looked at the sky and watched the clouds floating. I must have dozed off, for when I awoke, it was much later and there was a young shepherd taking his flock to a higher pasture. I heard the bells and the sounds of the flock at the top of the bank behind me, and I put on my sandals and climbed up there. The boy looked at me and smiled. As I took a few steps I realized that I had gotten sunburned and that my robes were twisted in disarray. I had put my sandals on the wrong feet. The shepherd boy could see my sandals were on the wrong feet and he began to laugh.

I now had a decision to make: whether to visit my friend in the village or to go back home. I decided to go back home; I didn't feel quite ready to see my friend. I was afraid I might tell her about my fears of being pregnant and I couldn't imagine quite how I would explain it. I walked rather briskly back toward my home.

After a while I got very hungry, so I sat down under a tree and ate the remaining food that I had brought. Once again as I was sitting there, I felt the presence sitting beside me. There was a breeze blowing and it made me sleepy. At first it was just a sensation and then the presence spoke once again, and said, "Mary, Mary, we are very pleased with you. You are a faithful daughter. We call you, Mary, to bring forth light. You carry in you now brilliant, brilliant light, a light so bright that it covers the world. You Mary shall bring forth this light. Do not be afraid, you are safe from all harm. We will show you the way. You have been chosen, Mary, because of your purity, and by that purity, we mean that the light within you is so strong and full that you can see that light in everything. This is why we have chosen you."

Then the voice asked me if I had any questions or anything to say. To be honest, I was speechless. I had never felt chosen to be anything. My mind began to reel; I felt the opposite. I felt different from everybody. I spent so much time alone with the nature spirits that most people, including my parents, laughed, and thought I was strange. I had been betrothed at a very young age, maybe ten or eleven, to the carpenter's son, Joseph; because my parents worried that I might have trouble finding a proper husband. They felt he would be good for me because he was very practical and had good common sense. He was able to keep his feet on the ground and accomplish tasks in a timely fashion. They felt my mind was always so far away. They thought Joseph would be the right person to bring me back to earth. Now I wondered what my pregnancy would mean for him.

When the presence asked me if I had anything to say or any questions, I couldn't form a single word from all these thoughts, and I certainly didn't have anything to ask. I felt the voice was laughing a bit to itself, but in a nice way, and it said to me "Oh Mary, your purity is truly enchanting. You, above so many others, will pierce the world's heart with your love. Like the most beautiful crystal, your joy reflects eternally. Now come, let us go back home. Your condition will soon become known to your family, but fear not, dear child. All will be taken care of and you shall be protected." I felt the presence taking my hand and leading me back to the path. It felt as if I flew back home. Arriving there, I hardly remembered the walk.

I arrived just before nightfall and my mother was glad to see me. She gave me food and drink and asked me all about my trip. She asked me about my friend, Leah, and I bit my lip not wanting to tell a lie. So, I told my mother I had fallen asleep by the water's edge and that it had gotten so late I had to hurry home. My mother just shook her head, laughing, and said, "Mary, Mary, you're such a faraway girl. Your head is always in the clouds, but I love you very much. You are my special Mary, and always will be."

I went to bed and had a good sleep with many dreams, but dreams that did not awaken me. In one dream, I could see the presence that I had only heard earlier. It said again, "Do not worry, Mary, we will take care of everything. Sleep easily child, all is well."

CHAPTER 5

Now, you remember that as I hurried away from the lake where I had fallen asleep, I heard a voice telling me that I had been chosen because of my purity. I would like to speak a bit about that purity. Many people misunderstand the purity of "the Madonna." You see, dear children, all creatures are pure, for everything in the universe is made from the most pure and exquisite light of God. Within the light of God is all sound, all color, all shape, all form. It was not just I, Mary, who was pure, but all things, in all times. Everything is pure, composed totally of God-light and love. This is truth. It is.

Now, when I heard the words that I was pure, I was puzzled, for you see, there are times when purity is forgotten. Why is that? Because of fear, dear friends. Very simple—it is fear. What is fear? Fear is the absence of light. Fear is the absence of the knowledge that all things are pure. Purity is the opposite of fear.

There I was, a very young girl, and while I was very pure and very much in touch with this light, as a human being, it was natural for me to feel the sensation of fear. I felt fear inside for I knew I was with child. The voices had told me. I had not, at this time, told my mother or father. The more afraid I became, the more isolated I began to feel, and the more isolated I felt, the darker it became. So, you see, dear ones, I know the terrifying depths of despair and loneliness. I know how you may have felt. I know the sadness of the loneliest heart, for I have experienced it.

I often took walks to the lake to be by myself and to try to understand all that was happening to me. As I walked back home one evening, I trembled inside, knowing that I had to tell my mother. I was beginning to gain weight so much so that my clothes did not fit and my shape was changing. But how? How could I tell my mother something I did not understand? How could I tell my mother about the voices I heard? My parents wanted me to marry Joseph because they felt he was stable, and that I was so flighty that someone like Joseph, a steady and sensible carpenter, would be able to bring me back to earth, so to speak. But how could I explain to him my condition? He would never believe me. When I had that thought, I threw myself down in the grass and wept, for I felt there was no escape. I felt completely alone. I felt unbelievable fear. I felt the darkness of the worse night that anyone could possibly imagine.

As I lay there crying, an angel sat beside me and said, "Mary, why do you weep? Do not weep. You are safe; all will be taken care of. You have only to fulfill what has been placed before you." And then the angel took my hands, held them, and looked into my eyes and said, "Mary, do you believe what you have been told?" I hesitated for a moment, and then I said, "Angel, Angel, I believe, I believe. Yes, I believe." The angel smiled the biggest smile I had ever seen. Then it disappeared. In that moment, I understood and so I rose to my feet and went home.

It was sundown. My mother was sewing by the fire. My father was sleeping. My brother and sister were not at home. My mother smiled and greeted me, "Mary, where have you been? I have been worried about you. What took you so long?" "Mother," I said, "I have something important to tell you." There must have been something in the tone of my voice because she looked at me quite seriously, with a penetrating stare. "Come, sit here Mary, rest your head against my lap and tell me what is on your mind, dear child." I told her an angel had spoken to me. I told her there was a child inside of me. I told her I had been chosen for this work. I told her I believed and I understood, but I didn't know why this had come to me. Tears rolled down my mother's face. "Oh, oh, oh," that's all she seemed able to say. "Oh, Mary, oh my dear, dear child. What shall become of us? What shall become of you?" She slapped me, and then grabbed me very tightly to rock me in her arms.

I was so confused. There were many things spinning around in my head and in my heart. She told me to go to bed. "We will not think about this until the morning. We must tell your father. We must decide what to do. Go. Go to bed. I must rest. I need sleep. I cannot think about this now, Mary." I went to my pallet to contemplate my fate, for I knew my mother was disappointed in me beyond the words that she spoke. As I lay my head against the pillow, I wondered why it was that I had been so chosen.

CHAPTER
6

The next morning, I arose early before anyone else was awake. It was still dark. I put on my clothes and shoes and went outside. There was still a beautiful moon and a very soft breeze, and I felt drawn to go a little way from the house and sit under the trees. Long beams of light poured straight down from the moon, and as I went under the tree, the shafts of light came all the way around me, creating walls so that I was inside a room of light. Then I heard a voice. I didn't see anyone. I stood up. The voice said, "Mary, your destiny has been created, and the path for your journey has been laid out. Just as it is walking upon stones across a small creek, so is the pathway of your life's destiny. You are a serious and practical young woman, more than you yourself acknowledge, for your heart is very steady, pure, and totally connected with the light. This light that pours all the way around you now, this light of God, is the substance with which all creatures in the universe are made. You are bathed in this light and you will always be protected, guided and shown the way."

At that moment, I knew in my heart that everything would be all right. All my fears and concerns about my family evaporated, for I knew, and from that point on, I would never question the purpose of my life. I would accept everything, whatever it was to be, that would come my way. I now had complete trust in my destiny.

I was standing under the tree looking up at the moon and I saw my face staring back at me, floating. In that moment, I realized that not only was I walking with both feet on the earth, but part of who I was,

was also floating with God in the moon. Therefore, I could trust in my journey and my pathway, for I was both the person and the God-light. This concept, which I now experienced personally as a young girl, would transform me, and allow me to go through my life with a balanced and total trust.

By this time there was the light coming from the East, the sun had not yet risen, but I walked back into my house. As I came inside my mother was just getting out of bed. She looked at me. I must have appeared differently because something in her face told me that she perceived a change. She came toward me and put her arms around me and held me very close, almost rocking me like a baby. I was very glad for my mother's loving arms, for I felt in that moment, as if I were floating in the sea on gentle waves, knowing that she would always protect me no matter what.

I want to tell you something. The concept I learned as I stood in the moonlight, is that part of me was floating above looking down. This is true for everyone, for all of you who suffer, cry out, and struggle. You simply must know that whatever it is that you want has only to be called upon—"it" is there all the time. For all of you, each and every one is in part walking with two feet on the planet Earth and in part floating with the moonlight and God. Know that at any time you may call upon that source, that light, that part of yourself that exists within and with God.

You may ask, but Mary, you had terrible tragedy, sadness, fear, and sorrow in your life. How can it be as simple, easy, and joyful as you describe? I will answer you with all honesty and confidence: my pathway, my journey, was laid out before me and I simply walked over each stone, one by one, step by step. All through my life, it was a mystery perhaps, but I trusted that mystery, I gave myself over to it, just as anyone of you could do.

Think of these words when you consider the natural disasters, disease, poverty, and acts of war that characterize the world you see around you now. Remember that every person on the planet walks simultaneously through these difficulties just as they are walking with God. The balance of these experiences, whether they are aware of it or not, involves many dimensions. The more people are able to trust in their destiny, their energetic purpose, in the totality of God's influence, the easier these obstacles will be to understand

and transcend. What appears to be horror, death, or destruction on one level, viewed in the light of cosmic understanding, becomes an opportunity for transformation for those willing to put aside their overwhelming need for self-affirmation and recognition on an individual level.

The overall state of transition, including the climatic and geophysical changes in the Earth's atmosphere at this time are necessary energetic cleansings, due to many factors, and many of the living, breathing entities are in fact ready and willing to participate in that cleansing. Your planet, like a person walking across the driest desert, is thirsting for this knowledge. If you can picture, millions of little light bulbs on wires, all over the planet, you would see little light bulbs here and there, but some of them are not completely attached, so that if you flipped a switch, they would not come on simultaneously. Connecting all the lights is what we are trying to achieve.

CHAPTER 7

The next day, my mother and I took a walk quite a distance from the house. We strolled in silence. There was a path that we had often taken before, and we knew it well. There was a breeze. The leaves on the trees rustled, danced. The light of the sun danced through the leaves and on the grass. Flowers were blooming. It was beautiful. As we walked, I could see all of the creatures in the trees and flowers. Soon my mother spoke: "Mary, I don't know quite what to say to you, child. I cannot believe what you told me, but I must believe it, for I am certain it is true. Mary, how could you do this to our family? How could you do this to yourself? You are pledged to Joseph, and when he learns of this, Mary, your life will be in chaos. Dear child, who, who have you been with? I cannot understand how you could do this."

My mother looked at me quite fiercely and I realized how very, very upset she was, and yet I did not know what to tell her. I did not know who I had been with. I only knew what the angel had told me. I looked at her and I shook my head and I said, "Oh, Mother, Mother, what has brought me to this? I do not know. I have had dreams where an angel has appeared, and he has told me that I have a pure heart and that I have been called upon to do this work. I don't know what work it is. I don't know why I have a child inside of me, Mother. I don't know where this child came from. The angel said it is meant to be. This is all I know, Mother."

"Mary, do not lie to me, your mother. Do not lie! There's one thing I will not tolerate, Mary, and that is an outright lie! How dare you say you do not know how this came about. You must tell me." I thought my mother would hit me again. I didn't know what to say or do. "Mother, please believe me. Truly, truly I do not know what happened. I have no memory of things that happened to me, only of the angel's visit. This is the truth, my dearest mother. Never would I lie to you, ever, ever, ever. I am a good and faithful daughter. I have done nothing wrong, my mother. Dear, dear mother, please, please believe me."

My mother looked at me for a long time. She shook her head and we walked silently for quite a distance until we came to a small stream. There we sat, eating some cheese and bread, we drank from the stream, and we leaned against a tree. Soon my mother questioned me again, and she said: "Mary, I truly must know from your heart what is the truth. What has happened to you, child? You must tell me; I am your mother. You must confess to me, Mary. I cannot help you if you will not tell me what has happened. I command you; I implore you, Mary, tell me, who did this to you?"

My mother had her hands on my shoulders, and she did not let go of them, but held me very close to her face. I looked deeply into my mother's eyes and began to swoon. Seeing her angry and inquisitive face, I began to feel ill, light-headed, and quite dizzy; I began to faint. My mother shook me, "Mary, Mary, wake up, come back here," and she slapped my face once again, not to hurt me, but to try to bring me back from this fainting spell. She shook me but it did no good. I fell, and my mother gently laid me down into the grasses as I fainted.

My mother went down to the stream and took the edge of her skirt and made it wet and came back and dabbed the cool water on my temples and on my face to revive me from this spell. She did this several times before I came to. At that point, I began to regain consciousness and my mother was slapping my wrists and was quite concerned. She had lifted me up so that I leaned against her knees, and she put my head in her lap.

My mother was rocking me gently and tears streamed down her face. I did not know what to do. I felt so terrible; I felt I had really let my family down. I began to fear for my life because I knew what they did to young girls who got into trouble such as me. Many times, they were stoned. They were taken into a public place and stones were hurled at them until they were so hurt and bruised, and sometimes they died, depending on how angry the crowd became. It was a disgrace to the entire family. I knew I had not done anything wrong. I knew that I was innocent. I also knew that my word would not be enough to save my life. My mother rocked me, and she sang a lullaby that I remembered from when I was still a little child.

Through the trees there was a kind of opening among the leaves, and from that clearing appeared the angel, the same angel who had come to me before. My mother could also see him, and she exclaimed, "Mary, look! Look, through the trees! Do you see that? There is a . . . there's an angel!" The angel said, "Do not fear. I bring you tidings. I bring you tidings of joy, of light. Mary is with child, a child of God. It is good. It is right. She was chosen among many for her purity of heart and soul. Do not punish her. Help her, protect her, guide her, for she is innocent, and she is carrying within her the seed of the Lord. Preserve her for she has been chosen among many." The angel left, just disappeared like a mist, and my mother was so afraid that she began to tremble and shake, and she said, "I do not believe what I have seen. I do not understand what I have seen. Mary, what is happening?" I replied, "Mother, I do not know, but this is the same angel who came to me before. I tried to tell you." My mother, still in disbelief, said, "Child, let us pray." We bowed our heads. My mother prayed over me, blessed me, and reassured me that nothing could come between the love of a mother and her daughter, and that no matter what befell her that I would be cherished and protected with the Lord's blessing. We gathered up our things and went back to the path. Again, we walked side by side in silence until we were back home.

As we went inside, my mother said to me, "Mary, your father left this morning early. I did not tell him what you had told me, and now I must break the news to him. I do not want you here when I tell him. Please go to another part of the house, do not come out until I call you. This is for your own safety."

CHAPTER
8

While my mother informed my father of my condition, I waited outside the house in an area where we kept chickens. I felt nervous and afraid. My father would be so angry and disappointed with me. I could hear my father speaking very loudly, but I couldn't quite make out the words. It ruffled the feathers of the hens as I pulled pieces of straw from the nest between my fingers to play with, just to give myself something to do to relieve my anxiety. I couldn't pray. I couldn't think. I continued to play with pieces of straw between my fingers and I felt that the hens, sitting on their nests, somehow understood my plight, for they looked at me and though their feathers ruffled, they did not seem disturbed or try to fly away from me. They sat there calmly, and somehow with this calmness they helped me.

It seemed such a long time until my mother came for me; at last, the door opened, and she came outside and said, "Mary, come inside, child. Your father wishes to speak to you. It is time." I took a very deep breath and followed my mother inside. My father had on his prayer shawl, candles were lit, and he had opened the Torah and was praying when I entered. I paused and my mother stood beside me with her arms around my waist as my father intoned the prayer. I realized he was singing the prayer of the dead, and I began to weep silently.

His prayers intoned deeper and louder. My mother stood silently as he sang. I felt her arm enclose my waist, pulling me to her to give me some of her life force.

At last, my father finished his prayers, closed the Torah, and looked up at me. "Mary, sit." That was all he said. Very quietly, I slipped into a chair at the table and bowed my head, not daring to even look at my father. "You have heard the prayer. This is what you bring to our house, to our family, to our community, to our tribe. You bring disgrace worthy of death upon us. I have no other recourse but to make the prayer of the dead, for as of this day, Mary, you are dead to me."

I cannot describe to you the pain that I felt in my heart as my father said these words to me. It was as if I had become invisible, that I was not really sitting on the chair that somehow, I had disappeared into a thin vapor. I had no emotion. Time had stopped. I had no sense of where I was.

My father continued, "Mary, how could you have done this? How could you? How could you have disgraced us like this? How can you be a child of mine? You, my beloved daughter, in whom I placed all of my hopes and dreams. You have destroyed my life. You have destroyed my family, my community, and my tribe. You have disgraced me in the eyes of God." Then, he stopped. He suddenly rose from his chair, threw himself toward the opposite side of the room and slammed his fist into his hand several times, hitting his fist into the palm of his hand, smacking it, calling out for his ancestors. He called out for mercy, and he called out for lightning to strike our house. My mother remained behind a chair by the table, only her hands revealing her feelings as she gripped the back of the chair. I saw the knuckles on her hands were bloodless, white, then almost purple; she gripped so hard.

When my father stopped his ranting, he walked to the table, threw his hands down, leaned across very close to my face and said, "Mary, if you weren't my flesh and blood, I would kill you, do you hear me, I would kill you right now. If you were not my own flesh and blood, I would take you outside, throw you down, and take a knife to your throat. Do you hear me?" I was trembling but, again, I did not feel that I was really there. I felt as still as a vapor, not a person, as though I had no flesh and blood to injure. My father turned away from the table. He walked away, kicked open the door, and went outside.

My mother threw her arms around me intending to protect me from my father's wrath. I know that she feared my father would kill me.

At long last, my father's rage subsided, and he came back in the house. Now he was quiet, moving very slowly, very methodically, pacing. My mother went to my father and offered him some food. He turned and looked at my mother as if she had asked him to go on a long trip to another country; clearly food was the last thing he was thinking about. I folded my hands and began to pray deeply, silently to myself, a personal prayer, asking for forgiveness and help in my plight. At last, my father returned to the table. He called my mother over to the table and asked her to sit. "This is what I have determined we shall do: We cannot pretend that this situation does not exist. We cannot send Mary away. She will not be safe. I will not harm her; I will protect her. We must face what is before us. I must tell Joseph and his family. We must tell the truth and pray that Joseph will make the right decision." My father's voice broke. I'll never forget that sound. "It is not up to us, it is up to Joseph, his family, and our community. "I pray that Joseph, our brother, will open his heart to this situation. I will understand whatever he decides, but I pray that in his wisdom, grace, and understanding, he will decide to stay by my daughter." My father rose from the table and left without a word. My mother brought me a bowl of soup and some bread. I was shivering. She brought me a warm, wool shawl and wrapped me in it. She took a chair to sit by me and fed me the hot soup as if I were a baby, spoonful by spoonful. I was in a state of shock and would not have been able to feed myself. She put the spoon down and I felt her hand in the middle of my back, as her hand just rested there, I knew that my mother loved me very much. I had brought such disgrace upon our house and yet she fed me and comforted me. I may have learned more about compassion in those moments with my mother than at any other time in my life. Her actions taught me that among the greatest of favors from the Holy Father is our ability to feel and to show compassion even in what seems to be the deepest, darkest moments of desperation. My mother's courage and grace on this night will always remind me of compassion's power.

Morning came. I rose, and seeing the sunshine made me feel that perhaps everything would be all right. Something inside told me so. I went into the main part of our house and there breakfast was laid out for me. My mother and father were not there. As I walked toward the table, the angel appeared, beautiful and smiling, just as before. He reached his arm out to me, touched my hand, and said, "Dearest Mary, trust in our words, you will be safe. You will be taken care of. Do not fear anything or anyone. You are loved and the light of God pours through you, now and forever more." Just as he said "more," he disappeared. I sat down and ate; I was quite hungry. As I sat there, I heard the voices of several people talking outside. I looked out and saw my parents and Joseph's father talking, very animatedly. Of course, I knew what they were talking about. Joseph's father did not come inside. He and my father made some gestures toward each other. I could see my mother had put her arm on my father's shoulder as if to communicate that things would be all right, or to steady him. I felt so ashamed. Quickly, I got up and went into my room to dress. I wanted to hide. I didn't feel capable of facing them.

I heard again the words of the angel and I was glad for those words. I remembered my mother stroking my hair, wrapping me in a warm nightdress, watching me until I fell asleep. I felt at that moment that I was not alone. I was ready as I carried the beauty of what my mother had taught me the night before; it was she who gave me the strength to go on. I knew I, Mary, would sustain myself through this trial. I knew young as I was, inexperienced as I was, I could face this challenge, that I had the strength. I knew so in my heart. I began to breathe evenly, and I made a prayer to the Holy Father that no matter what lay before me with this pregnancy, that I could graciously go forward and meet whatever circumstances were to be my fate.

CHAPTER 9

As you know, there have been many sightings of Mary around the world. The reason I use the term Mary instead of saying myself is because the sightings and some of the words that people have heard have been their own desire to make contact with the greater vibrational spirit than what is now available to them.

We in the spirit world have been making preparations for an interglobal connection of visionary souls who have evolved to a higher consciousness but have not had the ability to make any specific changes in others, other than in themselves. This was as it was meant to be. For the process has been for pockets of individuals interglobally to quietly raise their own consciousness first. This has been going on now for almost twenty-five years in your time. I should say it has accelerated over the past twenty-five years, although the beginnings of this process were started much earlier.

Now the time has come when there are a significant number of groups of individuals who are light-filled and living in all the major areas of the world, as well as in areas not generally populated or visited by officials in high places. Now the time has come for these people to connect interglobally. The question is, how shall this be accomplished? And what will come of it? We want to make it clear that this is a spiritual process which is realized in the hearts of men and women. This is not a political or even a social movement. This is a personal realization that will take place within each person's heart. In this moment in time, the reason that many people have had sightings of Mary is because their hearts are crying for light. If you can picture a weeping *heart with tears of blood pouring down from this heart, this is an image that is felt the world over, and people are in despair. They do not know what to do. We in the spirit world feel these tears and we wish to bring the light of true understanding to those who are ready to accept this light, for it is part of the process started so long ago with my story.*

There is a part of my story that nobody knows, for I never told it to anyone. It was painful. I must be honest and say that my father hated me, once he realized that I was with child. At the time it seemed certain that he would never forgive me. His anger toward me was beyond words. I knew he wanted to kill me. I knew that if it were not for my mother and my aunt, that he would have killed me. My father was a very angry man. He saw the officials of the region as against our tribe; and was in constant fear that we would be attacked or driven out. He lived in a perpetual state of stressful readiness to flee. Personally, my father was also quite insecure. It was important to him how he looked to the fellow members of his tribe in all religious matters. He knew the letter of the law, precisely, and followed all religious traditions and rituals. He never failed in his duties to the synagogue or in prayer and rituals at home. His approach was stern, and we dutifully followed his command.

In sharp contrast, I saw in my mother's approach to the rituals and the laws a joyful sense of connection to something greater than herself, and while my father's stern prayers and singing of the hymns of praise were done in a dutiful way, my mother sang with a lightness of spirit and a happiness in her heart. Through her example, and, of course, my own nature, which you already know about, I saw God everywhere around me, in all living creatures. Although I tried to see God's spirit in my father, it was often hard, for sometimes he gave me the impression that he would burst apart with his own anger. Now that my mother had told my father that I was with child, his anger grew beyond words.

My mother left one afternoon to go to the village to pick up grain from the miller, who ground the wheat. I was feeding the chickens when I looked up and saw my father coming toward me. I froze with fear. He said, "Mary, you have caused me such grief and such humiliation that I cannot face the elders in the tribe." I looked at him and I knew that I could say nothing, for if I had said anything it only would have inflamed him more. I bowed my head and did not look at his face, only heard his words. I could see his toes tightening and tensing in his sandals. He yelled, "Mary, look at me!" I slowly lifted my face and saw in his hand a leather bridle that he used on his horse. He slapped me across the face with it, back and forth. I fell to the ground. He screamed at me, horrible words. He beat my back, my shoulders, my legs, until I was bleeding all over and fainted. I remember that he called me a filthy whore, a stupid filthy whore. He must have said it a hundred times as he beat me. Finally, he threw the bridle down and left.

I came to, what seemed like hours later. I could not move. I lay in the straw and the dirt. I thought I would die. I looked up and I saw a smiling face hovering above me. The face said lovingly, "Mary, live in peace, for what you have felt will show you the way to help others. Do not be afraid. There is a reason for all things, and it will be revealed. Live in peace, Mary." The face disappeared, and I lay there, wondering.

Much later I heard my mother's voice. She was calling, "Mary, Mary." I had no strength to answer her, and I knew she was looking for me. At last, I heard her footsteps approaching. The chickens flapped their wings as she came toward the door. I will never forget the look on her face when she saw me. She threw herself down and took me in her arms. She cried, "Oh, Mary, oh, Mary." She got up and ran to get water and a cloth to wash my wounds. She did not even ask how this had happened because she knew. She lifted me up and carried me into the house. She put me into bed. She stayed by my side and stroked my brow, sang, and rocked me and never said another word about what had happened. That was usually the way my mother dealt with conflict. She would sing to me and stroke me and rock me, as if to take away all the negativity through the sound of her voice and the power of her presence.

My heart was like the heart of so many others who live today: my heart was crying tears. I knew as I lay there and my mother sang that no matter what, I would be protected. I knew the strength of my mother. I knew that she would do whatever it would take to preserve my life. I understand the mothers of the world whose strength has gone unnoticed as the violence of men has caused a rampage of destruction in countless places all over the world. I assure you, mothers of the world, that your quiet strength which has gone unnoticed shall rise forth with the strength of mountains and will take command of the universe. Again, I want to make it clear that I am not talking about a political or a social movement. I am talking about a fullness of light penetrating the hearts of those who have felt powerless, but who have quietly maintained their belief and their knowledge. Let those who believe that they can continue to wantonly destroy know that the power of the tearstained heart shall pour forth its majesty. My words may seem to be an impossible utopia, for there has been so much blood spilled on the earth, but I assure you that for every drop of blood that has fallen into the earth, a precious jewel of light will be reborn.

CHAPTER 10

A few days passed after the incident with my father. A kind of eerie calm came over the household. Everyone acted as if nothing had happened and a tension pervaded the air, especially at the dinner table. My mother remained very alert at all times, and I don't believe she slept very much. My father seemed to be distracted and always had a furrow and scowl on his face, as if he were thinking very deeply about something. I was quiet, intent on my chores and trying to stay out of the way.

Soon the time was right to consult with Joseph. This was done without my being there. My father made a trip to Joseph's house to talk to him and his father alone. My mother told me that the men were making the plans and preparations.

One afternoon, about a week later, I looked out the window and saw Joseph walking toward our house. It happened that neither of my parents were home. I was quite nervous as I saw him approaching, but Joseph was a special man and I had known him a long time, so I was not afraid, only nervous to speak to him. I decided to go to the door and greet him. As he saw me, he waved, and I smiled. He called out, "Mary, come outside, it's a beautiful day."

I put my headdress over my head, and I walked outside. As I reached where he stood, I felt the wind rush and blow across my face and hair. I felt it whisper to me reassuringly, but as soon as I looked at Joseph I began to weep, realizing what trouble I had brought upon him. I fell down at his knees and cried. I felt his hands on my arms and I felt him touch my head. He lifted me up and wiped away my tears. He put his arm around me and said, "Come Mary, let's walk a bit."

I was very shaky and trembled so much that Joseph became concerned, and we stopped to rest. We were in a meadow where there were some rocks and high grass. We could hear the sound of the wind and the leaves rustling; we sat there quite some time without saying a word. Once again, I could feel and see the little creatures in the grasses all around me, but I dared not say anything about this to Joseph.

Finally, he said, "Mary, it has all been arranged. We will be married. You and the baby are safe with me. I will care for you."

When he said that, I broke into tears once again, for I felt so unworthy to be cared for by him. I had no explanation for my condition. All of the events of the last months were like a dream so strange that I could not possibly find words to even attempt to explain them to him. As I sobbed, he stroked my hair and he said, "Mary, I do not understand the nature of all these events, but know that I love you. I trust what I have seen, for a vision also came to me in the night and told me our marriage is the plan of the Holy Father. Although I cannot foretell what this plan is or why I am involved in it, I will gladly go forth with trust in my heart and love for you and the child that is expected. I must tell you honestly that there was quite a fervent discussion among the men about this situation. Many things were talked about, many things that I would not even tell you about, but all through that discussion I knew that I would stay by your side, no matter what the outcome. Therefore, I come to you this day to tell you this personally because I want you to hear it from me and me alone. There may be more discussion and idle gossip. As you know, people like to talk, but pay no attention, for it has all been decided and nothing can change the plans that have been set. I am by your side, Mary, and you can count on me to be there for you always."

I was overwhelmed by his words; I had not really known the strength of this man, who had always been as quiet as I. Neither one of us ever spoke very much, and this was indeed the longest he had ever spoken to me at one time. I could only communicate to him with my eyes and my hand, which squeezed his arm from time to time while we sat a while longer, just feeling the air blow across our faces. I leaned against his shoulder, and he had his arm around me. It was such a good feeling to have him by my side; I can tell you truly, that without him, I would have been killed. It was because of his love, and I know it was selfless love, one that comes from such a deep place that it goes beyond any kind of understanding in human form, that I was able to live. This is what Joseph gave to me.

Joseph turned to me and said, "Mary, let me walk you back to the house; I must go and work with my father. There is always much to do." I nodded my head and he walked me up the hill and at the doorway I turned and touched his face. He looked at me, smiled very gently, and said, "Mary, I will see you soon and remember my words. Bless you, dear Mary." I squeezed his hand against my cheek and bowed to him in reverence, for I knew that he was making an oath to me and I accepted my part in that oath. From that moment on, I never questioned or doubted Joseph's integrity. For such a man to exist on the earth with such grace and utter purity, I know now is very, very rare. I am so thankful that he was with me.

He looked at me once more, took a few steps away, and went off down the hill to his home. I watched him and then I went inside. I sat down at the table and said a prayer thanking God for my life. I think it was only then that I realized how narrowly my life had been spared.

It appears incredible today, perhaps, that something so simple as a pregnant girl could cause such a rift in the entire community, but in those times, relationships were considered sacred and much more valuable than maybe they are in some societies today. People in a community were interconnected and everyone understood the nature and necessity of that interconnection.

It was a form of survival on many levels: survival in a political conflict, overcoming diseases, predators, and other dangers. This is why committed family relationships, established to protect the community as a whole, were so very important. When a certain member of the community, such as myself, deviated from the normal standard, it threw the entire community into chaos and confusion. Most of the time that person would be killed. It was the only way that the community as a whole could feel protected. I know that it was because of Joseph's loyalty and willingness to speak out for me, because of his courage, that my life was spared. I take the time to explain this, so that you understand the utter significance of the man, Joseph, in my story. I want the world to know that strength and purity of heart often come from the quiet and the ordinary, and that many men like Joseph are present in the world today. Although they are not always in powerful places, it is these men who will soon be coming forth to guide us all.

CHAPTER 11

After my prayers, I was left with a sense of the importance of my own existence; I somehow knew that there was a great purpose in my life being spared. Much later, when my parents came home, I told them both what Joseph had said. My mother was very happy, and she embraced me. My father looked at me sternly and said, "You are indeed fortunate, Mary, for there was much discussion regarding your future. You cannot possibly know the trouble and strife you have brought upon our community. Many hours were spent in serious contemplation and reverent prayer to determine your fate. Be wise, young lady, and know your place from here on out, one false step and you shall pay with your life. Hear my words: Even though you are my flesh and blood, I will not tolerate any further mistakes on your part. Only through the goodness and charity of our community and the gentle Joseph, have you been spared. Never forget my words to you this day, for all eyes are upon you, watching you, following you. You will never be able to take a step without someone knowing your actions again. Now, I am going to bed, and I suggest the two of you do the same. Good night."

My mother looked at me, as if to say, you know the minds of the elders and you must obey them; but I love you, so, do not be afraid. She hugged me and said, "Mary, you are my daughter, I love you with all my heart and I love the child within you, as if it were my very own. Do not worry. Sleep peacefully with my love surrounding and protecting you."

Even with these words, I could not sleep. I sat for many hours in the room, just sitting, staring into space, feeling relieved that my child and I would not be killed, and yet feeling unclean because of my father's words. I felt a quiet fear inside my heart of what the future would hold. At last, I rose and went to my room.

As I lay down, I heard a voice that said, "Mary, Mary, we are here with you. We will never leave you. We will protect and guide you, your whole life through. You are safe, fully, completely, and everlastingly safe. Know this and hold these words fast in your heart. These words which we speak to you now, allow these words to live in your heart. Sleep now, gently sleep. Many, many days filled with joy and light lie ahead. Remember our words, dear Mary." Just as they were saying these last words to me, I slipped off into sleep.

The day rapidly came when the marriage ceremony was performed and which our families had decided to hold privately. The rest of the village was invited to a reception afterward. I was very happy, flushed, and excited as I walked toward Joseph. He took my hand. It was a quiet, gentle ceremony. At the end, we returned to my home, where my mother served a delicious honey-cake and very good, sweet wine. It was a strange celebration, for even though I felt warm and happy inside, I did not feel really welcome by my family. It was as if they were sleepwalking and they avoided me, except for my mother and my aunt. Joseph was very attentive and sang a song and made a toast to our future life together. I couldn't help but observe my father's behavior. He stayed apart from us and never touched the honey-cake, drinking several glasses of wine and strolling among the trees and talking intently with one of his close friends. He never embraced me, but he did shake Joseph's hand, and placed his hand on Joseph's shoulder. I felt a cold, icy air from him.

The party ended and all those who had attended, as was the custom, came to greet the bride and groom. One by one, they passed by me and Joseph, taking our hands, kissing our hands, kissing my cheek, one by one, until they had all left.

My mother and father withdrew. My mother took in plates of unfinished food and Joseph put his arm around my shoulder and said, "Dear Mary, you must be very tired. It has been a very long and strenuous week for you. I want you to know how much I cherish you. You are like a jewel that sparkles in the sun. Your radiance and beauty are reflected everywhere. I hold you fast, within my heart, and you shall always live there with me." He took my hands and kissed them so sweetly; I'll never forget the touch of his lips on my fingertips. He looked deeply into my eyes.

I said to him, "Dearest Joseph, the light in your eyes guides my every step. I follow your light with my heart, knowing that my love for you is expressed in all my words and deeds. I cherish you with all my heart and put my life and dreams in your hands. I know that I am safe with you, and you shall never have cause to distrust me in any way. I give my promise, my heart, and my life to you, dearest Joseph."

I put my arms around him, and we held each other tenderly. Then he said, "Mary, let me take you inside, for you must be very tired."

He walked me to the door of the house and bid me good night. In these days we still were not in our own home. Preparations had not been fully made, only the ceremony confirming our union. Joseph left and I went immediately to my room and lay down for I had some pain. I could feel the child stir within me as I fell asleep.

CHAPTER
12

Time passed and the day came when I was to bring this child into the world. There have been many stories about this, but I will tell you the true story of how my child was born. It is true that we traveled a long distance, so that the baby could be born in a place where it would not be harmed. There were several reasons for this. First, the political climate at the time had put our tribe in danger; we had to be very careful that the government did not take away our children. The other reason was that there was still anger and resentment toward me and some anger and resentment toward Joseph for having married me. Throughout my pregnancy there had been constant gossiping and bitter words hurled both at Joseph and me.

We made the decision to travel to a faraway town to bring the baby forth in relative obscurity. I was very excited to have the baby, for I could feel his kicking and movements inside me. I had become quite large, but never sick or weak; perhaps my youth made it possible for me to carry the baby more easily. We packed our things and Joseph helped me climb onto the donkey. We both laughed because I was so large. I looked rather silly as I had to lean back at such an angle with my robes pulled around me. I looked at least four times my normal size, and the donkey looked tiny in comparison.

We left early in the morning, so that we could have the entire day to travel. Once night fell, it would become quite cold. Joseph did not want me to become overly tired or chilled. Our journey was uneventful and as dusk descended, we were on the outskirts of a small village near Bethlehem. Joseph felt this would be a good place for us to rest. He was always attentive to my every need and frequently would take breaks so that I could climb off the donkey to stretch my legs or lie down for a little while. I remember that I was especially hungry for figs, which I seemed to eat constantly.

Joseph and I rode slowly toward the village. I was experiencing some pain and I became very uncomfortable. I tried to remain strong and not give in to the pain, for I knew that we did not yet have a place to stay. I did not want to worry Joseph, who was already worried and being overly attentive to me. The pains began to grow stronger and even though I tried to stifle any sounds, at one point I cried out very loudly. Joseph stopped immediately, and got off his donkey, came over to me and asked if I was all right. I was trembling and began perspiring profusely. The pains were coming very quickly now. We were really in the middle of nowhere. There was nothing around us. For a moment, Joseph almost became panic stricken that the baby would come too soon.

Up ahead, where there had been nothing before, we now suddenly saw some kind of light. Joseph took the reins of my donkey and walked beside me, fearing that I would fall off; I was doubled over in pain. We moved toward the light up ahead as quickly as we could. It took some time to get there, as Joseph continued to walk behind me and hold me up, so that if I should fall, he could catch me.

At last, we came to a public house where travelers stayed. There was much festivity: dancing, singing. People were drinking and very rowdy, a lot of activity and commotion.

Joseph saw this, and he wanted to take me away quickly fearing for my safety. There were fires going and yelling, fighting, cursing. Some men, who were very sweaty and drunk, were yelling things at me. Joseph grabbed hold of me and the side of the donkey and moved so forcefully through the crowd that he almost knocked several of them over. We kept going and never looked back. Soon we reached a clump of trees near a place where farmers kept some tools and animal feed.

By this time, I was nearly falling off the donkey in pain. There was no choice but to stop immediately in this place. Joseph carried me to the grass and laid me down. He ran back to the donkey and brought blankets to me, for now it was cold. He put the blanket underneath me, rolled me onto it and laid another blanket on top of me. There was no light aside from the stars and the moon. I remember looking up at a beautiful, crystal-clear sky, with stars everywhere. The moon was full and very bright. In the distance we could hear the music and dancing and the shouts of the people we had passed. Joseph brought the donkeys closer, partly to protect us and partly for warmth. I did not know what I was to do or how this baby was to be born. Joseph, before we left the tribe, had talked to one of the wise women of the village. She taught him some of the lessons of her experience in bringing children into the world.

As I lay there, it seemed as if time had stopped, and a sudden hush came over the night. Then the pains began in earnest. I cried out. I was afraid. Joseph came to my side and as I grabbed his hand, he whispered to me. "Dear Mary, I am here with you. Do not be afraid, we can do this. I learned from Baryta, the old woman of the village, she told me what to do. Now, you must breathe and let everything happen naturally." And so, it went like that. It seemed like hours of pain and sweat and yelling. Joseph placed his hands on my stomach. Baryta had shown him what to feel for to gauge the progress of the baby. At last, I felt the baby's head burst forth. Joseph told me that I needed to push very hard, for this was the end of it. Soon I could rest and relax again, but the hard work was now. He told me to push as hard as I could. When I screamed, the donkeys would move and flinch; there were some other animals around and they began to move and flinch, too. Joseph concentrated and kept a steady control of the entire situation. I pushed one last time, very hard; I felt my body rip and out came the baby. Joseph was there to catch him, in a blanket.

I sat up just enough to see this shining red, glistening, creature. As I fell back down Joseph said, "Mary, it's a boy. Look at him!" He was crying. I began to laugh and cry. Joseph wiped him off, wrapped a blanket around him, and laid him on my stomach. It was such a wonderful feeling, to have this little creature nestled up against me. I held him close, as Joseph cleaned me up, for Baryta had warned him of the importance of tending to me after the baby was born. He took water that we had brought with us and washed me and dried me carefully. He wrapped me in the blanket. By this time, I was feeling cozy because my baby was now nursing. He found the milk so naturally and he seemed to be so content.

Joseph looked relieved and he began to relax. He built a small fire to warm us and to heat some food. Joseph fed me with a spoon, so that I did not have to move my arms from under the blanket or from holding the baby. He stroked my hair and kissed my forehead. He said, "Mary, this baby is beautiful. He is very strong. I love this baby, Mary, and I love you. We brought forth this child, in spite of everything and everyone against us. Together, we brought him to life. I am proud of this moment. I am proud to be this baby's father. I am proud of you, Mary. You had the most difficult job of all. Now let us rest; you sleep, Mary. I will stay awake to guard you and the baby. You sleep now. Do not fear, for I am guarding and watching over us."

I began to doze off, with my baby sleeping at my breast, the donkeys nearby, surrounded by a beautiful starry sky and very, very cold air.

The next morning, I awoke to the sound of voices. Some people had gathered having realized that a new baby had just been born. There were various people from the village and a shepherd, also. They gathered around us, smiling, laughing, and talking, and showing great interest in the fact that we were just lying there, in this place where only animals stayed. Some people were moved to give us small gifts, just things that they had available to them. They gathered around me. One laid down some bread, another person gave a small piece of cloth, I think it was a scarf. One person had something that looked like a tassel, from the blanket over their horse. They tore it off and gave it to me as a gift for the baby, something for him to play with later on. Someone gathered flowers and set them by my head. One person offered to call the elder of the village to come and bless the new baby. Joseph agreed. The people seemed so friendly and so simple. It must have been quite a sight to see us there, practically in the field, so close to nature. I think it must have been a very beautiful picture; all the people seemed to be calmed by being in our presence. Even the people who we had passed the night before were respectful and knelt by my side.

They asked me the baby's name, and I told them that the baby's name was Jesus. Joseph and I had already discussed the baby's name; we liked the sound of Jesus.

The elder of the village came walking toward us. He had brought with him a round-faced, rosy-cheeked matron of the village—a woman who had strong hands and arms and seemed very experienced around new mothers and babies. He was a very jolly man and stepped toward us, saying, "Well, well, what do we have here? What is this that I see? Why, it is a newborn baby and a beautiful mother. Ladies and gentlemen, we must give thanks for this miracle that lies before us. Right in our own pasture! Last night, this pasture was bare, with only the stars and the moon shining forth on this miracle. Now, on this day, the sun smiles kindly on a beautiful, new baby boy and his mother and father. Sing praises, let us rejoice! I declare this a miracle of joy."

At that, everyone shouted, clapped, and sang praises and songs, dancing lightly, with much rejoicing and laughing. People picked the flowers from the field and threw them into the air. The elder from the village was dancing and laughing himself, for he seemed so genuinely pleased at this event. He was the kind of man who made everyone feel good and we could understand why the shepherd offered to get him; he turned every event into a beautiful celebration. I will never forget the moment he blessed our family.

The rosy-cheeked woman bent over to fluff up my blankets and picked up the baby. She jostled him and rocked him with such experienced arms, that I marveled at the way she handled him. She knew just how to hold him. She showed him to the rest of the people, before handing him gently back to me, saying, "Beautiful lady, you have brought forth a healthy and handsome child. The stars smile kindly on you, and I see a blessed future for you and for your family." She opened a basket of delicious food. She called Joseph over and told him that she had baked bread that very morning, a special kind of bread. She said that we would be the first to partake of it, for it was important for new families to break bread together after a child is born. She gave us this delicious bread, still warm from her oven. Joseph ate it with great relish. She had more food, and she fed us as if we were a queen and a king. The elder of the village sat down on a stone nearby, talking and laughing; he told stories and whiled away the time in perfect contentment. Throughout the day, people came and went, always in good cheer.

This experience left an impression on me that I have never forgotten, the utter love given to me by these complete strangers brought joy, laughter, and sustenance to my life. They wanted nothing in return, for it was the simplicity of experiencing a joyful moment that they wanted to be part of.

The rosy-cheeked woman advised me to stay in my bed one more night in this place because it was a good idea to stay calm and not move around, as a still-healing new mother. She promised to return early the next morning with some boys from the village and a small cart. They would take us to her home, where we were welcome to stay until such a time as I was healed enough to travel. I will never forget the kindness of this warm, generous, good hearted, strong woman, who treated me as if I were royalty and who took command of the well-being of myself and my baby. I could tell that Joseph was relieved, for I don't think he had any idea what was going to happen next. On this second night, we slept in peace, knowing that we were protected by the angels, just as they had said we would be, for the kindness of these people was truly angelic.

I went to sleep, knowing that my baby had the most beautiful reception into the world possible. I could not imagine having had my baby any other way. It was so perfect and so beautiful. I made a prayer of thanks to the Lord, asking that my husband and child receive all the blessings from above to protect and keep them safe from all harm. As I drifted off into sleep, I could hear the sounds of the animals and smell the scent of the flowers and the grass. I thought to myself that surely this was better than any palace. I felt so cozy, and warm, and cared for.

CHAPTER 13

The next day, the lady and the young boys came to lift me from the ground and carry me by cart to her house. There, they gently laid me on a soft bed of straw covered by a handmade cloth; there was a pillow of very soft feathers. I had several physical complications after the birth that took some time to heal. The woman had experience in how to handle these things. I knew that I was being taken care of in a way that would not have happened in my own village. I was surrounded by well-meaning people who seemed to be somehow directed in caring for me and my child.

Joseph remained in the place where the animals stayed, because he did not wish to put an extra burden on the good-willed woman helping me. He visited in the daytime and toward evening would return to the shelter on the outskirts of town.

Several days had passed when a messenger arrived summoning us to return home. There was an illness in my family and they wanted us to be there. You may wonder how we were found so that we could receive such a message. In those times, a person bearing a message was directed to go to the town, village, or tribe and ask by name; oftentimes they had a description of the person, and who their family was. They would ask someone at the well or a person who talked a lot, and sooner or later they would be directed to the appropriate place.

I had healed enough and although I was somewhat stiff and not quite completely myself, I was able to climb upon the donkey and hold the baby. Joseph made a kind of sling that tied the baby to me, with an extra tie to the donkey, so that if any of them came loose, the baby had two ways to be held before he could possibly fall. Joseph always thought about these kinds of details. He quietly and methodically observed each situation to find appropriate solutions for the simple tasks of everyday living. His thoughtful and considerate nature made my life and our child's life safe and secure.

I embraced the beautiful, rosy-cheeked woman, blessing and thanking her from my heart for all of her generous ministering to me. I told her that I would never forget her and that she would live in my heart for my whole life. I had tears in my eyes as I bid her good-bye, for I doubted that I would see her again. I knew this was the entire length of our relationship. I wanted her to know how deeply lasting her presence would be for me. She held me tenderly, she kissed my brow; she held the baby, and she blessed him and kissed him on both cheeks and on his brow. She took Joseph's hands and kissed them, for she said that we were now in his protection; she kissed and blessed the strength of his hands to guide us into the future.

Her husband came forward, bowed, greeted us, and wished us well as we began our journey home. I would like to point out that in those times, the ceremony of leave-taking had depth and meaning. It was important to express in words and in gesture the truest and clearest meaning of a person's feelings at that moment. It was not to be rushed or dismissed carelessly, but to be savored, enjoyed, and thoughtfully and graciously performed.

As we rode away, I turned back to take one last look at the woman and her family who had been so kind and so good to me. I will never forget her face, as the sunlight struck her cheek as she wiped aside a wisp of hair. The smile on her face, I carry in my heart through eternity.

Remember these moments, dear friends; these small, ordinary, perhaps seemingly insignificant moments; they brilliantly express the Light of God.

We rode for many hours toward our home. It was hot during the high point of the day and cooler as the day wore on. I had a cloth over the baby so that he would not be harmed by the sun, but I needed to carefully lift the cloth so that he would get enough air to breathe. Three times we stopped, so that I could feed the baby and rest. We would also water and feed the animals that we rode.

I should tell you also that Joseph was ever vigilant in his care of the animals; he was as attentive of their needs as he was to ours. He did not want them to become dehydrated or overly tired from pushing too hard on the journey. He had an innate sense of timing and how to perform simple tasks in a gracious manner. I always admired this quality in Joseph. Perhaps because he was a carpenter and worked with tools and wood, refining the wood and measuring it, he had learned to work with such precision and attention to detail. Perhaps through the discipline of carpentry, he had recognized the importance of details in everyday actions.

We rode for one more day and before long we could see our village ahead. The message had only said one thing, "Hurry home, your family needs you." It was signed by my mother, Anna. I tried not to worry, but I had a feeling as to what the message was about. Neither Joseph nor I spoke about it during the trip. Joseph never engaged in idle chatter or speculative thinking. It was not his way. He knew the message was important, and we would discuss it when we were home and could know the truth of what the message meant. I knew in my heart that my father was ill.

As we arrived at the front door of our home, my mother rushed out to greet us. She threw her arms around us before we could even get off the donkeys. She was very happy to see the baby.

We climbed down and she smothered us with embraces and kisses and tears. She did not know if the birth had gone well until this moment. She said, "Mary, I have bad news for you. Your father lies dying inside our home. There was an accident and he's hardly able to breathe. He is very ill and has a very short time to live. I want him to forgive you; I want him to truly forgive you before he goes. You know he is a very stubborn man, and he puts great store in his pride. I am hoping that when he sees this baby, he will be moved to open his heart truly to you and the new child. This is my greatest hope, for I have been sad beyond words with the events of the past year. Come now; let us go to your father. It is time."

I took a deep breath and looked at Joseph. At the same time, he took my hand and held it firmly. He then put his arm around me and said, "Mary, I am here with you, I will help you in every way. We can do this together. I am here." I felt the strength of his arm. He always knew when to speak and when not to speak. As a man of so few words, when he did speak, it gave me the grace needed to face the hardships of life with majesty of spirit that I never could have had alone.

Together we entered the house. The three of us as one, a family unit. My father could not help but see us making an entrance in this manner. My mother had entered before us to prepare my father for our arrival. I paused before his bed. His face was ashen gray; his lips were a bluish color. He was having trouble breathing. He was thin and very weak. He was not the father I remembered. I knelt down and very carefully and slowly unwrapped the baby and placed him before my father. The baby squirmed and made little cooing sounds and his little hands and fingers were moving ever so slightly. I said, "Papa, here is our baby. Isn't he beautiful?" At that, Joseph knelt down as well and again we made this picture together of a family unit.

My father just looked saying nothing. There was silence. At last, he lifted himself up on one arm. My mother went behind him to help. He said the following words, "Welcome home. I am glad you are both safe. You have brought forth a healthy baby boy. I bless him and offer words of praise and thankfulness for his life. Mary, my child, I do not have long to live. Can you forgive me for what I have done to you? I have not been a good father and my heart is sad beyond repair. I shall go to my grave...." and then he fell back. My mother was weeping and the baby, too, began to cry. Joseph picked up the child. I went to my father's side and took his hands, kissing them and laying my cheek against them. I could not bear to see him like this; for even though he had hurt me, he still was my father and I loved him. And now he was dying.

As I took his hands and kissed them, I whispered, "I forgive you, Papa. I forgive you, Papa." I am not sure that he heard my words. I felt that it wasn't so much that he wanted to hear me say that I forgave him, although I did say that, but rather for him to say it to me. I believe he left us with a clear heart and that allowed our family to make peace with all that had happened.

There was silence, only the cry of the baby and Joseph rocking to quiet him. My father was breathing very heavily and made groaning sounds as if he were in pain. My mother wiped his brow with a damp cloth. Some other people from the village came in to say their last good-byes to him throughout the rest of the afternoon. We waited; we made a vigil around his bed. Every so often he would open his eyes and say a few words.

Around midnight he left us. We were all gathered there to be with him at the end. He went peaceably. Each of us kissed him in turn and my mother laid a cloth over him until morning. My mother stayed by his side. Joseph lifted me up, for he felt I must rest after the journey and everything that had gone on that day.

An angel came to Joseph and me. The angel was beautiful, with the most peaceful face. The angel spoke and said, "Your father is with us now and he is happy. Know that you will soon leave your village and live elsewhere, for the safety of your family. Your father's spirit watches over you. You will know what to do and where to go from now on. Peace be with you, now and forever more." With that, the angel evaporated. I lay down and Joseph lay beside me. The baby was already asleep in a cradle next to us. We slept.

In the morning there were many preparations made for my father's burial. He was an important and prominent elder of the tribe. Therefore, there were many important ceremonial duties that needed to be performed. It was a day of much confusion and activity, people coming and going. There were rumblings of some political danger nearby; people were gossiping and spreading news that it was not safe for our tribe. There were still many who cast dark, sidelong glances at Joseph and me. Some people were outright cold and turned away when I came near, somehow implying that I had something to do with my father's early death. As always, Joseph was there with his quiet dignity, making his presence known among the tribesmen. Although Joseph was an uneducated and simple man, he understood how to strengthen his position by maintaining a dignified and quiet presence among people who chattered or spoke negatively. Joseph never feared these kinds of people, nor did he allow them to intimidate him or our family. He held his ground, so to speak, but he did it with grace.

The following day my father was laid to rest and the entire tribe came forth to honor him and to eulogize his life. There was much singing and chanting and speeches were made. My mother bore up under it all, but she looked very weary and strained. She was a strong woman, and she knew her duty. Drums resounded and cymbals brightly clashed as they laid him to rest.

By nightfall, all was quiet. The villagers returned to their homes and we to ours. It was quiet in the house and once again my dear Joseph did the right thing. He brought forth an old lute that he had played since childhood. He began to sing a soothing, lyrical song that lifted our spirits and brought life back into the house. It was just me, my mother, Jesus, and Joseph around the fire. The sound of his voice, accompanied by the old lute, at one point caused even mother to join in singing. Again, I learned something that I would never forget—precious moments with loved ones so dear will lift the heart in the darkest moments. The sound of the fire crackling, the baby's soft whimper, the creak of the cradle, and the soothing melody of Joseph's song wrapped us in a robe of love that we wore together.

From that moment on, the four of us were bound together in a way that we had never felt before. Individually, we wore that love like a robe throughout the rest of our lives. It comforted us, each one of us, in times of sorrow and sadness.

CHAPTER
14

You may ask why struggles come when they do or why you have struggled so much. It is the test for all humanity to grapple with fears that keep us away from the light. I chose the words "fears," for I do not want to use the fanciful images of demons. Using those images somehow disassociates the simpler truth that human beings are walking storehouses of fear. These fears separate you and me from God—absolutely nothing more than this. Every day we see the manifestations of fear; they are everywhere. The trial and the test for humanity is to play out these fears, or rather I should say to struggle with these fears, in the search for the simple realization that we are the Light.

It is just as you pass through the darkest night of your fears, that you reach the dawn. It can be frustrating as the night still hovers behind you, even as you can look into the dawn. This is where faith is tested; as you look toward the dawn you are also facing the unknown. Look at this state as an opportunity, the opportunity of a lifetime. You have come to the end of one journey, the darkness hovering behind your back, and now the dawn, the promise of a future, hovers before you. Many slip at this juncture, for their fears outweigh the promise. Know that even if you slip back, you will slip back with greater knowledge. Know that if you go forward, you open the door to the purity of the heart. Every member of humanity faces these moments, it does not matter who they are. They may be kings, they may be farmers, they may be beautiful, powerful women, they may be factory mothers, they may live in China, they may live in Idaho, and every person who walks the earth is joined together in this journey. We do not make light of what this journey entails, for it is always an arduous path.

Once the door is open, the miracles begin to happen. Imagine individual people, who after surviving an anguishing journey, reach the moment where their hand is placed upon the doorknob. Their arm pulls open the door and the light that is their very essence washes over and through them. From that moment begins the promise.

This image must be seen as individual pictures. Perhaps it is a farmer sitting on his tractor, and he opens the door. Perhaps it is a woman with a baby tied to her hip standing in a rice field and she opens the door. Perhaps it is a man sitting in a corporate board room, surrounded by his colleagues and he opens the door. Perhaps it is a mailman, delivering letters, and in one moment he opens the door. Imagine each of these people as a bulb on a string of Christmas lights, each connected, around the earth. A process like this is happening, one by one, the doors are opening. Like a string of Christmas lights, they will light simultaneously. This is the miracle; this is the hope.

After my father died, we stayed to help and comfort my mother. It was a great joy for her to have a grandchild. He was not actually the first grandchild, but he was the one, at his tender age, spending the most time with his grandmother. Something about the little baby's cheerfulness and tenderness helped my mother in those days after my father's death.

Around this time, there began a lot of political upheaval and unrest within the tribe and in the surrounding communities. It became clear that my mother could not live on her own. It was not safe. Joseph was concerned about our welfare as well. We had heard rumors of children having been killed in villages not far from our own. It is difficult to explain the political situation at that time, partly because I was simply not involved in it. I had no understanding of why people would want to harm others. Why, for instance, would someone in a town far away, who did not even know me or my family, want to hurt my baby, or my mother, or my husband? I could not understand this. Joseph tried to explain certain ideas about particular groups of people. Rarely did I ever find myself truly angry, but when he told me of their threats, and of course, I heard the rest of the tribe speak about it, I became angry. I thought about the interconnection of all things; I saw and heard the creatures of the trees and the grasses from the time I was a child. I wanted no part of this way of thinking or doing. My feeling was that, if anyone dared take my baby, then they would have to take me as well, for no one would touch my child without having me to deal with. I think Joseph was amazed at my strength as I told him this, for I had always been so quiet. In this matter, I took my rightful place as a mother.

Let it be clear to all those who hear this story: the strength of a mother's heart is so powerful that men in tanks and airplanes, with suits of armor or metal guns will fall at the feet of a mother. They think they have fought, even won; they continue to think that they are stronger than life itself. I assure you; their door will open yet and they will see.

We soon realized that we had to make preparations for our very survival. We sent my mother to live with her sister, in a small place, so far out of the way that they would be safe during this upheaval. Joseph, Jesus, and I were to leave the area altogether. Before we left, Joseph discussed our plans with his own family. They had taken us in after my mother had gone to her sister. The night before we left, we gathered there for prayers. Joseph's father seemed very saddened at our leaving, but he attempted to hold together the family traditions in the face of our being split apart. That, for me, was the most agonizing aspect of our departure, was seeing this old man, filled with dignity and love for his family and his tribe, seeing him through the force of his will and the depth of his faith, hold the family unit together in the traditional way. He made the prayers, he chanted the songs of praise, he passed the cup, we made our covenant, and we renewed our bond of trust to each other and to the Lord.

I was angry. I felt like a hunted dog. What had I done, a mere, simple woman, with a small babe at my breast? What had I done that I had to flee in the night to save my baby's life? As I said, Joseph had never seen me like this. I had a strength that I believed could have held back armies. I want you, the mothers, to know that this strength is real. The force of that strength has been diminished by the illusion of fear, but that is only an illusion, an illusion that shall evaporate, for life is the clarion call and it will be heard.

Now the time came when we had to move quickly. We gathered our things and there was barely time to say good-bye. We moved out through the night in a hurry.

Joseph was like an animal; all his senses were at the ready to guard us. I knew that he would kill, if need be, something that Joseph would never think to do, something he would be driven to do only by this madness of fear unleashed on an entire people, a fear which continues until this day. We traveled with a sense of fear and foreboding, but we were guided by our belief in the Light. Neither Joseph nor I ever, ever lost our belief in the Light. We clung to it. We held it fast, inside our hearts, and therefore we were guided safely through a perilous countryside.

At last, we came to a place where we were received by distant relatives and other members of our tribe who had moved to this place sometime before. We had developed a network of points of safety, connected by messengers, who went from place to place at great danger to their own lives. I repeat that you cannot know the fear, the animal-like behavior that we were reduced to, simply to survive. Believe it or not, I, Mary, survived because of my anger. It gave me the strength to live through these terrible times.

I saw other mothers cave into the sorrow and the sadness. They were so overcome by grief; I saw their very lifeblood flow out of them as they screamed in agony and misery. It is hard to imagine what it would be to see your baby's throat slit in front of your eyes, and the blood of your child that you brought forth, gush into the very earth itself. The wails and the sound of soldiers' boots were the sounds that people slept through and awoke with. Even though we were in a town that was allegedly safe from the scourges of these despicable soldiers, we had to remain hidden. They were sending scouts to the outlying regions to uncover those who had escaped as we had. I hated these days; I despised this inhumane treatment. It went against everything that I knew to be God.

Now, you may ask me what went through my mind during these times. Did I lose my faith? Did I question the existence of the Light? Did I accuse God of abandoning us, throwing us into a sea of snarling dogs? I tell you, truly, never once, and this may be hard to believe, never once did I lose sight of the Light. I know it to be the very source of all existence. It was my anger that helped me to differentiate between the madness of fear and the utter purity of the Light. I knew somehow that the Light could never be dimmed. I chose to believe that the madness of fear was only a temporary spell that would be broken.

Do not be afraid, my friends, of your emotions. The emotions of strength, that come from a righteous understanding of injustice, will carry you like the wind carries a seed from a flower to another place. That little seedling will land in the middle of nowhere and create new life.

Time passed, and the danger passed as well, leaving the blood of thousands of babies and the tears of thousands of mothers and fathers, many of whom died in agony and anguish with their hearts broken into millions of pieces. But, like the tiny seed that lands in the middle of nowhere, life begins again. We entered a period of relative calm, that is to say, Joseph and I found a place to begin a homelife. Joseph worked as a carpenter. We brought forth more children. Our children were healthy, we had enough food, we were safe from the elements, and even though we kept an ever-observant eye on the political situation, we could sleep at night. By this time, Jesus was four years old. He was a very vigorous, fast-moving child. He seemed to be everywhere at once. With an insatiable curiosity, he wanted to touch, taste, smell, and hear everything. In some ways, he reminded me of myself as a child. He seemed to see and hear the spirits of all living creatures also, just as I had done. Fortunately, I could understand him, whereas the adults I had known had been puzzled and perhaps even fearful of me.

Sometimes, I looked at him and I wondered, where *did* he come from? I had repressed these thoughts so many times, having no answer. It was like a deep memory that would not come fully back into consciousness. I thought of what the angels had said and knew that Jesus was special. The rest eluded me, sometimes teasing my consciousness. I looked at this child, this curious child, and just wondered. You could say I marveled, too, though usually I put these thoughts aside. They would give me a heaviness of spirit and heart, and as there had been enough of that, I preferred not to indulge these feelings to any great degree.

Joseph, on the other hand, was much more accepting, and far less questioning. He was always a sunny, cheerful man, and not particularly contemplative. That is not to say, however, that he was in any way frivolous. Joseph was always prepared in all matters of protection and survival for our family. When there was the possibility of peace and quiet in our home life, he took full advantage of it and enjoyed those moments to the very fullest as a father, husband, and member of the community. Joseph was known for his ability to give thoughtful counsel and many,

many people came to Joseph with their problems to seek his guidance and wisdom. Joseph was always generous in the care that he gave to these people. He sometimes talked to me about their particular situations and together we would discuss them. We prayed together for the Light to manifest in the hearts of these people. We felt this was the best prayer to offer; it allowed the individuals to arrive at the solution from knowledge and light in their own heart, from their own relationship with God.

Joseph always made this belief clear to the people he advised. He, himself, did not have the answer, but, through prayer and heartfelt concentration upon their own hearts, they would receive guidance.

CHAPTER
15

This part of my story took place when Jesus was seven years old. At this age, I took him with me on all of my daily errands and shopping and he accompanied me in performing daily tasks. As he was the oldest child, he would give me a hand carrying various things or occasionally watching the younger children while I went inside a shop or market to get something. Sometimes, he would deliver a message to a neighbor. Sometimes he stayed with his father, but Joseph did not wish to have him around the working men because Jesus had a way of getting under foot. Joseph was worried about his safety with the sawing and hammering and the heavy mallets they used in the carpentry shop. He preferred to have Jesus spend time with me. They had much work to do, and Joseph could not keep his eye on him all the time.

You have to picture Jesus as a very active, you might even say, overactive child. He was absolutely, positively curious about everything. He wanted to know about everything. He would ask me millions of questions, questions I couldn't even begin to give adequate answers to, because I, myself, did not know the answers. He wanted to know everything about the rainfall, for instance. He asked me over and over again where did the rain come from, where did the rain live, and why didn't it rain all the time. He loved the rain and when water poured from the skies, there was no stopping him from running out to jump up and down and play in it, racing around. He picked up things and threw them in the puddles. When the rain stopped, he said that he felt the air speaking to him. He said the air told him how good being washed by the rain felt. He made me laugh with some of the things he came up with. He said the leaves on the olive trees whispered to him about how good they felt after the rain. Now, mind you, I did understand what he meant, because I also heard voices from the grasses and the trees, as I have told you. As I got older, though, I became less and less able to hear those voices I remembered from childhood.

One day he came to me and said, "Mother, the other children are laughing at me. They heard me talking to the leaves. A small group of them were hiding behind something and they overheard me talking to my favorite tree. They began to throw things at me, sticks, stones, and pebbles, calling me names, telling me I was crazy."

As he was telling me this, big tears were welling up in his eyes. He looked at me directly and said, "Mother, is there something wrong with me? I don't feel like the other boys and girls. I do talk to leaves and trees and grasses and flowers and birds, I even talk to the wind, Mother, and I talk to the rain. I talk to the air and to the sun. Mother, what am I to do? Something is wrong with me."

He put his little head down on my lap and cried softly. I knew just how he felt, for I remembered when my uncle had taken me to task for the very same reason. I knew that my words at this moment would shape the way he felt about himself and his specialness. I knew the importance of my words for him at this time in his life. I stroked his hair and allowed him to cry, for I had learned in my own life that it is important to allow the free flow of feeling. I would not deny my little child his feelings; they are real and very serious to a child and, in fact, to anyone at any age. I waited before I spoke. I simply stroked his hair and stayed with him.

At last, he quieted down. I picked him up and held him on my lap, which was something I could not do very often anymore. He would rarely sit still long enough for me to hold him. But, today, he was sitting in my lap like a little angel, with his arm around my neck.

This is what I said to him: "Jesus, there are many beautiful creatures everywhere. Everywhere you look; there is something beautiful and interesting to see. You, my special and beautiful child, see everything. This, dear Jesus, is a gift. You have a gift, a very special gift. It is something that belongs to you and that was given to you by the Lord because he loves you."

He looked at me inquisitively and wrinkled up his nose and replied, "Mother, I am happy for this gift, but those around me are not happy. They think something is wrong with me. They throw things at me and tease me. They won't play games with me. I do not understand this gift, Mother. I thought a gift was to make everyone happy. I don't want this gift, Mother. I don't want it anymore."

He got off my lap at this point and ran out the door. I stood in the doorway watching him run off, feeling a very deep pain. The feeling that a mother has for a child who is in emotional pain is indescribable. I felt helpless, inadequate, and in some way responsible for his pain. I knew that he had inherited these traits from me. On the other hand, I truly saw these abilities as a gift.

It is not easy, my friends who read this story, to know, to see, to feel, or to experience all the beauty of the Light when those around you cannot see it. Many times, we feel utterly alone in situations where we are in tune with the beauty of God's creation in all its minute articulation because those around us may not see it at the same time we do. This is hard. I had this experience and now my son, Jesus, at age seven, had experienced this, too.

Very soon thereafter, Joseph came home from a long day, anxious to wash and have his dinner. When he asked where the children were, I told him what had happened. I also told him of my frustration at not being able to adequately answer Jesus' questions. I told Joseph that I was worried that if Jesus kept going on this way, he might not have friends. He could even develop a reputation that would be harmful to him. Joseph listened quietly and then he spoke. "Mary, my beautiful Mary, our son has a gift. He is sensitive in a way that other children his age are not. Let us embrace his sensitivity. Let us cherish it. Let us hold it close to our heart and thereby nurture his gift. Like a seed planted in the field, his gift needs watering and tending. It will blossom in the right way, have no fear of that. Put your fears aside. I will talk to him later and see what I can do to help."

The next morning, Joseph asked Jesus to accompany him to the carpentry shop. He told Jesus that he needed some special assistance and hoped that his son could help him that day. Jesus was very excited and proud that his father had asked for him to help. They went off together hand in hand.

Later, Joseph told me what transpired. At lunchtime, he and Jesus had gone for a short walk near the shop to eat their lunch together underneath the trees. Joseph told Jesus. "My son, I am very proud of you. I see that you are an observant young man with an intense curiosity about all things. This is admirable and pleases me greatly. I encourage you to keep your mind and heart open to all living things, regardless of what other people may say, for you my son, have a tender and sensitive heart and you must cherish this and hold it dear and close to you. You shall come to know, dear son, many things because you have cherished the tenderness of your heart. I know how much you love the leaves of this tree under which we sit. I know you hear its voice. I know how much you love all the living creatures around you. Someday soon you will find that kind of love in the people around you. What you have learned from the leaves and the air and from the rain and the sun will teach you about the hearts of the people around you." When he finished telling him this, Joseph scooped Jesus up and hugged him very hard and said, "Come on now, let's go back to work!"

It was in this way that we, together, helped Jesus through his first, I suppose you would say, emotional crisis. After that, we both observed Jesus finding ways to talk to the bullies who had been teasing him. Somehow, he managed on his own, to find ways to win them over one by one. We watched this and looked at each other with a smile of warmth and understanding. Together, as a unit, we had been able to help our son.

Once again, Joseph had taught me something I never forgot. He chose to love and enhance a quality within a person that very easily could have been punished with harsh words and fearful demeanor. He could have stricken this beauty from our child. It would never have occurred to Joseph to punish Jesus, or to suggest that he try to be a different way to make the other boys like him. He provided a light from the outside. As Jesus looked to Joseph's example, he saw the beauty and the truth of his own light as it was embraced and reflected back to him. In his wisdom, Joseph had seen that encouraging these qualities would brighten and enhance the inner light of our child. That is what had happened. Although I understood what Jesus was going through, from experience, it was Joseph's beautiful wisdom that gave Jesus permission to be himself.

It was after this incident that our little boy began to blossom and to take his rightful place among the other children and within himself. My love for Joseph increased a thousandfold; I was overcome with awe at his wisdom. I made a prayer of thanks that I was blessed with a husband so wise and kind, so good-humored and hardworking, and who was so deeply thoughtful in all things. I cannot express to you the wonder of my life with Joseph. In all things that were to come, Joseph was my anchor and my helpmate. I knew that I was a woman blessed and I gave thanks to the Lord for this magnificence in my life.

Please know the significance of loving and embracing all those who cry out in fear, hurt, anguish, bewilderment, puzzlement, confusion, and despair. Embrace and love them, by doing so it releases the inner light of the person. As this released light begins to shine forth and is reflected back to them, they become whole. Punishments, words of recrimination, words that generate fear, threats, physical abuse, mental and emotional torment, all these kill the light within. It will blacken their hearts; it will squeeze the very blood from their veins. What they send forth will be darkness and despair, a river of fear. And that will be reflected back to them, and their light will be dimmed, darkened, and sometimes extinguished. The sadness generated from this cycle is felt by every leaf, by every molecule of the air, by every living entity. Each feels the dimming and the extinguishing of light. We need to learn, very simply, how to love.

My message is to teach and to show the art of expanding the capacity and the breadth of love. It may appear that the task is too great or that it is impossible to erase the fear-motivated cruelty that runs rampant over the earth. I assure you that there is nothing impossible in love's light. I assure you that lights dimmed, blackened, and extinguished have only been so in appearance. This light that appears to be gone in so many places, I assure you, will shine brilliantly in each and every one of you, each and every one of you. The love that I am talking about is so great and magnificent that each and every one of you will know this light. It is your gift; hear the music of that gift.

CHAPTER
16

*T*he time is now here for the bearers of light to step forward and become known. Many who have suffered in darkness are now ready to open their hearts to the light. They suffer now, even as we speak, for they do not know what it is that they are looking for, they do not know the path out of the darkness. They remain isolated and alone, frozen in fearful anticipation of what is to come next. They long for a way out of their circumstances. That is why it is time for the lightbearers to step forward, to become known and to light the path so that others see the way to the heart of love and fulfillment.

Rest assured that these lightbearers are being guided to build bridges upon which the path of light will travel. There are many who have patiently listened to the quiet within their own hearts, even while experiencing their own difficulties and daily struggles. They have heard the call and have prepared for the coming of love's demonstration. For as I have said before, there is a revolution taking place and continuing to take place around the world. It is a revolution of inner knowledge and the embodiment of the light of the heart. All beings living at this time are lightbearers, and in time, each of them will know all that they are. The world has been brought to a crossroads, where the choice of what path to take will become clear. No matter what atrocities have occurred in the past, in the present, or which lie in the minds of those who walk in darkness waiting to inflict them upon the innocent and unsuspecting, they will never take away the magnificence of life itself. For now, a way appears out of the cycle of atrocity.

Many people believe there is no way out, that these things are inevitable, but I tell you there is another way. Suffering is not inevitable, and things are about to change. The vision of love, which the Holy Father created, will manifest. The magnificent artistry of that vision requires those believers of love and light to assist in that manifestation. We are all intertwined and part of one magnificent vision. Those who sit in fear and darkness, who work so hard and fight so desperately against joining the giddiness and lightness and lovingness and laughter-filled joyousness of the light-bearers, will be coaxed, gently prodded, and brought forth by the loving arms and gentle whispers of love-filled messages that move with the wind around their heart.

They shall be drawn ever so gently, step by step, with one foot placed in front of the other, onto the path of love. Make no mistake, there is no going back; we have come very far, and this mission will be accomplished. Do not be fooled, we are not without strength and majesty of spirit because we speak of love and light. Love is not small. Love is not weak. Love is not a quiet voice. Love knows all things. Love's voice is louder than any thunder that rages through the universe. Love's arms reach over mountains, down through valleys, and over the waters of the ocean to reach and wrap themselves around all living things. Let me assure you that love's strength is the greatest just when it appears to be stamped out. When you are surrounded by the hundreds of thousands of examples and images of despair in your world, love is at its greatest strength. You might ask me, "How can that be? How is that possible? How can love be at its greatest strength when it appears to be stamped out?"

That is the genius of love. This is a very difficult concept for those living now to comprehend. Love is so great that it allows the darkness to overtake it, with the full knowledge that it can never be overtaken entirely. You see, love is so great, and indeed there is only love, that even darkness fulfilled is held within love itself.

I understand that this concept requires illustration and that there will be many questions concerning this idea. I bring it forth at this time because there is energy about these ideas floating around in fragmentary forms; those who are ready will be happy to receive this information for it will assist them in piecing together their thoughts. How few understand the word, idea, concept, realization, and manifestation of love. I'm sure that if you asked many people to name all the things that they could talk about in detail or know a great deal about, the word "love" would rarely, if ever, be mentioned. It is simply not understood or practiced. This will change.

In those days as Jewish people, we lived outside the majority of the population. We were considered outsiders; we were not respected as part of the established order. We were different; we had our own customs, our own language, and our own religion. We were foreigners wherever we lived. We did not own our land. We settled in places and when the ruling people decided they wanted this land or wanted to use it for some other purpose, then we were no longer allowed to be there, and they would raid our villages and chase us out by violent means. When these attacks happened, they were totally by surprise. It was better for these ruling people to kill us and burn us out, because if they just moved us, then we would still be on their land and in their way. So as long as we were in a place where they didn't see us or when we were on a piece of land that wasn't valuable to them, we were safe; but when they wanted that piece of land, they wasted no time in attacking us and driving us out. So in the case of our village, word came at the last minute and only the strong ones were able to move quickly. Joseph was able to get us out, but those who were weak, sick, and elderly, or those who didn't have fast horses were not able to leave. That is why it was so hard for me because my friends and neighbors didn't have the capacity to escape. We were young, and Joseph knew these terrible things could happen and he was good in making preparations in his mind, for them when they did happen.

Joseph came running home from the carpentry shop. He was in a great deal of distress and told me we were to gather our things, call the children together, and leave immediately. I asked him what was wrong, and what had happened that we would need to flee. I resisted and said to him, "I don't have the strength to do this! Please, Joseph, must we go?" He took my arms and squeezed them. Looking into my eyes, he said, "Mary, we must go now!" I did not ask him any more questions; I took action, gathering up essential things and putting them into baskets as quickly as I could. I had an ominous feeling and was choking back tears. I couldn't bear the thought of running again with the children, of being without a household, of trying to find another safe place. It was almost too much for me to bear.

Joseph was outside gathering the horses, taking enough feed for them, filling up water bags. I had no idea what was going on. I gathered up all four children. Jesus was the oldest at age nine; there were the two girls and one younger boy. The children were asking me questions—all except Jesus. He saw my emotional condition and as he was becoming a mature young man, he understood immediately that there was trouble. He threw his little arms around me in an attempt to comfort me and to give me strength. He looked into my face and said, "Mama, it will be all right. I promise you." He kissed my hands and then he ran outside to help Joseph with the animals.

I scooped up the children and the baskets and the bundles. By this time Joseph had prepared three horses. Jesus and his sister rode on one horse, Joseph took the youngest son, and I took the youngest daughter. There wasn't a single wasted action. Joseph was curt and every gesture, every movement that he made was intended to get us out of there quickly. He yelled, "Children, pull yourselves together. Don't look back, for we have work to do. We must ride quickly. We must move fast. We can do it and we must stay together. We must concentrate—let's go!"

Away we went as fast as possible on our horses, moving across the plains with the children hanging on for dear life. Even while riding at this swift pace, we heard an awful noise behind us. We saw that the village was being set on fire. The flames, the screams, the sounds of horror were everywhere. We did not look back for long; we didn't have to look at all, as the sound of it was enough to tell us what was happening. I saw the arms of the children grasping even harder to one another. They knew the danger we had escaped.

We rode as hard and as fast as we could. Joseph led the way on his horse and set the pace for us to follow. We rode for what seemed to be hours. Joseph was intent on getting as far away as humanly possible. We came to a river that was too wide and too deep for us to cross. We rode along the bank, hoping to find a shallow area. Joseph felt that it was essential that we continue on in this direction, even though it was getting dark, and the journey had been a lot for the children to handle. He simply said, "Now, children, we are all looking for a good place to cross the water. Let us all look together. Whoever sees a place first, call out." Once again, I was in awe of Joseph's ability to pull the family together and even make a game out of our very survival. Joseph was truly a great man among men. My love and admiration for him grew and grew.

Before long, one of the children did cry out, "There Papa, there's a place we can cross." Sure enough there was a place, and Joseph said, "Yes, you are right! This is a good place to cross. I will go first and behind me Jesus, and Mother will follow. Here we go." He took his horse into the water first to test it, to make sure it was safe. We managed to cross the water, one by one, and reach the other side safely.

As we climbed up the embankment to the other side, Joseph turned to all of us and said, "I am proud of each of you, we have done well. You have concentrated and used your energy in a good way. I know you may be tired and very hungry, but we must ride further. I know you can do it. Let's take a moment to thank God for bringing us safely to this point. We have the Lord to thank for our arrival here." Then, Joseph sang a song of thanks and praise. The children joined in, and it seemed to revive everyone, including myself. I kept seeing the faces of my friends and loved ones in the village. As I was thinking about them, I looked up and saw Joseph staring at me. He said, "Mary, my love, we are alive, and we must carry news of this attack to those who need to know. It is our duty to carry on. I love you and I cherish our family. I know you will have the strength to carry on." He called the children closer and told each of them to take a small piece of bread and to taste each bite, savor each bite, swallow it down and give thanks for the bread that would give us all the strength to ride farther. In a short while Joseph motioned for us to leave, and away we went. Joseph had an uncanny ability to judge the amount of time that any particular task would take. When that time was completed, he immediately began the next task at hand, without hesitation or lengthy transition. He simply began and we followed him in complete faith, never questioning his judgment or abilities.

We rode and rode for what seemed forever. At last, we came to a small village, actually much more of an encampment than the village where we had been living. We had known about this place for some time. Never knowing when it would be necessary to flee suddenly, Joseph, throughout our entire lives, always made certain that he knew the safe havens, how far away they were, and how to get there. I can say truly that if it had not been for Joseph's abilities and wisdom, I would not have survived. After a point, I did not have the strength to plan and prepare for these events.

You never knew when these events would take place and so after many of them, our tribes became more prepared to protect ourselves and we developed what we called soldiers. These were men who were trained to get word, to follow the ruling people. We had spies to learn when our enemies wanted our land, then we developed enclaves in out of the way places which the Romans did not value, where we would have what we called safe havens. So many of us had been killed, and there were so many times when we did not know what was going to happen. We always had to live on the alert. I understand so well the terrible genocide and the terrible things that are happening all around the world in your time. When that village was burned, Joseph and I and our children were young, and we had the strength to run for our lives. But many of the people of the village did not have the strength, so even if they had been warned they could not have managed to escape.

As I told you, when Jesus was a baby and we fled, my anger gave me the strength to survive that incident. In this case, I was overcome by emotion, knowing that my friends and probably most of the village had perished. It was only through Joseph's strength that we lived. Had it been up to me alone, I don't think I could have been able to escape.

These were my thoughts as we rode into the encampment. Immediately people came to greet us. They were aware of what had happened. Almost without words, they gathered us together. These devastating incidents were so common in our lifetime. In order for people to survive them emotionally, they spoke very little about them. Communication through the eyes, the touching of hands, made it so that no one had to exchange long and lengthy descriptions of events. So many people had had loved ones murdered in front of their eyes. It was not necessary to talk, but rather to comfort each other. In many ways, words were too much to bear.

We were gently received, and our hosts knew that we needed to eat something and go to sleep immediately. Our horses needed water and food and we all needed to know that we could sleep in safety. All of this was communicated and given to us. It was clear there were our soldiers guarding every inch of this encampment. The word had spread, prior to our arrival, of the massacre of our village. Joseph, in his wisdom, knew that it was important for us to sleep well. By sunrise we would need to know what to do next. He did not, therefore, engage in any lengthy discussions with the other men, and instead went right to sleep.

This incident was very hard on me. I had grown to love the village where we had lived and had believed that we were truly safe there—how wrong I was. I prayed, "Oh most Holy Lord, I am sad beyond compare. My heart cries out. I am afraid. Oh Lord, fill me with your love. I know your love will never leave me and that although it feels as if it were gone, I know in the deepest part of my heart, your love is even stronger now. I don't know how I know this. I don't even know why I believe this; I only know that you are there. I can hear you whispering to me not to lose heart in this dark hour. I thank you, oh Lord, that we are alive, that my children are with me and that my husband is here. I praise you and hold fast to the promise of your love's total fulfillment."

With that prayer, I fell into a deep sleep.

Beloved children, please take the time to wrap your arms around your own heart, to love and cherish the light in you and know that it is God's light. For your happiness is a journey inward. Where it becomes a conflict and source of frustration for many, is the mistaken belief that it comes from somewhere outside of you. There is a tendency for some of you, my children, to want something supernatural to land at your feet with some inscription written upon it. This is not what really happens. When you find yourself wanting something to tell you, to show you, to direct you even, take those thoughts and turn them inward. Ask your own heart, through prayer, to give you the light that you seek. The love you carry within you is so great, simply know that. Know that the love you feel for others is the love that you are. You are that love; that is you.

Perhaps some of you believe that it is somehow not right for you to feel love for yourself the same way that you love others. You must see that this idea constricts the totality of the meaning behind the word "love." Many people wish to limit, define, and cast their own interpretation on the totality of love. We assure you this is not possible, for love is all things. All living things, all energy, everything in the universe is made of the substance of love. You can use the word light as well. Much effort is spent by many, many people who wish to put their stamp of approval, if you will, on the meaning of "love." Recognize that you are already love; see it, believe it, embrace it, and breathe in the substance of life, which promises you everything. Perhaps the promise of everything glitters so brightly and brilliantly that the fear which controls so many of you will not allow you to take it in. We understand this. We see it as a process of building the bridges and lighting the light, one by one, step by step.

CHAPTER 17

The next morning, Joseph and I awoke early. I don't think either of us slept very well. For me, I had slept fitfully, alternating between dreams of floating in water and nightmares of running from a burning fire. I felt close to giving up. To be truthful, I surprised even myself; I had not realized that I could fall so completely into the feeling of despair and anguish. I could not erase memories of the faces or voices of my friends and loved ones from our village. I felt guilty that we had survived. I could not understand why we had lived and others had perished. I felt sick to my stomach. I felt weak and even dizzy.

Joseph saw that I was suffering. He put his arms around me and held me tenderly. He did not speak, but held me close and allowed his breathing and the beating of his heart to communicate what could not be put into words. As he held me, I found myself remembering moments from my childhood. I saw myself running through the meadow, playing in the grass, seeing all the spirits and creatures, just as I had once seen them as a child. As he held me, his breath and his heart helped me to strengthen my own breathing and the beating of my own heart. He took my face into his hands, and he looked into my eyes and he said, "Mary, you are the very essence of life itself. I cherish you with all that I am. My love for you goes higher than the stars and deeper than the waters of the ocean. I need you, Mary. The children need you. You must trust the path that has been put before us. We must walk upon that path together, for we have made a sacred vow to each other. I need you, Mary, I need you to believe and to carry on. I know we can do this together." Then he kissed me, and in that moment, it was as if a fire had been lit inside of me. My own life, which had begun to dim and fade out, flared up, charged up and I felt the energy and the life-force flowing through my veins again.

I looked at Joseph, took his hands and said, "I will never leave you. Let us go forward now, together. I am ready. I can do it." All of a sudden, Joseph smiled. He lifted me up, lifted me off my feet, twirled me around and began laughing. He said, "Mary, Mary, Mary, how wonderful you are!" He kissed me again. With each kiss, and each embrace, I felt the fire inside of me growing stronger and stronger.

He said, "Get the children ready. Let them eat, while I speak to the others. We need to make preparations. I will return with a plan." He took my hand and kissed my fingertips, just as he had done on the day that he told me that we would be married. That day, I knew that my life had been spared, because of Joseph's love. Now, once again, I knew that because of Joseph's love I would live.

It was then that I realized that though we think, believe, and act as though we are by ourselves, the truth is that we are intertwined, one with another. We are not alone, ever. Joseph taught me that love can restart the heartbeat and imbue another person with the breath of life. How is that done? Through love, my friends. Our son, Jesus, in later years, healed many people of leprosy, mental illness, and spiritual sadness, through the same mechanism by which Joseph healed me.

The children woke up and were very hungry. To them, this was an exciting adventure and so, in spite of myself, I became caught up in their enthusiasm. Their little faces, their questions, and their loving arms around my neck brought the light dancing back into my eyes. They were so tender and joyous and innocent.

Before long, Joseph returned. He said that it was wise for us to stay in the camp; things had died down, but traveling was still ill-advised. He assured me that according to the scouts and seasoned protectors of the tribe's system of communication, we were in the safest place that we could possibly be at this time.

Later in the day, there was to be a gathering for prayers, chanting, and communal grieving. There were to be prayers for the souls of the dead, and prayers of praise and thanks. It was our custom to pray in praise and thanksgiving, even in the darkest of hours. Until then, Joseph suggested that the children go off and play with the other children of the tribe and for me to relax, to take a walk, or visit some of the other women. In fact, he had learned that there was someone there who knew my mother. Joseph took me to be with her while he continued discussions with the other men.

We stayed in that place for almost a month. It was a strange feeling for me; I never could settle down there and I was the kind of person who needed familiar surroundings to quiet my heart. All during that month, I was nervous and edgy, very much unlike myself. I felt neither here nor there. I was rootless, without a real home. It had been a long time since I had seen my mother, who now was quite old. It seemed as if one day went by and then another and then another, all without meaning. It was very hard.

Then one day, Joseph came into the tent and said, "Mary, we have received word. We are going to move on to another area, a far distance from where we are now. There is a larger community with soldiers who will protect us. We can go there and establish a home. The children have had a month to rest and grow stronger; they will be able to manage the trip. Once we are in our new home, we can settle down again and live in peace. Don't worry for our safety. Others are joining us to make this trip, and we have seasoned soldiers accompanying us across the plains. We will be safe. We must leave early in the morning, after a good night's rest. Let us call the children together, tell them the plan, and give thanks and praise to the Lord for protecting us."

Joseph gathered the children together in a circle, as we always did; both Joseph and I offered prayers of thanks and praise. We all sang together, which the children loved; it seemed to unify and comfort them. They felt a part of something. They would snuggle up to each other and to us. It was very warm and comforting.

The next morning, we made our way across the plains. Joseph had predicted that it would take four or five days of travel, perhaps even longer, depending on the weather. He prepared the children by giving them things to think about and little tasks to do, which helped to focus their concentration and kept them interested in the journey.

Before we left, I made a last visit to the old woman with whom I had become very close. In some ways she reminded me of my mother. She had dignity and wisdom that I longed for. In her face and in her eyes was a clarity of vision that seemed to be unshakable. I remember her saying to me, "Mary, my child, I am old, and I have seen many things, many things that I do not understand and will never understand. But Mary, I know that these mysteries are a dance of wonder and intrigue, and that it is not necessary to know or understand all things. We are asked only to listen, to hear, to see, to feel, to cherish, and to remember the important moments. It is the wise one who knows what to remember." As she said this, she placed in my hand a small, beaded bracelet. She said, "This is for you, Mary, each bead represents a moment to remember. When you wear this bracelet, you will remember me and my words. We will never see each other again, but you will remember." She leaned over and kissed each of my cheeks. I took her hands and kissed them, placing them against my forehead and bowing to her in reverence. Although I did not completely comprehend the depth of her meaning at that time, I knew that she was giving me a gift that I could perpetually contemplate and consider. With this experience I began to grow as a human being. Until this experience, I was a follower. After this, I began to lead with my own heart.

The more I thought about what the old woman had said, the more I understood about patience and forgiveness. Just as in nature, there is a season for everything; there is also a season for hearts to heal. We cannot know all things, and that can be a liberating and at the same time, frustrating reality. It is the wise one who knows what to remember, what to see, and what to know. Therein, what appears to be mysterious becomes clear. Although we do not understand every action, there is a way through anything, and this is what each and every person is learning.

At this time, there are many things occurring that will quicken the process of the heart's flower opening to those who have hurt or harmed us on a personal basis. As each hurt is healed, it is possible for more and more healing to take place. Like a stone dropped in the water, the ripples go out and out and out. What is a difficult, if not impossible concept for those who exist at this time to understand, is the incredible potential for love that perpetually exists within every heart of every living being. Even when a person who someone has loved has also hurt them deeply, love is still present within both of them. That is the mystery and the majesty. For I assure you once again, the healing I speak of, in the form of an overall opening of the heart, is a manifesting reality that will bring forth a new day. There is no turning back. The promise is here, but there is much to be done.

CHAPTER 18

We traveled to the distant village, our whole family, along with numerous other families and the soldiers. We felt that we could begin new lives here in relative safety. I use the term "relative safety," because seemingly no matter what we did or where we lived, there was to be an ever-present concern for the safety of our community. But as I told you before, as I experienced anger and despair, ultimately, I also experienced growth-producing realizations about myself from living through these experiences of being hunted down.

Many people, regardless of what time period they live in, suffer similar experiences. The old woman who gave me the bracelet set off inside me a spark that ignited a deeper sense of myself: myself in relation to other people, both close family members and friends, as well as the outer world. On this journey to new land, I began to hear a deeper voice inside of me, calling me to listen more intently, to my deeper thoughts, to trust in my own counsel, and to feel stronger and more courageous. After our village was burned to the ground, I faced a crossroads within myself that only on this journey was I able to look at in some detail. I now realized that I had come to a fork in the road, wherein I had made a decision to live despite the uncertainty in our lives and to go on, to persevere in believing, in hoping for the vision, which somehow we all know exists, even if it has not yet been fully manifested.

I made the decision to live. Even though I had desires to let go , to give up, I listened to my inner voice, and I relied upon the love of my husband and children to support and encourage me. But it was *my* decision to go on.

As we rode across the desert plains, and as I looked before me and around me and listened to the *clip-clop* of the animals' persevering feet moving forward to carry us to a new land, I knew that I had made the right decision. With that realization, I found myself uplifted, and even felt my shoulders and body physically lift up. My chin raised with greater dignity, for I had chosen life. I had chosen a life of good things to come, not of bitterness, despair, or anger at the lot that so far had been presented to us. I believed that life would enfold just as it was meant to.

In partnership with the powerful voices of light and hope inside me, this was a turning point in my life. During this journey, many thoughts came back to me. I remembered the angel who had told me as a young girl that I had been chosen for the purity of my heart and that my life was laid out before me like stepping stones over a small creek and that I had only to step upon the stones, one by one. I remembered those words, and renewed my courage and faith that indeed this band of people was following the path of stepping stones, one in front of the other, into a new life, a new land. I felt good, I felt content. When night drew nigh and we stopped for a rest, I gathered my children in my arms and lay by my husband's side in peaceful tranquility with this certain knowledge. Before, I had still felt like a girl, but on this journey, I reached womanhood quietly and through contemplation and deep counsel with myself.

As I lay there, I looked at the starry sky above me. The air was cool and crisp. The only sounds were the sounds of animals moving about; otherwise, it was perfectly quiet. I took a breath and feeling so at peace, I prayed: "Oh, holy and radiant light of love that lives inside me now, that comes from You, the holiest one, I rejoice in the radiant illumination of thee and praise the magnificence of your stars that glimmer and gleam throughout the entire universe for all to see. I rejoice and sing praises for my life and my children's lives and my husband's life and all living beings. Oh, beautiful light, I am yours."

The next day, we arrived in the new land. It was a good place to be, was protected by a mountain, although not a huge one, on one side and a river on the other, which provided us with much-needed water and additional protection. As soon as I saw this terrain, I felt fortunate that all of us had made it through the journey safely.

We lost no time in each family finding an area that suited them; somehow that process happened naturally. There was no arguing or debating over who should have which piece of land. We each followed our natural instincts and somehow it all worked out quite equitably. The elders asked us to unpack our things and to convene later in the center of our newly created village to give thanks, to sing praises, and to honor the holy Lord for bringing us here safely. These community gatherings of celebration, thanks, and honoring were essential rituals of our tribe, not only for our physical survival but also for our emotional survival and healing. As we came together as a community in the heart of the village, we felt bound and connected to all other members of our tribe. If there was any heaviness of heart or those of broken spirit, we were able to recognize those emotions and to lay hands upon our friends and neighbors, to assist them and help them in their hour of need.

Our son, Jesus, was very sensitive to those in need. Both Joseph and I observed this tenderness in him, even as a child. At this ceremony, there was another boy about the same age as Jesus. He had been saved from the village by a quick-thinking neighbor, but his parents had perished. This child was now an orphan. Jesus discovered this. At the end of the ceremony Joseph and I were walking with the other children, and we saw Jesus comforting the boy. As it was a private moment, we stayed back so as not to interfere. The child was crying, and Jesus was sitting by his side, holding his hand and every so often, placing his hand on the boy's head. We observed that Jesus allowed the child to cry as many tears as he needed. Jesus did not attempt to shush him or to explain anything away. He simply sat with him and listened. We decided to walk by; we felt that Jesus was able to handle this and that when the time was right, he would come to us. We returned to our tent. In a little while, Jesus came home. He came to Joseph and me and, without a word, hugged us tightly. His embrace communicated something to me that I had never felt from him before.

He said, "Mother, Father, I met a little boy whose parents were killed in the village raid. His heart is sad and lonely. He grieves for the loss of his mother and father. I listened to him, Mother. I felt his tears, Father. I comforted him as best as I could. I promised him that I would be his friend and that we would play together, and he could come and visit us. I prayed that his parents would be happy in God's love. I told him that they were watching over him and that brought a smile to his face. I don't know how I know that—it just came to me so that is what I told him."

We both leaned forward and hugged him, simultaneously. He then said, "I love you both, I don't understand why it is I have a mother and father while he doesn't have his parents. Why is that? I do not understand." He looked at us both with a very quizzical face, asking one of those questions that children have a right to ask but are terribly difficult to answer. It was Joseph who replied.

He said, "My son, you ask a very deep and important question. I must tell you the truth, for I love you and honor you. I truly do not know the answer to your question. However, this would be my suggestion to you, to all of us: Let us pray about this question, individually and together. Let us think upon this question and take time to reflect. We will discuss it again. Let us see what comes to our hearts and minds as we ponder it. In the meantime, my son, I want you to know that it is all right to not always know the answer. It is quite all right to ask a question and to meditate, pray and ponder it with others who are doing the same."

Little Jesus looked at Joseph for a long time without saying a word and then he said, "Father, I hear your words. You have spoken to me honestly and sincerely. I wanted you to give me the answer and instead you have shown me how to seek the answer. Thank you, wise Father." He hugged and kissed us both before crawling next to his brother and sisters to sleep.

CHAPTER
19

This may come as a surprise to you, but the most important person that you can reach is yourself. You may have some resistance to uncovering your deepest motivations and feelings. However, it is only through the deepest journey inside of one's being that the light needed to reach others is found. You may feel frustrated at this time because you want results that you are not prepared for. You want to jump over the fence before you are big and strong enough to do it. Take time to quietly and truthfully acknowledge to yourself, in some detail, the strides you have already gained. Look at each one, lovingly and carefully, so that you may understand your own growth. Then, ask yourself, what does my heart ask me to pay attention to, that I am running away from? By worrying about the reality of others, it is easy to deflect the important issues within your own growth, within your own heart. You want to rush ahead and do more, more, more but by so doing, you miss the beauty of the present. You miss the depth of experience and feeling of the now. Not only that, but it helps to submerge any pressing feelings that may be knocking at your heart's door.

Imagine this: You are standing in a field of freshly plowed earth. Your feet are burrowed deeply into the dirt, the sky rises above you, you are breathing deeply, your shoulders and arms hang freely, even as your feet are planted, rooted firmly and deeply in the earth. You stand there in the field, your chest and shoulders wide open and you exude and breathe in and out the feelings of being grounded and knowing joy. Is it difficult to imagine this? In this picture, you have tended and nourished the earth, field, and sky that is you. You have *watered your own seeds, feelings, and thoughts. Therefore, you stand firmly, joyfully and in a state of thankful and grateful satisfaction. Well-developed habits of moving forward too quickly happen because it conveniently takes the focus off the deeper (and in some cases painful) feelings which you still need to explore and have been put aside. It is necessary to allow yourself to live moment by moment in the now. This can be a hard thing to do. While you are moving too quickly, or inversely staying stuck in the past, the whole experience of the present goes by. And you wonder why am I not happy? Why do I not feel satisfied? Why am I not doing more? We wish for you to know that this is an illusion. It is not your truth. You have allowed it to become your truth, but indeed, it is not your truth. We send you love and light and courage that you may follow the present yearnings, feelings, desires of your heart in the present, in the now, moment to moment. You can do this, you can. It will require a planting of the feet down in the earth and tending ever faithfully to yourself. Don't run from yourself, it is a hopeless endeavor. You are not alone; there are many others, all around the planet, who spend their precious lives at too hectic a pace. They are miserable and do not know why.*

Begin with your own light. Feel the beauty and magnificence of that light, cherish it, nourish it, nurture it and you will soon see how that light will permeate far-reaching circles.

Understand as I continue my story, I will tell how my son, Jesus, went into the deepest parts of himself and only through this process were his thoughts, ideas, and depth of feeling, communicated to many others.

The time came when Jesus was turning eleven years old; this is an important time for a young man in our religion. Boys his age studied the ancient law, learned the rituals of the Elders, and spent hours in prayer and contemplation. On a daily basis, Jesus, along with the other young men, were tutored by the Rabbis. Jesus, as I told you before, always asked a million questions. He questioned everything and as he questioned, he also thought deeply.

You have to understand something about human nature and that is simply this—people in high places do not always appreciate challenging questions, especially the millions of challenging questions from a child. Jesus developed a reputation for being a rebellious troublemaker.

It started out slowly at first. The Rabbi would stop by our home and in a smiling, slightly joking way would say that Jesus had disrupted the lessons by asking too many questions and by putting forth his own points of view. It was clear to Joseph and me that he was asking us to somehow squelch this enthusiasm in our son.

After one such visit, Joseph and I sat down to discuss this matter, for both of us took it quite seriously. Joseph said, "Mary, I must tell you that I am rather surprised about what I just heard from the Rabbi. I did not expect him to discourage a young boy's inquisitive mind. I feel somewhat at a loss as to what to do in this situation."

I looked at Joseph; he was rarely at a loss for ideas on any particular subject and I realized that this was a critical moment for him, as a man. Caught between the leadership of the village's religious community and his feelings regarding his own son, he was wondering how this conflict would reflect upon himself. I understood these feelings, as I was a woman and not as involved in the politics of the village's leadership, I could more easily side with Jesus without reservation.

I answered, "Dear husband, I see a spider web in which we are all ensnared. On one hand, you and I, together, fervently believe in the inquisitive mind of our son. Neither one of us would ever wish to dampen his curiosity." Joseph nodded his head in agreement. "On the other hand, however, it is clear that the Elder Rabbis—dare I say this, Joseph—seem to be threatened by the young boy's questions. How is this possible? He is only a child." We looked at each other and quite honestly, in that moment, I had a sense that this was only the beginning of many conversations. At the very least, as we sat across from each other at the table, we both sensed that this would not be resolved quickly or easily.

I said to Joseph, "Perhaps it is wise for us to tutor Jesus here at home, where he may have the opportunity to ask his questions. We can discuss things together and by so doing, when he goes to his classes, he will not ask so many questions." Even as I said that, both Joseph and I laughed. We knew that there was no stopping his questions, especially when he sought to receive the answers from people who supposedly knew the answers.

Joseph shook his head, "Mary, I don't know what to do. For the first time I feel angry at the Elders. I see nothing wrong, personally, with my son asking any questions that come to him. Perhaps we should bide our time, say nothing, do nothing and see what happens. I cannot in good conscience ask my son to inhibit his mind's natural curiosity." I agreed that this was the best course of action.

A day or two later, Jesus came home looking upset, so I asked him what was wrong. He sat down and said, "The Elders refuse to answer my questions. They cut me off before I even finish. They ask me to be quiet; they tell me that I am disturbing the other boys' learning. I am a good student. I read and study and think and pray. My questions come from my heart. I thought we could all discuss them, the way we do here at home. They don't seem to want me to think or to question. They only want me to memorize the Law and to repeat it back as it is written. This I can do; I have memorized the Law. I have learned every word, but in so doing, questions have come into my mind. Besides, I see people's faces and I observe people's experiences. These Laws do not always answer or explain them."

Having told us all of this, he broke into tears. We allowed him to cry, and we made no attempt to comfort him. His tears were tears of frustration, confusion, and anger. In a short time, he wiped his tears away. "Mother and Father," he said, "I must listen to the Holy Father, my real father, for it is he whose voice I hear inside of me. I must listen to his words." Joseph and I sat in silence. What was there to say to such clear-headed understanding coming from an eleven-year-old boy? Joseph broke the silence, "Let us pray. Oh, Holy and miraculous voice, heart, and mind, we pray together for your deepest wisdom, to open our hearts and minds and the hearts and minds of the Elders. We pray that they will hear and see your light, its greatest majesty, and that we may grow individually and as a community through honest study and discussion. Be with us, most Holy One, and shine your Light upon our each and every step that we may walk closer, ever closer to Thee. We give thanks and praise. Amen." Jesus got up and he came to each of us and hugged us, resting his head on our shoulders before leaving the room.

Joseph took my hand. Looking into my eyes, he said, "Mary, our son is special. We have known this from the beginning. We cannot hold back the powerful waterfall of his growth and even though it will cause controversy, we cannot do anything to control, or stop the free flow of his heart and mind. These gifts are great forces, and we would only do ourselves and our child harm by tampering with them. Therefore, it is our duty to allow Jesus to unfold unhindered. I will go tomorrow and discuss what exactly has been going on with the Rabbis further. I feel, Mary, that this is not something to be taken lightly."

I nodded my head and said, "Yes, I agree with you entirely. We must face this issue together. This is not something small."

I lifted up the candle and as we held hands, I blew the candle out.

CHAPTER 20

Jesus continued his studies after the conference. With Joseph there was an increased if temporary calm regarding our son's activities. For a time, Joseph and I felt that all was well and that whatever fears or concerns that the Rabbi had when he spoke with us had been resolved. However, this was not the case. Once again, we were visited by the Rabbi. He requested that we come to the temple and meet with all of Jesus' teachers. We were to gather to determine what was to be done regarding Jesus' questions and preaching that apparently disturbed the young men's lessons.

Joseph and I went directly to the temple where we were greeted and asked to go into an inner chamber along with our son's Rabbi and the scribe of the training sessions. I remember that the room was rather dark and there was a damp chill in the air. The door was very heavy and closed behind us. I felt as if the room lacked enough air for us to breathe and in addition, I was quite afraid.

Three elders peered intently at me, and they seemed to be saying, although not directly, what kind of a mother would have such a rebellious upstart for a son. Although Joseph appeared calm, I could tell that he was keenly alert. As I have told you in the past, Joseph was remarkable in his ability to deal with danger, crisis, and confusion.

One Rabbi began by saying, "We welcome you both here today to our holy temple, blessed and venerated by our forefathers, dedicated to our people. The Holy Father has made it possible that we may sit here together today." He then introduced our son's chief Rabbi and teacher, and the scribe, who assisted the Rabbi and was a scholar of Jewish law and the ancient scriptures. He then proceeded, "I believe that you are aware of the reason for our meeting today. As you know, it's been several weeks since I visited you in your home and since that time, I regret to inform you both, the situation has not improved. In fact, it has worsened. It has come to my attention that Jesus is causing a severe disturbance among the other young men. This is something that I cannot allow. I am sure that you understand my position. It is my hope that we can, together, come to an understanding and find a satisfactory solution." Then he smiled and became more informal. He added, "Well, you know, we have all been young once, haven't we? I certainly remember when I was your son's age. I myself had many thoughts and questions. The difference in my approach, as compared to your son's, is that I kept my thoughts and questions to myself. You see, I did not feel secure enough to bring forth these thoughts and questions when I was still learning the letter of the law and the ancient scriptures. I had respect for those teachings! It never occurred to me to question, as a mere youth, the teachings of my elders. I must say to you, in all honesty, it would never, and I repeat, never have occurred to me to challenge the authority of my teachers, learned men, who studied, prayed and sacrificed years of their lives in fervent dedication to the laws of our religion and the commandments of our Lord."

He heaved a sigh and again smiled patronizingly at us. He continued, "Let us, today, find a way to help your son. I believe that it is in Jesus' best interests to spend more time in prayer and contemplation and less time questioning, arguing, disrupting, and disturbing our class. I'm sure, as concerned parents you would agree with me that Jesus . . ." Just as he was about to say something, there was a knock at the door. It was an assistant to the elder Rabbi with a message. He entered the room in a bit of a hurry and whispered in the Rabbi's ear.

The Rabbi frowned as he dismissed the messenger, and as he did so, shot a glance across the table toward Joseph and me. At that moment, I felt a piercing pain shoot through my heart. I believe in that moment, I somehow foresaw the end of Jesus' life. I felt coldness, an icy chill that caught me by surprise and almost took my breath away. I now knew my son's life was in danger. I just knew it. He was only eleven years old. I must explain that this warning came in a flash, so quickly that I did not grasp the full impact of what I felt and a part of me would never want to grasp the full impact of what I felt.

As the messenger left the room and closed the door, the Rabbi continued, "I have just received word that your son has gathered together a group of the young men and he is, and I cannot believe this, he is preaching to them and turning their minds away from the letter of the law. He is attempting to eradicate the very teachings that we have spent day-in and day-out, in holy dedication, teaching our young men. This is an outrage! I will not tolerate this behavior from your son or from any young man. This behavior threatens the very foundation of this community. This is a slap in the face of the most holy teachings of our ancient forefathers, and of God. It is unfortunate that I must now make a decision that I had not expected to have to make, but it has come to this."

He put his fists on the table, leaned over, and spoke quietly, but intently, "I am forced to do something that I wish I did not have to do. Your son is no longer allowed to attend our classes. He is banned from these lessons. Perhaps, in time, if he can come to his senses and recognize the error of his way, we could consider, in the future, allowing him to re-enter the program. For the present, however, he is no longer welcome!"

At that, the scribe closed his book. He took his hand and was rubbing his forehead agitatedly. They all appeared infuriated beyond any reasoning.

The Rabbi stood up from the table and took a few steps away, his hands folded behind his back. He turned to us and said, "Do you have anything to say to us regarding this matter?" There was a long silence and a very uncomfortable tension in the room. I knew that Joseph was very carefully weighing the words that he might say in reply.

At last, Joseph said, "Most learned and distinguished Rabbi, it is a great honor that you have invited us here today. My wife and I humbly thank you for the time that you are devoting to this matter. I find myself as concerned as all of you and, therefore, I am in agreement with your plan of action. My wife and I will make every effort to understand our son's actions and come to a resolution within our own family. As it is not our intention to cause any further problems for you or for the other members of our community, we believe that we can handle this matter best in our own home. We hope that in the future our son may re-approach these very important studies. Once again, I thank each of you for your concern. My wife and I regret any difficulties that our son's inquisitive and overzealous mind has caused. We know our son well and I assure you that his heart is in the right place. It is our task as his parents to guide him in the proper way and therefore, we accept all responsibility for his behavior and actions."

Once more there was silence in the room. Finally, the elder Rabbi spoke once again. "Joseph, you have spoken well, and I hear the sincerity and concern in what you have said. I shall let the matter rest in your hands. I also wanted you both to know today that I have spoken to your son briefly about his behavior and his reply to me was this—he said to me directly, 'I speak to you the words of my Holy Father, for I know him through my prayer. He speaks to me, and I hear his words. His words are different from the law in these books. I am confused and I have questions, but I must believe the words of my Holy Father, for it is he whom I love and trust above all others.'"

As I heard what the Rabbi was saying, I knew indeed that those were Jesus' words. I knew my child well. The Rabbi concluded, "One last comment. In all my years I have never heard an eleven-year-old boy speak in such a way. It is truly unbelievable. As his parents, you must discipline him and teach him respect for those who have built the foundation upon which he now stands. I know that you both will take this matter seriously and will find the proper way for a favorable solution. I believe that we can now adjourn knowing what we each need to do. Go in peace and blessed be all those who serve our community. Praise be to our Father on high. Blessed be He, creator of all." We rose from our seats and left the room, escorted through the temple by the messenger, a nervous and wiry man with long, slender fingers.

Joseph and I, arm in arm, walked down the steps of the temple and proceeded to our home. We walked in silence. I was so glad to be back in the sunlight. I never liked the dark, inner part of the temple. It always made me feel sad for some reason. When we arrived at home, Joseph turned to me and said, "Mary, I feel quite tired right now. I need to rest and think about what has happened. Would you excuse me? I don't like to leave you alone at this time, but I really must lie down. I feel so very tired." It seemed that he had grown older before my eyes. My ever-vigilant Joseph suddenly seemed to have aged and grown weary. I touched his face and said, "My beloved, please rest. I am quite all right and when you wake, I shall have prepared a good and nourishing meal for you." He kissed my hand and went to sleep.

I walked into the garden and sat in the remaining sunlight and I prayed, "Blessed Father, hear a mother's plea. I pray for my son's well-being. He loves you with all his heart and only you can protect him. Watch over him, guide him. He is your son, gentle and loving; he praises you in all ways. I ask your blessing and to give my husband much-needed strength and wisdom. Amen."

I rested my head against the wall of the house and dozed off, feeling the light of the sun across my cheek and a soft wind, a breeze, gently blowing.

CHAPTER 21

Jesus was puzzled, hurt, and extremely upset when he learned that he was no longer welcome in the temple. It was, according to Jesus, a very short, abrupt pronouncement that the Rabbi had dismissed him without any further explanation. He said, "Mother, Father, I do not understand. Why have they banned me from school? All that I have done is to think, to study, to observe, to ask questions, to talk with my friends and to discuss with them things that I do not understand. I have prayed, I have developed closeness with my Father in Heaven, whose voice I hear. He speaks to me inside my heart, and I feel very close to him. I do not understand why I must be banned from continuing my studies with the other young men. Mother, Father, what have I done?"

I felt helpless in providing him with a logical answer. I did not understand why the Rabbis were so disturbed by his questions. I did not know what to say to my son. I waited for Joseph to speak, but, for once in his life, he too seemed to be without words. A silence hung in the air, and Jesus repeated, "Mother, Father, please tell me what have I done. I do not understand!"

Both Joseph and I wanted to answer him in a way that would allow him the ability to be true to himself and at the same time would shed light upon the situation. I said, "My dear son, this is a difficult time. It pains us to see you suffer the consequences of a curious and thoughtful mind. We, ourselves, are indeed puzzled as well. Your father and I understand your feelings of confusion and hurt. Jesus, it is difficult for me to say this, but I feel in my heart that I must encourage you to continue your prayers with the Holy Father and to continue to listen to His words that come to you within your own heart despite any consequences. I could not be an honest mother if I did not continue to encourage you to listen, to pray, to think, to question, and to be a part of the unfolding plan of our most Holy Father. Sometimes, for reasons we do not understand, certain people, people in high places, may not understand and, perhaps, may even be afraid of an inquisitive mind such as yours. I feel that this is the situation and that by asking questions and offering your observations, you may have unknowingly threatened the prescribed teachings. It is clear to me that the Rabbis do not want this kind of controversy. They have asked you to no longer attend the school unless you can do so as a quiet, unquestioning, studious boy. As this is not your nature, and they know this, they have chosen the route of least resistance and simply banned you from further study. Do you understand what I am telling you?"

Jesus was silent, for a while. He then took a deep breath and said, "I understand what you say Mother, but I must be about my Father's business, for my Father calls me and I cannot turn my back to Him, to His words. I must pray about this situation and ask my Holy Father what it is that I am to do. It is His work that I must fulfill. This I know in my heart, and I cannot turn away from what I know in my heart. I cannot."

Joseph took Jesus' hand and placed his other arm on Jesus' shoulder. Then he said, "My son, today you are a man. Only a moment ago you were still a child. With these words, you have stepped into the shoes of a man. Continue to pray, to read the scriptures, to contemplate, to discuss, to listen, and to follow your heart and calling from the Holy Father. As your father, here on earth, it is my job to support and encourage you in fulfilling and realizing your destiny. I speak for your mother and myself in shining light, love, and blessings upon you. We will be by your side and do for you whatever we can to guide and assist you in your journey. I know in my heart that you must find the way on your own and that you *will* find the way on your own, through prayer and meditation.

"It is your feet that will walk upon your path and only you can fulfill the mission of your light. I release you from any obligation to satisfy manmade rules and ask only that you truly listen to the words of your heavenly Father. If all your words and deeds emanate from His source, then you will have fulfilled your destiny. I see, in this moment, that there are many things to come that will be out of our control. This we must accept. I see this now, as I have never seen it before, and I believe that I understand now what the past twelve years have been about. My son, I love you with all my heart. I cherish you with all my heart. I bless you and hold you fast to my heart, binding your spirit with my own. We have watched over you, with light and wisdom, as best we could, but today you have grown in stature. Choose your friends wisely, pray deeply, and listen closely and you will make me proud. Bless you, son. Bless you."

Jesus stood there gazing at us both. It is difficult to describe our feelings and thoughts in these moments. It was as if we had turned our son over to someone else, to himself, to the work of the Holy Father, to his destiny, to the future. We released him and allowed him with our permission to be true to himself regardless of any adversity.

Jesus drew us toward him and said, "Words cannot encompass the breadth of my feeling and love for you both. I promise to fulfill my Father's work and I will never turn away from my destiny. I would like to walk now and to be alone, that I may ponder all that we have spoken of. You have both given me jewels that reflect thoughts and ideas. I will hold these jewels close to me and I will need to think deeply before I speak further. Thank you, for your infinite wisdom and compassion. I am truly blessed among men to have such parents as I have in you."

Then he laid his face against our hands and touched his forehead in honor and reverence to us. Without another word, he went outside. I looked at Joseph. He was shaking his head. He said to me, "Mary, let us have a glass of wine, for this is truly a day of great significance. Let us break bread to praise and bless our union and our son, for today is a day never to be forgotten. A day that has been forever sealed upon our hearts, a bond between the three of us that shall never be broken by anything, any person, or any situation. Come; let us sing praises, for it is clear who we are. Hallelujah, praise be to the Holy Father on high. Hallelujah, praise be for the light of the Lord reigns eternal, forever and ever and ever. Praise, praise, praise. Amen."

From this point, Joseph and I considered our jobs as Jesus' earthly mother and father complete. That is not to say that we did not continue watching over him, but from that night his life began. Joseph and I accepted his path and knew it to be the will of God. I don't think that we ever doubted our decision but perhaps to some people; it might have even appeared to be a cruel one.

The night was clear, pure, and bright. Joseph and I walked in the garden together. We looked up to the sky filled with brilliant stars, lighting up the galaxy. I could not help myself and I burst into song, praising the magnificence of every speck of light that I had ever seen or felt in the universe. I sang and sang and sang. Joseph joined in and we danced into the wee hours of the morning. We understood the mystery and the majesty of God and the universe.

Before we went to bed, I made a prayer: "Oh, holy light, shine so bright, and dance eternally through the night. Beautiful stars that light up the sky, lead our son, and grace his life, that he may know the majesty of all that is. Now and forever more. Amen."

Joseph and I went back inside. Even though it was late, very late, we were not so tired, as much as we were complete. We went to rest with satisfied hearts, knowing that we had fulfilled our mission.

CHAPTER
22

Jesus' expulsion from his rabbinical studies was a painful, as well as an enlightening experience for our whole family. We became well known in the village as a family that was, shall we say, different. I know that people gossiped about us. Many times, as I walked to the well in the center of town to fetch water for the family, I heard other women talking about what had happened to our son and even elaborating upon the story. Some people who I thought to be close friends drew away from us. Others shunned us entirely. You see, it was not common to be different in those times. As I have said earlier, for the village to survive in times of social unrest and political strife, it was necessary to band together. Differences were not generally tolerated.

When the word got out that our son had been expelled from rabbinical studies, our family suffered the slings and arrows of public opinion. My husband's carpentry business suffered somewhat. There were certain people in the town who no longer wished to associate themselves with our family. The word had spread that our son was a rebellious troublemaker.

My daughter was at this time eight years old. We called her Rachel Anne, after my mother. She was quiet and ever vigilant when it came to looking after my welfare. Even as a young child, she was very protective toward me and always wished to keep stresses and trouble away from me. At eight years of age, she knew enough to understand that her brother was being talked about by the other children. She also understood that the older women in particular were saying things about our family.

One day I was preparing some vegetables outside in the courtyard where I did much of the food preparation. Rachel came over to me with a troubled heart and said, "Mother, they are saying terrible things about Jesus. I hear them talking. Sometimes when I pass by, they laugh and whisper things that I can't quite hear. This hurts me, Mother. I don't understand what it is all about. Besides, Mother, I have noticed that you are not as light-hearted as you used to be, since Jesus was expelled. I'm angry at him, Mother. He has brought shame upon our family and he has caused you to be unhappy. Even Father seems quieter and doesn't sing songs to us like he used to. Mother, tell me, what are we to do?"

I looked down and saw such a grown-up person in that tiny face. I said, "Rachel, my daughter, I love you so and I am thankful that you show concern for me and the family. It shows me that you are considerate, sensitive, and observant. Your brother, by following his own heart and his personal communion with the most Holy Father, has listened to Him closely and must follow what he knows to be true. He is accused only of asking questions, thinking about the words of the Torah, and contemplating their deeper meaning. In the mind of our family, we see nothing wrong with this. We have all been taught to study diligently, to pray and meditate upon the scriptures, and to have open discussions about their meaning. We are sorry that the chief rabbis see things differently. It is my duty, as a mother, to encourage the inquisitive minds of my children. Therefore, although many people disagree, I must remain steadfast in my understanding of the truth and support my son in his quest to understand truth through prayer and serious contemplation. My dear child, these may be large-sounding words to you, but I believe that you can feel the spirit behind them. Your brother loves you, and I hope that you will feel comfortable talking to him directly. It is always better to talk openly and to share your feelings. This brings understanding and light to any subject."

At that moment, we could hear Jesus' footsteps as he came through the house to the garden. Rachel loved her brother and looked up to him with admiration. She ran over to him and threw her arms around his neck and hugged him. She said, laughing, "Jesus, we are talking about you."

Jesus replied, "Oh, is this so? And what, may I ask, are my esteemed mother and sister talking about regarding me?"

Rachel answered, "Well, Jesus, everybody is talking about you—not just Mother and me. All the boys and girls and the women at the well talk about you, too. They think that you are a troublemaker, Jesus."

Jesus responded, "Me, a troublemaker? Is it a troublemaker who prays daily, who reads the Torah hour after hour, and who sits for hours under the olive tree to think and meditate? Is it thus that I am a troublemaker? Come, my little Rachel, I will tickle you until you find a new name for me."

He picked her up and twirled her around, tickling her until she screamed with laughter. She threw her arms around his neck and hugged him, saying, "You are my great Jesus, my big brave Jesus." She hugged him tightly.

Before long, the family was gathered for dinner together, in the courtyard. All of us were laughing and talking and singing. We loved to sing together as a family. Everyone had their say, as we had always shared discussions. No one was ever left out and everyone could say what they thought. It seemed that everyone was particularly hungry that day and we ate and ate. Little Rachel sat protectively between myself and her big brother, Jesus, whom she adored. From time to time he would put his arms around to hug her and her little face lit up, like the rays of the sun.

Our family pulled together and expressed our feelings truthfully, without censor. This was always our policy. We found that our children thrived in this atmosphere.

CHAPTER 23

Time passed and our children grew, and for a time things were uneventful. I enjoyed the small everyday tasks in my life. I found pleasure in watching the plants grow in my garden. I enjoyed preparing food for my family. I lovingly baked bread for my children, as I had learned to do from my mother. I sang to myself, for me these small, ordinary aspects of my life were a source of great enjoyment and beauty. I never tired of looking at the sky. I never tired of hearing the birds. I never tired of watching the buds and leaves grow and bloom.

One day while I was working in my garden, I was surprised to once again see the small creatures that I had seen as a child. They spoke to me, "Mary, do you remember us? We've been with you ever since you were a child. We never left your side; we chose to follow you, for we feel so close to you. We feel the tenderness of your fingertips when you caress our leaves. We love your singing and all that you are. We have chosen to stay with you your whole life through."

I got up, and as I did so I felt dizziness come over me. It had been such a long time since I had seen the creatures and heard their voices. In those moments I felt myself lying underneath the tree where I had fainted so long ago. As the sunlight poured down on my face, I began to dream.

In the dream, I stood on a mountaintop surrounded by a misty cloud. From this place I could see water, sky, and long expanses of beautiful flowers. I began to walk through the cloud toward a pool of light.

There I saw the face of God. I fell to my knees and this beautiful light was everywhere. I could no longer see the mountains, the clouds, or the flowers. I bathed in that pool of light and felt as if I were floating. When I woke up from my dream, I was sitting on the bench in my garden with my head leaning against the wall. The hot sun was beating down on my face and for a moment I was not sure where I was. I stood up and took a few steps, only to sit back down again; I was still too dizzy. I did not know what was happening to me, I was disoriented and could not get my bearings.

Again, a voice spoke to me, "Mary, hear our words. Listen closely, for you must know what lies ahead. A path has been put before you and even though this path becomes narrow and filled with thorns and briars, you will continue, no matter what comes your way. Follow your path, Mary. Be faithful in your journey. Dark hours will come, but never turn back. Remember your dream, as you stood on the mountaintop. You saw the light. Hold fast to that dream."

Then I sat, for a moment, just feeling the wall and my head against it. It was like a kind of daydream, something in the back of my mind that unexpectedly came forward. I did not place any particular significance on this message. I took a deep breath and shook my head, as if to shake myself back into reality. It had been a long time since I had experienced anything like this. I felt out of shape, out of practice, as I realized how long it had been and how much of the beautiful, light-filled atmosphere that I could see so clearly as a child, I had forgotten. I had lost that capacity and here in my garden it had come back to me. Now, I was suspicious of it and did not have the joyous feelings or the complete understanding that I had as a young girl.

I suddenly began to feel sad. I thought that if I took a walk, it would lift my spirits. I followed a path that was familiar to me. It led to a particularly lovely part of the countryside. It was a beautiful day. Although I had work to do, I decided to follow my feelings and my heart's calling. With each step, my spirit began to rise. I felt a lightness come over me and I breathed in deeply. My arms began to swing back and forth, and I felt younger, even carefree. I realized as I walked that I had retained the naturalness and ever-hopefulness that I had had in my younger years. In the intervening time I had become burdened with fears, worries, and concerns. I had lost the light that I had thought would burn eternally in my heart. As I walked, I felt it rekindle inside of me. I felt joy come back into my heart. I felt goodness spreading through my whole body. I knew that everything around me was filled with the light of God and that his spirit was everywhere. I felt free and as light as a bird. I shouted with joy and ran down a small embankment to the river below. I was a little timid at first as I dipped only my feet, but no one was around so I threw myself in. The water was usually cool and yet, by the edge, where the sun had been beating down, it was warm. I played in the water, floating, and splashing for quite a while. It had been such a long time that I had taken time to be with myself, to renew my spirit. Cares and burdens had come over me like a heavy blanket. I wore this heavy blanket day in and day out and did not even realize that even in the midst of a beautiful, sunshiny, summer day, I was still wearing a heavy blanket. As I floated and splashed in the water, my heart grew even lighter, and the blanket seemed to evaporate.

As I climbed back onto the embankment, suddenly I remembered the day that the shepherd boy had seen me climbing up the bank in my wet clothes. I laughed out loud, because I remembered so clearly the look on his face when he had seen me so long ago.

I twisted the hem of my dress to squeeze out the water and bent over and ran my fingers through my hair to let the air and sun dry it. Everything about these actions was so joyful and easy. I sat down for a moment and leaned back. I felt the sun embrace me with rays of warmth and love. I thought of how miraculous it was, the tenderness of the sun, its love for me, as it shone down and to dry my hair and clothes.

I arose and began to make my way back home. I waved to some of my neighbors, greeting them happily. I came into my garden and there was Joseph, with the children. He was reading to them. He loved to read to them; I did not want to interrupt the story. I looked at this beautiful picture. Then Rachel saw me and called out. Everyone looked up and such beautiful smiles came across their faces. I ran to them, hugged each one, and kissed Joseph. We sat together as Joseph finished the last lines of the story. I brought out fruit, bread, and cheese, and we ate together and talked and laughed until the sun went down.

When the children were asleep and Joseph was sleeping by my side, I sat up in bed. As I put my hand on my heart, I felt the flame burning brightly, "Praise thee, oh most Holy One, thy light is eternal and ever-present. You show it to us in every blade of grass and ray of the sun. Sometimes the darkness overcomes us, but your light lives forever inside of us. The flame may dim but it never, ever dies out. It was my dream of the light that burns in my heart. I will follow you forever. Amen."

Many of you who hear my words understand what I say, but are afraid. Put aside your fears and follow the spirit and you will soon see, and you will never have to be afraid again. Don't let fear hold you back from the source of your life. It is only fear that causes the darkness, the dimness, the dying out of the light. It is an illusion, for the light is ever-present, it never dims, but the belief in fear causes the illusion of dimness and all the sorrows emanate from that. That is why there is no greater work than the demonstration of the nature and the manifestation of the spirit. Do not shy away from the bringing forth of your heartfelt, hard-earned knowledge. Listen, hear, and follow your heart's call, your spirit's cry. You shall soon see the manifestation of all there is.

When one is in full understanding of the spirit, there is no differentiation between giving and receiving. For in the fullness of the spirit, there lies only joy, ecstasy, creation, love, integration, complete understanding, and all those who walk upon the earth are on their individual pathways to total spirit. May you hold fast to your heart's dream. See it, hear it, follow it. Through your spirit, you understand how to do it; you did not always know. You know now, now it is a matter of action. Act upon your knowledge and you will see miracles before your eyes.

CHAPTER
24

The next part of my story comes a few years later than our last chapter. Our family made a journey into a larger town where a religious festival was being celebrated. This was a magnificent time for the people of all nearby regions. They gathered together to celebrate and carry out religious rituals. There were special dances, singing, and food preparation. People came from miles around and there was joyfulness and communal spirit. We had decided to go, primarily so that the children could have the opportunity to experience such a well-known event and to participate in a religious celebration that was very meaningful to the Jewish community.

Jesus was particularly excited to visit the temple. He had never been to the large tabernacle. He had been faithfully studying on his own with the help and advice from Joseph and myself. He was beside himself with excitement. He talked about it for days, even weeks before the event. He got the other children excited, too. We packed up our things, taking with us food, water, and a few essential items that we might need for the trip. We took one donkey, which the smaller children rode upon. The rest of us walked. It was a beautiful time of year, and we enjoyed the journey. There were many others walking alongside of us. As we got closer to the city, they grew in number. For us, coming from a small village, it was overwhelming.

At some point, I became fearful that we would be separated from each other. Joseph was in a jovial and happy mood and told me not to worry, that this was a very special occasion, and that God was watching over us.

We followed the road into the town and everywhere people were sitting by the roadside, eating, drinking, talking, and laughing. Some were dancing; there were drums and horns. There were colorful flags and ribbons that represented some of the regions from which the different people came. Rachel, my daughter, was ecstatic to see all the sights, sounds, and colors. She couldn't believe her eyes. She was looking and watching and listening to everything. At one point we stopped to have something to eat and drink and Jesus begged us to hurry, for he wanted to go to the temple as soon as possible. He kept leading us forward, and his enthusiasm and intensity spurred us on to the center of the city. At last, we arrived and stood before the great temple of Jerusalem. None of us had ever been here and we felt great wonder and some fearfulness at what we were seeing.

Jesus said, "Mother, Father, I must go in immediately! I must go now! This is something that I have waited for my whole life. I will find you later, but now I must go." Before we could say anything to him, he ran up the steps at such a pace that we could not have possibly stopped him. Besides we had the donkey and the children, so we could not follow after him.

Joseph turned to me and said, "Mary, it's all right. Let the boy go. He will be fine, and he has work to do."

I must say that I did not feel so confident and was quite worried about finding him in this huge crowd. By now there was a loud cry of trumpets rising from all the hillsides, calling people to gather around the temple. You cannot imagine the force of the large crowd which had gathered there. The trumpets' calls stirred up the crowds. The people gathered even closer and tighter together. I grabbed hold of the children; I felt a little bit panic-stricken, for I was not used to this kind of an experience. I confess that it was not to my liking. I felt us being pushed and shoved every which way. I cried out for Joseph, who was himself being shoved and pushed. He stumbled and fell; several people tumbled over the top of him. I was holding on to the donkey and the children, so I could not really assist Joseph. He managed to get up and I reached out my arm toward him. He grabbed the donkey's rope and hung onto it, leading us out of the frantic crowd. As soon as we were out of the way and could breathe again, I told Joseph that I did not want to stay in the center of the city any longer. He comforted me and said that he understood. We would go to the other side of the temple, where he thought there would be fewer people gathered.

Rachel wanted to know where Jesus was. I had a terrible feeling in my stomach, for I had no idea where he was or how we would find him. We went down a small hill and began to climb up a larger hill that at one point became quite steep and I realized that Joseph had been right. There were far fewer people here because the climb was more difficult. We were used to walking in the hilly terrain of our village, so I preferred approaching the temple from this vantage point to being packed in by so many people. Again, trumpets rang out from all the hillsides. Joseph said that when the trumpets rang a third time, that would signify the slaughter of the goat. We hurried to be closer to the temple stairs to see this symbolic act of forgiveness.

Days before this journey we began preparing our hearts and minds to be forgiven and cleansed of all our transgressions. We hurried up the hilly path and came within sight of the back of the temple, just as the trumpets blared out. Upon the third call of the trumpets, we fell to our knees. We knew at that moment that the blood of the animal had been spilled and his body thrown over the cliff to the rocks below. At that moment all our sins were washed away. We prayed in thankfulness.

Colorful flags were unfurled across the different hillsides and down the temple stairs. Beautiful sheaves of color appeared, as drums and trumpets and rams' horns and other instruments resounded from hill to hill. People began to chant and sing, and many of them rushed up the steps to the top of the temple. We stayed below because there was nowhere to go once you reached the top and besides, the donkey was with us. This chamber was not open to the public; it just offered a better view from hilltop to hilltop.

Rachel squealed with delight and hugged her brother James, crying out once again, "Where's Jesus, where's Jesus?" Now, I was frightened, and I said to Joseph, "How are we going to find him?"

"How will he find us?" Joseph answered, "Mary, I feel that it is all right. He is safe, and besides we are going to stay here for the night. If we don't find him before sundown, we will surely find him in the morning."

His words did not satisfy me at all, but I did not know what else to do. We began to walk into a grassy, hilly area below the temple. Other people were pitching small tents; some were roasting food and selling pieces of it. We found a place to pitch our small tent and sat down on the grass to eat the food we had brought and to rest from our journey. People came by and spoke to us, as this was one opportunity to exchange news. People asked each other about friends and families in villages that were far from them. There was always someone who knew someone else, and people were very generous with their food and bread and offered whatever they had to each other.

Now the dancing began in earnest. There were fires built, over which meat cooked. Whole groups of girls and boys began to dance around the fires. One by one the older people would join in. They would clap their hands and sing, and there were tambourines and drums and laughter.

Joseph insisted that we dance. An older couple camped near us offered to watch over the children. It had been a long time since we had danced in this way. Some special dancers from one of the villages far away had dressed themselves in elaborate clothes. They were dancing wildly and so expertly that the rest of the crowd drew around them to clap in rhythm to their dance.

The celebration and festivities went on into the night, and at last we bundled up to sleep. Before I lay down, I walked around for a period of time to see if I could find Jesus, but he was nowhere to be seen. I reluctantly returned, knowing that I would have to sleep through the night not knowing where he was.

The next day I rose early, but Joseph was already awake and had gone. The children were sleeping peacefully. I stirred the coals in the fire to heat some water that we had brought with us. I looked for Joseph, assuming that he was looking for our son. Before long, Joseph returned with a huge smile on his face. "Mary, all is well. Our son has been found. He is in the temple preaching to the rabbis. I saw it with my own eyes. They were listening to what he was saying with rapt attention. They put many questions before him, to test his knowledge. Every question he answered, and they were amazed at his knowledge. One by one, they questioned him on points of the law, and he answered, not only the exact point itself, but also offered all of the history and context that had created it. I heard one of the chief rabbis murmur that he did not believe his ears and that although his eyesight was very poor, it was clear to him that this boy had more knowledge than anyone he had ever heard speak. I did not want to interrupt our son, so I left a message with one of the scribes telling him where he could find us when he was through.

"Mary, you would have been amazed. Just as the rabbis in our village had been so angry at Jesus, these elders were completely amazed and in awe of his learning. I did not realize that our son could speak publicly. I've only seen him talking to boys his own age. Let us give thanks, Mary, for perhaps now our son will be embraced by the elder rabbis and no longer treated as he has been. I know what an important day this is for him and for us as well. This day confirms our belief in guiding him to follow his own heart and to listen as the most Holy Father spoke to him. I am amazed, Mary. We are from such a small town. Who would have thought our son would speak at the largest temple in the land?"

Then we went about gathering our things and packing up. As we were putting the finishing touches on our preparations for leaving, we saw Jesus striding toward us. He walked tall and came toward us with a great and energetic stride and he cried out, "Here I am. Mother, Father, I am here." Rachel went running up to him and he scooped her up and hugged her tightly. We all gathered around him.

"I received your message, Father. I had a most interesting day. I met some of the rabbis and they invited me to their council. It just happened that a point of law came up, a tenet I particularly knew well. The rabbi I had been talking to earlier encouraged me to speak. It was a lesser known and understood tenet and I was suddenly listened to and questioned. They asked me many, many questions. I answered in the best way I knew. This went on for quite some time. Many elders spoke to me admiringly and marveled at my knowledge. They asked where I had learned all of this and at what school did I study? When I told them that I did not attend school, they did not believe me and thought I was trying to trick them. I told them that I studied on my own with the help, the guidance, and the love of my Holy Father in heaven. I told them that He spoke to me through my heart and that I pondered each thing that I read in the Torah. When I have questions, I ask the Father directly and He answers me. They thanked me and wished me well in my studies. One rabbi was very kind; he patted me on the shoulder and said that I was a very special young man. I thanked him for inviting me to the council. He said perhaps we would meet again in days to come. And now, I am here."

I said, "Oh, Jesus, I have been so worried about you. I am so glad to have you back. Come, let us start for home. I long to be in our village." We began our journey home, laughing and talking, teasing each other, and feeling very brave for making such a long trip from our small village. When we arrived safely at home, we all gathered together and held hands while Joseph prayed in thanks for our safety and in gratitude for the celebration and for our atonement. We were all thankful to sleep in our own house, especially me.

CHAPTER
25

When I called the Author to my house, I asked her to please tell my story. She opened her heart and felt the needs and feelings and fears and desires of many other hearts. I called her for I knew that she would have a pure and unbiased approach to my story. As we had known each other in my earthly life, and she had been my daughter, I knew that she would be able to tell my story in its fullest personal expression. My daughter, Rachel, gave her life in order to make my life easier and more blessed. She sacrificed her own happiness and well-being to protect me and to take care of me. I wish in many ways to return that love that she gave to me.

Many of you now living on the earth do not know the full understandings of what it means to truly love. For all loving relationships between people and indeed, between animals as well, are eternal.

You may think that when you supposedly die that that will be the end of a particular relationship. That is not the way of the spirit. Relationships are eternally bound and live eternally through the spirit. The spirit is ever alive and continues to blossom and grow. Depending upon in which dimension the spirit is functioning, it will take on a particular form. Many of you walking on your planet now have a very small and limited understanding of the incredible beauty, majesty, and playfulness of the spirit. When I use the term "Spirit," I mean that to be the breath of God that lives in each and every one of us.

If only you knew the length and breadth of your relationships truly, you would all feel happier and more fully satisfied. You would understand that you are eternally bound and connected to all those whom you know and love. For that matter, you are just as bound and connected to those who cause you *confusion and anguish. There is no running away from eternal relationships. They are ever-present, waiting to be seen in the fullness of what they are: the love and the light of God. Many of you who now walk upon the earth do not see or know of this light, and you remain fearful, lonely, and sad. That is why those of you who do have an understanding of the eternal nature of the spirit must find ways to bring this knowledge forward through the daily and ordinary routines and tasks of your lives. I am calling to all those who can hear me to step forward into the light and to bring your heart into all that you do in your everyday lives.*

Those who can hear know what it is that I ask. You know that I am asking for your memory, your soul memory, to activate now. For too long, too many people have been sleepwalking through their lives. The pain, loneliness, and sadness have been too great. The time is nigh approaching for those who have been asleep to awaken and to breathe in the very essence of the soul and the spirit. No longer will there be any misunderstanding about the nature of existence. Enough people will have awakened and through their daily routine of living will communicate to many others, the eternal, loving, nature of all relationships.

My daughter, Rachel, was one such person, who through her ordinary life revealed the truth of love in everything and everyone she touched. I remember when Rachel was fifteen years old; she truly walked in the sun. That is to say that wherever she went, she brought a joyful, loving spirit and allowed that spirit to pour forth in a natural, and lighthearted way.

One day she was walking through a rocky part of the countryside. She came upon a group of beggars and sick people who, in desperation, were living far away from the village. They called out to Rachel to come to them, to help them, to have pity upon them, for they were sick, hungry, and in need. Rachel could easily have passed them by. The road that she was taking was a road well-traveled by many others and she was not in real danger from these people. Instead, when they called out to her, she stopped her journey. In fact, she walked away from the road that led home. She walked off the road and went directly into the area where this group of people was gathered. Many of them were lying on the ground, some were leaning on each other, a few were sitting on rocks, and others crawled toward her feet.

Rachel called out to them in a clear voice. She said, "My friends, my beautiful friends, how wonderful it is to see you all here, gathered together, on this day. How fortunate I am to have been called by all of you that I may stop here by your side and rest from my journey. What a blessing it is to see you here. I have been walking a long distance and I am pleased to rest awhile with you."

At these words, the beggars were amazed. The ordinariness of what she said to them rang so clearly in their ears and in their hearts that they responded to her as if they were well and in normal circumstances. They welcomed her, saying, "Thank you, Miss, we are glad to have you here. It is indeed a beautiful day. Won't you sit with us and talk to us? Rarely does anyone ever stop upon the path to speak to us. Your words have lifted our spirits and lightened our hearts."

They began to gather closer together. Rachel simply smiled. The thing you must know about Rachel is that she always saw truth reflecting and sparkling like sunlight in the eyes of all those she met in her life. This was natural for her and her special blessing. As such, she smiled upon this group, which many, many others, in fact, most others would have fled from.

She was carrying bread, some cheese, and bits of fruit. She opened her satchel and said, "My dear friends, would you please be so kind as to share this bread and cheese, which my mother made for me with her own hands. It would please me greatly if you would accept my mother's bread, for I know that it would please her greatly to know that I was able to share it with so many new friends." At that, she broke off pieces and distributed them to every single person gathered there, one by one, until everyone had received some of what she had brought with her.

Rachel told me later that she had never seen such beautiful faces. Within that moment, that tiny brief moment, those beggars and even very ill people forgot, simply forgot their plight. They sat upon the rocks in the sunlight and under the spell of Rachel's beautiful and ordinary tenderness. In that moment, they were beautiful and happy and content. One person had stepped off her path, had walked among them, and had spoken to them with the warmth of sunlight.

Each of those gathered that day, one by one, came to Rachel, looked her in the eyes and said something special to her. Like a chorus they told her "What a pretty face you have," "My, my, your mother certainly makes good bread," "Be careful now upon your trip back. Stay upon the middle of the road. It's a smoother, less treacherous path." "What a lovely voice you have, young lady. I feel better just hearing your words."

They said simple, ordinary things to Rachel. One by one, they all said something to her that Rachel carried in her heart.

There was one very frail, bony, wizened, old lady. Her hair was stiff and white. She called Rachel over and asked her to take her hand, which Rachel did. Kneeling down, Rachel held her hand and looked into the old woman's eyes. As she did so, a smile grew upon her face. The old woman looked at Rachel and let out a loud and long breath of laughter. She said, "Oh, my dear child, seeing you this day, I see what I will be tomorrow. What a vision! What a sight! Look at you! I'll be just like you tomorrow." At that, she squeezed Rachel's hand and laughed and laughed, until Rachel herself broke into laughter. In fact, all those who were watching and listening, chuckled, and laughed in spite of themselves. For indeed, this very old woman became younger and younger as she was laughing, and the delight in Rachel's eyes poured forth upon her.

Rachel rose up and said, "Oh, my friends, bless you all. I will stop by again on my next trip. Until then, may the sun shine bright on each and every one of you. I shall remember you all."

They cried out, "Yes, yes, do. Don't forget us! We will be here, come again. Remember what we said: stay in the middle of the road. It's safer there. Be careful, young lady. Thank your mother for her bread."

"Bye," Rachel called out, and off she went toward home. As she walked, a storm cloud came up and it began to rain. She continued walking in the middle of the road, just as her new friends had told her to do. Sure enough, it was wise advice. The rain fell so hard and strong, she thought afterwards that if they had not warned her to stay in the middle of the road, she might have been hurt. Ordinarily she walked along the side of the road. It was only on this particular day, after meeting her friends that she stayed in the middle and therefore made it home safely through a very treacherous storm.

Now, my dear friends think kindly on those ordinary moments, tasks, and people. Remember that behind, and in, and through the ordinary is the eternal relationship that binds us all. Rachel simply shined a young girl's sunlight upon these sick and aged beggars. In return, they poured their love and wisdom back upon her. Imagine this scene, like a painting in your mind and heart. Fill it out in detail and color, as you see fit.

You see, it is not that Rachel was some extraordinary, enlightened being. She simply followed her spirit and her heart's calling to share the ordinary aliveness that was hers to give. That aliveness that she gave, freely and easily, is the gift that we may give to each other at any time.

Rachel came home, drenched from head to foot, hungry as a bear, and happy as a lark. She had quite fallen in love with those people, and she talked and chattered and drew pictures of them, for days and days. She insisted that Jesus come with her the next time. She felt that they would like him. After all, he was her older brother, and he had a very special way of talking to people. She wanted them to meet each other. That is how Rachel thought of things. She never put more onto any task or subject than was obvious. That was her brilliance and her genius. Later, in the evening, she sat down and ate a huge dinner and went to sleep right afterward.

I chanced to walk by where she was sleeping, and I looked down into my child's face. I paused there, gazing upon her form and her gentle smile as she slept. I placed my hand on her forehead and brushed her hair away from her face. In my heart, I thanked those sick beggars by the roadside for bringing my daughter safely home to me. As I expressed that thankfulness in my heart, I somehow felt their spirits all around me. Instead of seeing them in that moment as sick beggars, I felt the warmth and glow and beauty of them as people.

Rachel stirred and opened her eyes for a moment. She muttered something, something like "tomorrow I'll be just like you" then she kind of laughed a little, rolled over, and went back to sleep.

Thus ends this chapter about my daughter, Rachel.

CHAPTER 26

Blessed are those who walk upon the earth at this time, whose hearts cry out for guidance, who have suffered without answers in times of dreadful darkness; my story will guide you and lead you into the magnificent pool of light that is your birthright. I call you, children of God, to hear my words that you may know who you are, that you may receive the blessings and guidance to open your hearts. Know that my love for you is so great; when you read these words, feel this love penetrate your heart, surround you with the deepest understanding and guide you faithfully step-by-step to the innocence and purity that already resides in your hearts and lives forever.

Dear ones, I have spoken to you before regarding the eternal nature of all relationships. You shall soon see how you are all bound together in the magnificence of the spirit, and experience the glory manifested by the collective of those of you who have truly opened the valves of your heart chambers to compassion. I speak to you using the heart as the symbol, psychically, for it is the emotional doorway to visions of heaven on your earth. Only through the chambers of the heart and the exploration and the ferreting out of each and every heart on your planet, can you possibly bring forth the most magnificent vision ever thought of by the Holy Father.

You all must understand that for this vision to live, the Holy Father and you must re-establish your oneness, your complete oneness. Only a universal symphony of music could fully capture the true reverberations of this experience. Know, my beloved ones, that this experience lies within your hands. It is as close to you as your very own hands, which can lay tenderly and gently upon your heart. Know, my beloved ones, that I shall never leave you. I am with you each and every moment. I am beside you, tenderly calling you, gently watching over you. I hear your cries. I see your agony and I know what it is that you suffer. I feel the frustration, the rage, the fury, the madness, the insanity, the horror, the unjust, and unbelievable outrageous acts occurring as I speak to you now. I know what you have suffered and what you have seen. Trust my words, as I tell you all things are possible for those who love and trust in the Holy Father.

I shall fervently assist you, my beloved children, for I am your Mother, and shine a Mother's love through and around each and every one of you. You are not alone, even as you feel alone, abandoned, or deserted. The loneliness and blackness of the darkest night has swept many of you away from the bosom of your mother and father of the Light. We have come back to reclaim you, children. We have come back to hold you lovingly in our arms, so that you may through our nurturing know your value, for my dear ones, we need you just as you need us, and just as you need each other.

I must tell you a story that is painful to me.

Joseph fell ill. It came upon him suddenly. He was struck by a terrible fever. No matter what we did nothing could take this fever away. We called doctors and healing experts to his bedside. Nothing relieved the burning heat on his brow. I laid cold compresses all over his body. I prayed over him. I never left his side. I rarely slept and as the days wore on, I became delirious from exhaustion and utter fear. Joseph was the most important person in my life. I could not imagine living without him.

Some days passed and his fever broke; it appeared that he would come around. He could eat some mashed fruit and drink some water, but he was so weak that he could barely sit up, even with the help of his sons. We all gathered around him at this time. He spoke, saying, "Let me see your beautiful faces, your eyes reflected in my eyes, let me touch each of your hands. I feel that my journey here has come to an end. I don't want to leave you, but I feel that I am being called home. My beloved children, my wife, you have been everything to me in my life. I will protect you, just as I have done these many years. I did not expect to leave this early; I thought I would be here to see grandchildren, but that is not meant to be, and I accept the path that the Father has set out for me faithfully."

At this point, he was too weak to speak further, and he fell into a deep sleep. I was nearly crazy for grief, lack of sleep, frustration, agony of spirit, and anger. I was angry and I did not allow the anger to be a secret, for in my delirium, I raised my fist and cried out, raged, screamed, tore at my clothes, and cursed. The children knew better than to try and contain my unleashed emotions. I, Mary, who loved and trusted the Holy Father in all things, fell victim to a rage that nearly consumed me. I passed out from this fit of uncontrollable grief and woke up in the middle of the night, with my son Jesus, who had come to minister to me, by my side.

He took my hand and he said, "Mother, I am here with you. We must go on, Mother. It is God's will. There is more for us to do; we must fulfill our purpose here. Father has completed his purpose and shall return home where he will watch over us. Give him the strength to complete his journey, Mother. He needs you. He can't do it without you. You are eternally bound to him and he to you; therefore, you shall be together again, Mother. Know that. God has counseled me to tell you this. He knows that this is a terrible and dark hour. Come now, Rachel is tending to Father and we must go to him for the end draws near."

At that moment, Rachel cried out, "Mother, come now, come quickly." Joseph opened his eyes. They were very clear and very focused. He looked at each of us, one by one. "My loved ones, it is beautiful here and I embrace and hold you close. It is truly beautiful here." With that, he slipped away and left us. He was gone. We closed his eyes and laid a blanket that had been in the family for generations, over him. There was silence, no one said a word. The feeling in the room was as if a new baby had just been born. Time slowed down and a quiet surrender took over. Everyone just breathed, consumed by their own thoughts. We sat like this until dawn.

As the light of the day grew, we felt a lifting of our spirits; we knew Joseph had reached his new home safely. We could feel it. We loved him, he was truly one of the most loving, wise, and generous men who ever walked on the earth.

The whole community was devastated by Joseph's early death. He was not young, but he certainly left at an age that was too soon for a man of such vigor and strength. Many songs and words of praise poured forth, not only from our community but from many, many communities far and wide. Joseph had been a leader in protecting the Jewish communities through a network of messengers and a council of men who watched over the political situation. People traveled from far and wide to pay homage to him.

Rachel and Jesus were very worried about me, for I did not speak to anyone for many days after Joseph died. Then one morning, I called all of us together and said, "Beloved children, I am your Mother, and I shall not leave you. I must go on, for it is what Joseph wants me to do."

My love for Joseph compelled me to reach inside the deepest part of myself to find strength and to continue my life. "We must band together, my children, we are a family unit, and we must watch over each other, guide and protect each other. I want to follow in Joseph's footsteps, for he prepared the way for us to carry out his work and to live fully and completely, remembering his wisdom, tenderness, and kind heart, his clearheadedness, his lightheartedness, and his steadfast and never-ending love for all of us. This was his legacy."

I recall Rachel singing a song that Joseph had taught her. Hearing it, it was as though he were with us in the room.

I must confess that I, in the face of losing my husband, lost sight of my purpose, my path and my trust in the Holy Father. I know there have been times when this has happened to you. Joseph taught me many things, and in his death, he taught me the greatest lesson of my existence. Once I let go of Joseph in life, I learned what eternal life really means. I don't think I really believed it, but Joseph made it clear that physical and spiritual lives are actually one and the same. Never did a day go by that I ever felt that he was completely gone. It is something that is difficult to put into words: I simply knew. It was his gift to our family to carry this knowledge intimately into our own hearts. Because Joseph had lived his life in a simple, uncomplicated way, the power of this lesson that he taught us is all the more fully felt. Therefore, by his leaving us when he did, he strengthened our family in such a way that from that moment on we each of us had no longer any fear to fully fulfill our life's purpose.

We went on living. We could feel his hands embracing, holding our very hearts, and giving us the strength to be fully who we were.

CHAPTER 27

The day came when Jesus came to me to confess something that had lain heavily on his heart. It was evening and I was sitting outside our courtyard, where there was a large, old olive tree. I was sitting there in the twilight, putting the finishing touches on a basket I was weaving. I did not at this point need a lot of light to see what I was doing, as I had become adept at weaving by the feel of the reeds between my fingers. I was thinking about Joseph and remembering how we had sat here together so many times before. As I told you, although Joseph was not with us in physical form, the strength of his spirit and the simplicity of his approach to life made the difference between living in physical form and living in spiritual form seem equally joyful and powerful. As I sat leaning against the olive tree, remembering my Joseph, I could feel him with me, and I did not feel alone.

Jesus came forward quietly, walking slowly from the courtyard entranceway. I knew immediately that something was wrong. He said, "Mother, I must speak with you. I really don't know where to begin. This is very difficult for me, but it comes up over and over again in my mind."

I said to him, "Jesus, please sit down next to me and tell me what is on your mind."

As he sat, he suddenly burst into tears. By this time, he was a grown man. Even so, he wept and wept. I allowed him to cry, for I know how important it is for emotions, when they pour forth, to be allowed to run their course. I placed my hand on his shoulder to remind him that I was there, but I remained silent.

At last, he spoke, "My dear Mother, I do not want to bring sadness or hardship upon you by asking you these questions." I knew immediately what he was going to ask me. I had known for many years that this day would come. I waited for him to finish. "Mother, from the time I was a child, I have heard rumors that Joseph was not my father, that you and he were married after you were already carrying a child. As I am the first born, I know that child was me. I don't know who I am, Mother. You have never told me, nor did Joseph, who I loved as my dear and true father. All my life, Mother, I have felt different. I have not meant to be different, but I have felt different. In all my life, Mother, I have loved you deeply and have tried to be a loyal and good son to you. Now I have grown to manhood, and I feel a pulling within me. I see so many things around me: sick people, poor people, political strife, cruelty, people in pain and suffering I want to help. I want to be a servant. I want to make life better for people. I don't know how I am going to do this, Mother. Rachel and I talk about things, for she feels this way, too. At the same time, I feel distracted by this uncertainty about the truth of my birth. Inside of me is a terrible unrest, for I do not know, Mother, who I am. Now, I come to you to tell me the truth. I promise you that whatever it is that you tell me I will hold sacred I will not castigate you or chastise you in any way. I only wish to know the circumstances of my birth and who I really am."

He looked at me with open and innocent eyes and I laid my hands against his face, stroked his hair and his brow. I said to him, "My child, I have not told you because for so many years I did not remember what had happened to me. The story lay buried inside of my mind. Events occurred when I was very, very young, that in many ways, are almost unexplainable. I will try to explain them all to you now even as I have begun to remember them myself.

From the time I was a child, Jesus, I saw and heard the voices of all living things. I could hear the leaves speak, the winds, the trees, the sky, even the air. I could see them running through the grasses. I talked with them, and I played with them; they were real to me. You remember, Jesus, when you were a little boy, you came to me and said, Mother, the other children are laughing at me and making fun of me because I can see and hear voices in nature. I knew exactly what you were talking about because I had been the same way.

Many times, since then, Jesus, I have thought about why I was able to see these things, when I knew others could not. I must tell you what I really believe in my heart. I can see these things, because my love for all things living and their joy is so strong. As I grew older, I felt even more a part of nature. Sometimes, I felt myself able to transform as I ran through the meadow. Sometimes I felt like the grass growing. As I would swim in the streams, I would feel as though I was the water. When the birds and the butterflies spoke to me, it was natural; it seemed that that was the way life was meant to be. Sometimes I would see visions. I don't know what these visions were, Jesus. The closest thing I can compare them to would be angels—beautiful angels. During this period, I was about eleven, twelve, or thirteen years old, I would often sense them around me and frequently see them. The sightings were often triggered by my mother's singing. I must be honest with you, my son; I began to question my own sanity. I knew other people were not experiencing these things. Something told me to keep my own counsel, to trust myself."

"Now you know that at a young age I was betrothed to Joseph. Through the wisdom of my family, my Joseph was chosen for me. Even at a young age, he exhibited a kindly and generous nature. Our two families came together and determined that we were a perfect match. I was a dutiful, spiritual, and loving child prone to fantasy, while Joseph was a strong, sensible, level-headed young man and together we would create a union of our qualities. Indeed, our families were wise, for through all our years together, Joseph and I admired and enjoyed each other. Now, my son, please take my hand while I tell you what I could not remember for so long."

"I want you to know this, before I tell you. About three months before this incident took place an angel appeared to me and said, 'Daughter Mary, you have been chosen for the purity of your heart and the love that lies within you for all living things. You shall be the mother of a child and his name shall be Jesus and you will bring forth a son and his light will fill the world. It is you, Mary, that God calls. We will be with you every step of the way. Do not be afraid. We are with you always' I did not know what this meant, but I held this experience closely to my heart. One day, my mother had left the house to go to the orchards with some friends of hers and I was all alone. I was fifteen years old. It was a very hot day. I was inside our house. Suddenly, I looked and there, standing in the doorway, was a man, a very tall man, with dirt and dust all over him and he appeared to have traveled far. He wanted something to drink and to eat. I was alone and not accustomed to strangers, so, I told him that I would bring him something to drink out in the yard. That did not satisfy him, and he came into the house. He said something to me about having a pretty face and he came toward me, and he kept coming toward me and I put my arms against him to force him away and he hit me and I fainted."

At this, Jesus dropped his head and put his face in his hands. I did not have to explain in detail. He understood what had happened. He began to cry. For myself, I remained somewhat numb, as there was a kind of real and unreal quality to that experience. I never remembered anything that happened to me after I fainted.

I put my arm on Jesus' back and stroked him. At last, he looked up at me, he took my hands in his, and he said, "Oh, Mother, I am so sorry. I did not know what you suffered." We looked at each other in silence and I spoke to him saying, "My dearest son, I do not understand this mystery, but I do know that I was told by an angel that I was to bring forth a son to be the light of the world. I know this to be true, you are my light, and you will be the light of the world, just as the angel told me. God works in mysterious and wondrous ways, and I have put my complete trust and faith in the path that lay before my feet. I have never questioned it, I have rebelled, I have cried out, but, I have always returned to the vision and the wisdom of the Holy Creator. We are eternally bonded, you and I, by the mystery that lies within God's heart. I can tell you Jesus, that as your mother, I have loved you with every breath of my body and that Joseph loved you with his entire being and from the depths of his heart. You are and have been and always will be our cherished, firstborn son, whose pathway is to lead to the Light. I don't know anything more than this, Jesus, but I know this much to be true."

By now it was quite dark and there was a very bright moon and its rays poured down through the leaves of the olive tree, highlighting the tears on Jesus' cheeks.

Jesus took my hands and laid his face against them. He kissed my hands. I took a piece of my veil and wiped his tears. He said to me, "Mother, I don't know who my father is. Who was that man? Where is he now? Could you recognize him? Was there anything about him that would tell me who he is? Please, Mother, tell me. I must know this."

I almost could not bear the agony in my son's voice. I could understand his questions and why he would want to know. I thought, perhaps, from the sandals this man had worn, for I remember seeing them clearly when he struck me and I fell to the ground, that he was a Roman soldier. Otherwise, I had no way of knowing who he was. He was not from our tribe or our people. He was foreign.

"Mother, I must take this into my heart. I don't know what I think or feel right now."

I took his face, looked at him directly, and said, "Jesus, you know who your father is. You know the father of all of us and you know what the angel told me. I assure you, as though my life depends on it, that what I have told you is true. Therefore, know that you have been chosen, you have been called, you have been created to fulfill God's plan. I don't know what this plan is. We, you and I, must live out that plan one moment to the next and trust the vision and the pathway that the Lord has made for us. That is all that we can do. What is done cannot be undone."

Jesus breathed very deeply. He looked at me, nodded his head, and even smiled. "You are right, Mother. I must contemplate, pray, and meditate about all that I have just heard, for this weighs deeply upon me and I have much to think about. Thank you for telling me the truth and for not hiding anything from me. The truth, regardless of what it is, brings a liberating feeling for me. I cherish and hold you in highest esteem. I love you with all my heart and I always will. It is clear to me why our destinies have been intertwined and I will pray that I may soon understand what my own pathway is to be. I find myself in a state of confusion about things and I must be alone to think this through. Do not worry about me. But I must go into the mountains alone to pray and to contemplate. I will leave early in the morning and shall return when I know what it is that I am to do." Jesus stood to go inside and offered me his hand to help me up.

"I think that I shall stay here a few moments longer. I bless you and may the Lord keep you safe and wrap his loving wisdom around you. The spirit of your father, Joseph, is with you and he will be with you in the mountains. He will be there with you, as I am with you always."

"Good night, Mother."

Jesus went inside. I pulled my veil more closely around me as it was quite chilly. I took a deep breath. I felt the powerful rays of the moon wash over me and I was relieved that this day had come; the day I had wished never would have had to come. I took a moment to say a prayer, "O, Holy Vision, creator of light, cleanse my heart, my soul, my spirit, and bathe me in light. Be with my son, our son, show him the way so that he may hear and follow. I am forever yours and will follow thee in all ways. Amen."

I picked up my basket, rose up, went inside to my bed, and slept deeply.

CHAPTER 28

My son did go to the mountain to pray and to think about the things that I had told him. He was gone for many weeks and during that time many thoughts and concerns came into my heart. There were times when I thought to take the donkey and follow him into the mountains, to find him and to comfort him. Each time that I had those thoughts, however, I knew that I would be disturbing him. It was important for me to allow him the complete freedom to realize his own independence, and to communicate with the Holy Spirit. Just as I am sure he was meditating and praying in the mountains, I did the same in my garden and on the long walks that I took. It was during this period that I came to understand that my son had truly been called and that I needed to encourage him to fulfill his destiny.

One day, I was walking away from the village and as I came to the bank of the river, I noticed the sunlight dancing upon the water's surface, making brilliant reflections like jewels. I found a smooth, warm stone on the bank and rested there, happily gazing into the light-filled water. As I did this, I saw an image of my son sitting and weeping at the crest of the mountain. I heard him cry out to the Holy Father, saying, "Oh Lord, I am your son, but who is my father? Why was I brought into this world by a nameless, faceless man, who violently set upon my mother? Why? Why? I pray to you, Holy Father, to enter my mind and spirit and reveal to me the meaning of this devastating and confusing event. I have been a faithful son to you, Oh Father, I have studied the scriptures and all the teachings of the scribes. I have prayed and meditated upon each point, and I have come to you for wisdom. I am not able to understand the deeper meaning of this conflict. Oh, Father, I call upon you now with all my heart, to shed your light on me and reveal the meaning of this awful event." As I sat on the bank, I came back to my senses and felt compelled to rise up and to walk farther along the river's edge. I could feel my son's suffering. I knew he was experiencing deep confusion and feelings of betrayal. As I walked along, I could feel his distress.

Soon, I came to a small hillside covered with trees, shrubs, and flowering vines. I had never walked in this direction before, but that day I followed a pathway leading to the top of the hill. As I made my way up, I could see the length of the river and portions of the village in the distance. As I climbed higher, I could see a beautiful expanse of the land below. My steps took me faster and faster to the top of the hill, until at last, I came to the very top. I heard a voice saying softly, "Look all around you, Mary. See the world from this place, look far and beyond, in every direction, as far and as wide as your eye can reach. That is how far our Light can reach. As you turn and see the world from every vantage point, know that your son will carry forth the words and the love that surpass understanding, that flow within and penetrate the hearts of every living being. You are a part of this plan and have been from the beginning, for as you stand upon this hilltop, the love in your heart flows to all living beings."

"Now, Mary, fear not about your son. There are many things still to come to pass, many events that will take place. This is as it was meant to be. Your understanding and trust will make it possible for you to experience the events in such a way as to bring forth a depth of understanding and wisdom. Go now, for your son will return today and he will reveal to you the inner workings of his mind and heart. He has reached a full and complete understanding of the true origins of his existence. Go now, for by evening he will return to your home. Prepare to be with him."

Without another thought, I made my way down the hill in anxious anticipation of reuniting with my son. I hurried along the riverbank, moving quickly. Before long, I arrived home and began preparing dinner. Just as twilight came and I was placing food upon the table, I heard my son's footsteps. He called my name, and I ran to embrace him. He was sunburned, his hair was long, and he had grown a beard. In his eyes there radiated a peacefulness that I had never seen in him before.

"My son," I said, "I am so happy that you have returned home. Come, I have made a supper for you, of all your favorite things. Sit at the head of the table, for I am sure your appetite is strong after so many weeks in the mountains."

Jesus smiled, laughed, and said, "Yes, indeed, Mother, many, many times I thought of your special dishes, the delicacy and tastiness of the foods you always prepare for us. You knew I was coming today, did you not, Mother?"

"Yes, my son, I was on the hilltop taking a walk and I knew that you would return this evening."

Jesus replied, "Yes, Mother, I know."

"Let us sit and give thanks, for a mother and her son and for the magnificence of this food."

Jesus ate every bite of food with relish. Eating second and third portions, we laughed and talked. I set a plate of fresh fruit on the table and as it had grown quite dark, I took a moment to light candles. The other children were away in other places and so it happened that we were by ourselves.

Then Jesus spoke seriously, "Mother, you know why I went to the mountains. I want to tell you what I learned there. There were days and nights when I was so agitated, angry, and disturbed that I did not know which way to turn. I felt betrayed by the Holy Father. I felt confused by the events that brought me into this world. I could not understand why this had happened to me or to you. I prayed and meditated but no answers came. I walked and walked and walked. I cried out. I questioned my life's worth. What terrible character traits may lie within me, from a father unknown, nameless and faceless? I threw myself into the dirt and wept, beating the ground with my fists. I thought about killing that man who came to you that day so long ago. I fantasized about seeking him out and slitting his throat for what he had done to you, and then throwing him into the center of the town for everyone to see. All these thoughts and feelings raged through me. I felt so unworthy, unlovable, devoid of human feelings and compassion, like an animal only fit to be kicked and beaten. Then, I saw your face, Mother; I saw the light and the love in your eyes. I heard your voice call out to me. I felt your arms embrace me and sing tenderly to me. I felt sunlight penetrate my heart, for I could see and hear you, Mother, and my heart began to heal."

"I called upon my Holy Father, and this is what I heard:

'My Son, hear my words, feel my heart entwine with yours, and know that you carry within you the seeds of all human experience, every feeling, ever experienced by anyone. All that I am lives inside of you. All of my children need to know this. Many believe that I am somewhere else, in another place, in another time, but this is not true. Knowledge of the nature of your conception has opened a place inside of you and allowed you to know this fully and with complete understanding. Without this event, there would not be a way for you to experience this fully and completely, for each of my children walks upon the earth, and I cry out in loneliness and need for them, to know me, who I truly am and you, my son, will help me. You will help me to bring us all together again. It is time to bring us all together.'"

"Mother, from that moment, I felt differently. I cannot put this into words, but I know that you understand. I know now, Mother, events will occur, and I will fulfill a plan. See, Mother, I was so fully imbued with the Light, that the events that will occur, in a way are in my mind; although I know they are real, there is a feeling of unreality, that the fulfillment of this spirit that I feel inside, this light, is so great, that whatever is to come my way, is simply a series of events to bring us home; therefore Mother, I take your hands in mine and I give thanks for this homecoming this evening and as I look into your eyes, Mother, I simply know all, all."

We sat with no words exchanged, and the candles slowly burned. The stars shone brightly and as we sat, into the night, we heard every cricket, felt every breeze, and from that day on we lived in the grateful awareness of who we were and who all others were.

Now, my beloveds, we bless you, and call upon each and every one of you. Like my son, you will hear, wherever you are, whoever you may be, no matter what you feel you have done, the Holy Spirit calls you home.

For many people, the greatest obstacle to being called home is trusting the power each of us has to communicate with God. This is where people stumble and fall, where they fight and resist, pull back, run away, proclaim loudly, develop intellectual treatises and important documents proclaiming otherwise; establish theories and systems of externally proclaiming God everyplace but within. I understand this resistance. The hardest idea for man to know is that God lies within and that we are one, but it comes, my dearly beloved ones, it just simply comes. In his presence, it is eternal. When you call out, God really does answer you.

Give yourself joy and beauty—you need these things more than anything—and we would add to that, enjoyment. When you give yourself all three, everything else will flow naturally as a result. This is an opposite concept for many people, for they would think in terms of hard work, sacrifice, or hardship. If you give yourself truly, truly, what you long for, dream of, and desire so fervently, if you give yourself these things, you will see miracles happen. You will see a flowering, an expansion, an incredible fulfillment that far exceeds your wildest imagination. When it is hard for you to achieve what you wish to achieve it is not because you are not working hard or long enough. When you tend to the needs of your spirit, all physical or material manifestations flow naturally from that.

I ask you not to simply believe this because I have said it, but rather to try it and see with your own eyes what it is that we describe for you. Indulge your desires for joy, beauty, and fulfillment of your heart's dreams. Do not postpone. The time is now.

CHAPTER 29

The day came when Jesus left our family home to go into the villages and over the mountains to other regions where he was beginning to gather like-minded followers. At first, I did not want him to leave our village to travel so far away for such lengths of time. I feared for his safety. During this time there was a great deal of political and social unrest. But, I also knew that my son had an inner journey to follow and that it was important for me to honor this and to support him in his life's calling. Although I had the worries and fears of a mother, I kept them to myself and encouraged my son to follow his heart. By doing so, I maintained a closeness with him and developed a clear understanding of the ideas behind his work.

From the time he was a child it truly saddened him to see people in desperate need, who had no way to find relief from their despair. My son was very aware of the political entanglements and the power structures that existed in our daily lives. He knew the fear, the violence, and the laws that were used to control and manipulate the lives of the common people. Even so, my son sought daily guidance and light to be shed upon his path through daily prayer and meditation with the Holy Father. Knowing this about him made it a little easier for me to let him go.

My son spoke to groups of people wherever he found them. Sometimes they would be at a river's edge, in fishing boats. Jesus would walk among the men, sometimes taking up the net in his own hands, to work alongside the other fishermen. He made friends easily and he always found the right words to say in just the right situation, using words that everyone could understand.

I must tell you that during this time of our lives, the average person labored long and hard to provide food for their families and that consumed the bulk of their time. With the government using violent measures to keep the people under their control, it made what Jesus was doing even more dangerous and would later expose him to their scrutiny. Imagine, a personable young man who walked among the common people, beginning to talk and to paint word-pictures that engaged their minds, opened their hearts, and allowed them to think in ways that they had never been allowed to think before.

It should come as no surprise that not every person was a willing listener. Sometimes, people spat at him and yelled or booed and hissed at the things he had to say. It was during these times that Jesus became aware of an inner power that gave him the ability to create what some would call miracles.

One such instance involved the feeding of a multitude of people who had gathered to hear him speak by the river's edge. There were hundreds upon hundreds of people. They came from far and wide, mostly on the spur of the moment, many of them dropping their daily tasks to make their way to the gathering place. It soon became clear that this large mass of people would go hungry as there were no places nearby where they could buy food. Many of them had traveled long distances.

Jesus later described for me the energy in that crowd. The strength of their presence, the look in their eyes as they listened intently to his words, opened up his heart in a way he had never felt. He called upon the Holy Father to open the heavens and to provide a way to feed these people. Just as he made that prayer, a group of fishermen appeared close by in the harbor with boats laden with fish. As they were followers of my son, they gladly offered to feed the people with the fish they had freshly caught.

Suddenly, a man appeared out of nowhere; he strode directly toward Jesus and said, "Master, here is wine for the people to drink. There is enough for every person." Jesus gave thanks for he knew that these people had appeared in answer to his prayer. He knew that the love of his Father in Heaven was made manifest on earth through the generosity and the coming together of the people gathered to hear him speak.

My son, throughout his life, remained an ordinary, caring, loving human being. He never lost sight of who he was and the simple purpose of his existence. That is why he reached the hearts of so many people. Anyone who met him immediately saw and felt his simplicity, honesty, and capacity for love. In many ways, he was like a child. He never thought to manipulate, to be greedy, or to seek power. After so many years of suppression by the Roman soldiers, the kings, and governors, riding on lofty horseback and bedecked in their finest clothes, it was a great shock to the ordinary person to be in the presence of my son who was so clearly a leader and yet so simple and humble a man.

While many people found these qualities refreshing and gratifying, it was these same qualities that also irritated and infuriated others. They assumed that this was all a sham, to cover up my son's real goal of taking over, of claiming power. This frightened, indeed terrified many people in high places, both in the government and in the temple. My son soon became an object not just of ridicule but of suspicion.

Those against Jesus would sometimes lay traps by planting agitators in the crowds; people paid to ask Jesus all sorts of questions in an attempt to have him say something that could be used against him. But they could never manage in their efforts. My son's simplicity and greater vision lifted the hearts of even these people, who stood in awe of his ability to take every question put before him and bring forth a clear and meaningful reply, understandable both to the intellectual and to the simplest, uneducated mind. In fact, the more these agitators laid these traps for him, the more followers he gained. All those within hearing distance were spellbound by the beauty and the insights that came from his words.

One evening Jesus was called to the home of one who had recently died. His family was weeping and crying in grief. They had tried to reach Jesus earlier in the day to come and perform a miracle over the man who had been their son and brother. He had died before they reached Jesus, and when they found him, the family surrounded him, crying out in sorrow and pain. Jesus asked them, "Why do you cry? Your son is not lost. He lives." They lamented, "No, Master, he is dead. Gone from us this very morning. We will never see him again."

Jesus replied, "Weep not, for your son does live. Come, let us go to him and I shall show you."

They approached the grave and there was their son, who stood up and greeted them. They all dropped to their knees and instantly their hearts were open; they gave thanks to my son, who immediately lifted his hands to the heavens and cried out, in praise and thankfulness to the power of the Holy Spirit.

"Remember this day," cried Jesus, "for you have seen a living demonstration of the power of the Holy Spirit, made manifest in this man, who stands before you, fully healed and blessed by the spirit. Know that this miracle that you see before you came from the only power in this world or any other. Do not be fooled, dear people, by grand displays and fanfare. See and recognize today that the true power, the only power is the magnificence of the Light of God that brought this man fully to life. By recognizing this power in you, each and every one of you who stands here today will carry this Light, like an eternally burning candle that illuminates each and every heart, for now and forever more." There was much rejoicing and celebration, and many people, including many of the wealthy people of the villages, bowed before Jesus asking forgiveness for their greed. Some of these very people would later become his disciples.

Sometimes, Jesus would become exhausted and to gain perspective and to strengthen himself would go into the mountains to pray and to meditate. He needed this time alone, away from all those people who needed him, in order to reclaim for himself the resolve needed for his work.

This was not something that his disciples could always easily understand. They did not all possess the same inner quietude that my son had. Therefore, these periods of retreat were very difficult for them, and it was during these times that they felt the most confusion and sense of doubt. It was one thing to see Jesus as the leader and speaker before hundreds of men, women, and children. It was quite another thing to see him a quiet and lonely man praying in the moonlight in the cold air of the mountains.

One day I was in my home, preparing food in the courtyard, when I heard familiar footsteps. I looked up and there I saw Jesus, who came toward me smiling and embraced me and lifted me up off my feet. He twirled me around and laughed heartily, saying, "Oh, Mother, dear mother, how I have missed you. I have come home to you, for I need to be near my mother's heart, to hear her wisdom, to steady me and to hold me close."

So, we ate and laughed and talked.

When Jesus told me of these miracles, he also shared with me many doubts, fears, and questions that he had held closely inside his own heart and mind. He knew that the word about his work had spread to the highest officials of the land and that his life could be in danger. This concerned him not so much because he feared death, but rather he feared he would not have time to complete his work. He asked me what I thought about this.

You can imagine what a question like this can mean to a mother. What was I to say? One part of me wanted to say to him, stop, stop this ministry, give it up, turn back, and take up the occupation that your father taught you. One part of me wanted to encourage him to stay in the village and continue to preach and to stop his traveling. In my heart of hearts, though, I knew that I had to speak truly to him. It was clear to me and always had been, that my son had a task to fulfill, a mission to complete, a journey to travel. So, when he asked me what my thoughts were on this subject, I simply said, "Son, do as your Father bids you. Do not turn back or away from what you know to be your calling. Continue to pray and to receive the spirit which guides you. Your pathway will be lit by the light of God. He has never forsaken you, Jesus, nor will he ever. Your father, Joseph, was a living example of this. If he were here now, he would encourage you, my son, to follow the light within your heart in spite of all obstacles. You have always received encouragement from us here at home, to follow what you know to be true. You have wisely returned home to anchor yourself and to gain strength so that you may set out once again with greater insight and energy. You will fulfill your destiny, given to you by your Holy Father. His power is greater than any force you are facing on this Earth. He will be by your side every step of the way, just as he has been by my side every step of the way, in my own life."

And now, dear ones, I pray that your hearts will open to the destiny that lies within each and every one of you. For it is God who speaks within you if you only have ears to listen and a heart to feel and see. The happiness that awaits you is glorious. I pray that each and every one of you will open your heart this day to the light within that is the Holy Spirit. It is what connects and binds each and every one, for no one is separate; we are eternally bound through the Spirit. The opening of your hearts will bring about a glorious revelation.

CHAPTER 30

Time passed and life became steady, clear, and fulfilling. My children had grown, and they were healthy. They married and had families of their own. I was blessed with many grandchildren, who gave me many happy hours. Only Jesus remained unmarried, for it seemed that he was so driven by his work and his need to travel to other regions to preach. Where many others would have dared not go, Jesus always forged ahead, following the visions he received through prayer and meditation. He never questioned his purpose, but rather followed his inner guidance, which he received from the Holy Father.

My daughter, Rachel, was now herself a mother, having brought forth six children of her own. She was a strong and courageous force in the community; she was outspoken and energetic in helping the sick, the feeble, and the aged. Her heart warmed those in truly desperate conditions. She understood their needs and always tended to them as personal friends, with great dignity. While most others saw these people as desperate beggars, clinging to the fringes of existence, my daughter, Rachel, saw each person as a very special, beautiful, human being. Rachel was unafraid and never worried in any way about going among this group, although many of them were often quite ill.

She became known throughout the countryside, particularly for her ability to heal the spirit. She sat with people, told them stories, sang to them. She touched their hands and faces when no others would. She fed them and bathed them. She had a talent for preparing herbs and poultices.

Much of this was self-taught; Rachel seemed to simply know many of these recipes. She experimented. She had a natural understanding of what to do and she did it, every day. Singing always as she approached them, she brought them flowers or anything that she could find that was beautiful in color. Rachel went throughout the village to collect bits of cloth or anything that she could find of color or having a shiny surface. She would string these objects together, sometimes sewing them, to make banners that she would attach to poles. These she would carry with the help of some of her friends, to the places where the aged, sick, and feeble lived. She would place the poles around where they were lying, thrusting them into the earth and placing rocks around them to hold them up. These magical banners, as she called them, helped by the wind, made beautiful patterns of light, color, and sound. In many she had sewn in small bells, or objects that would make tinkling sounds in the wind. The tall banners could be seen for miles around and were greatly admired not only by the people themselves for whom they were intended, but also by the villagers.

There were some people who did not understand the purpose of Rachel's magical banners and started rumors that she was not just eccentric, but crazy. They tried to plant suspicions in the minds of the elders of the community. Her banners were attracting so much attention because they were unusual and therefore threatening to some people. This tendency toward unusual expression within our family would present a recurrent problem in our lives. It has always been the case that when one follows the joy within oneself, acts unquestionably out of inner soul searching, when one follows fully and truly one's destiny, this ability will call up within others their deepest fears, insecurities, yearnings, doubts, and ultimately bring forth jealousy, violence, and aggression. You may ask why? How can this be when a person is simply following something good within themselves? Why should it be this way?

This is why: the desire for the light within is so great, that when one does not have it, or is blocked from receiving it, and when one sees others who have the light, it invokes an energetic rage that can manifest petty manipulation or outright violence. Between their desire to have the light and their inability to find it, that raging energy can take many twists and turns. Many, many times the person who is following the light will become the victim of those in most desperate need. This, my dear friends, is the condition of the world in which you live. Make no mistake; this is ever-present in your lives as you know it.

My dear Rachel never questioned her life's pursuits. For her, everything that she touched flowered and bloomed. It was a natural extension of her spirit. She never forced it; it simply was. As her banners floated and danced in the wind, she sat with her people and told them stories. She knew them all by name. Many people under her care were healed and returned to their homes and families, grateful to be alive, never expecting this second chance at health. Others continued to live in this community of beggars, but the quality of their lives grew richer and deeper. Many within that community grew strong enough to help others who were less able. In this way, Rachel was able to have assistance in her work.

The people who had been spreading rumors that Rachel was crazy and had evil powers, came one day to her door with a written edict proclaiming that she was no longer allowed to go among the sick and administer to them in any way. The reason they put forth was that she would bring disease into the main village, a threat to the well-being of the healthy villagers. She was to cease from any further association with the community of beggars who lived among the rocks on the outskirts of the village. This edict was given to her on a scroll stamped with the seal of the elders of the village.

Rachel came to my house immediately when she received this news. She said, "Mother, two soldiers delivered this edict, only moments ago, I have it here in my hand, signed by all the elders, proclaiming that I am never again to go to my friends. They say that I am a threat to the health and well-being of our village, and that I will bring disease to the healthy, to my own family. Mother, what am I to do? The encampment depends on me, I cannot leave my work. I will not stop, Mother."

I looked at Rachel's face and in my heart, I knew that no edict would stop my daughter from her mission. It was clear. I said to her, "Rachel, as I see it, you have no choice but to follow what you know to be the most important thing in your life. We must devise a way around this edict. I would recommend that you let a few days go by and visit your community of friends during the night. Under the cover of darkness, you can still help them, but hopefully not be seen by those who are so concerned. I recommend this path for the current time."

This pleased and satisfied Rachel, for she always had a sunny approach to any obstacle that came her way. Rather than dwelling on what could not be, she immediately invested herself, with full energy into this new plan. For a while, it worked, but, like so many times in life, the day came when our alternative methods were found out. A tribunal was formed, as they had learned that Rachel had continued her work in secret and against their orders. The elders decided that action must be taken to rid the village of Rachel's presence and the accompanying potential threat of disease. They dispatched a soldier on horseback to snatch her from her bed at night and to take her miles and miles away, where she was thrown into an unfamiliar den, a den of diseased people, people without families or homes. In order to punish her for her insubordination, they threw her into the worst known area for lepers and thieves.

With a friend of mine, I went to the elders and to the head of the tribunal to plead my daughter's case. I was met with such harsh words, such arrogance, such unfeeling cruelty, such utter hatred, and scorn. It did not help her that her brother Jesus with his preaching and healing already was a renowned troublemaker, a rebellious revolutionary. I could do nothing to persuade the tribunal; they had made their decision and it had been carried out. They did everything but spit upon me. I was lower to them than the lowest animal and without husband I did not even have the authority to plead my case.

My friend and I returned home. We knew that they had taken Rachel miles and miles away and that she was heavily guarded by armed soldiers. I prayed, asking for direction and guidance. I was comforted by one recurring thought: I knew my daughter would not turn back, no matter what. She was not weak, but now she could no longer make her magical banners or take her bread and herbs and poultices to the people. Surely now she was in need of these things herself. At the end of my prayer, I vowed that nothing would stop me from finding her. In the morning, I, with a friend, would depart from the village to find Rachel.

Rachel's husband had disowned her in the name of safety for his own family and kin. He told me privately he had to do this, or the lives of their children would have been in danger. You see, my friends, it is never easy to follow that path, the difficult, winding path of the light. Now my daughter, who was so filled with light and joy, had lost her family, her husband, and children, because her community turned against her.

I rode for two and a half days over rough terrain. Even in this dark hour there were, in fact, signs of hope along the way. Word of my daughter's beauty and true spirit was known through the countryside by many, many people. Talking to them lifted my spirits; I soon realized that for every negative person who was filled with dark energy, there was an equal abundance, if not more, of those who knew the truth. The difference being that they were not in places of power.

We rode on and at last came upon a prison where I had been told my daughter Rachel was being held. It was a horrible place filled with cries of agony, of death and dying. There were no magical banners here, only sorrow. The soldiers were resting in the hot, noonday sun and paid little attention to the gates. I walked past them, unnoticed, and I came to the top of a hill.

There, I saw Rachel. She was sitting on the highest rock, with only her white undergarment for clothes, with many people gathered at her feet. In the heat, the terrible heat, their faces seemed transported. The soldiers seemed hardly to care whether she sang or danced. There was a fence between me and Rachel and the people, and the one guard who was leaning against a tree. I managed to slip behind him, quietly, so as not to disturb him. I drew closer. Rachel was very thin, but amazingly she did not look ill. My worse fear was that she would have become ill. What I saw was something I can almost barely describe, for I did believe that she had transformed into an angel. She was luminescent with light, her hair flowed down around her, and she was amazingly untouched by sunburn or by dirt. Her voice rang out like a bell. I watched, hesitant to disturb her work. At last, she climbed off the rock and went among the people. Instead of distributing food or herbs the way she used to do, she distributed blessings to each person individually.

When she had completed her task, I called out to her, "Rachel." She lifted her head and she looked in my direction. She ran to the fence and cried out, "Mother, you found me; I knew you would find me."

We hugged each other. I said to her, "I must take you from this place."

She replied, "No, Mother, my destiny is here. I will be killed if I leave. It is better for me to stay. I have been befriended by that soldier at the tree. He watches over me and will not let anyone harm me. I must finish out my days here, Mother, unless it is God's will for it to be otherwise."

I told her about her children and husband, I thought it best that she knows the truth. She was not angry, but instead was glad that they were safe. She had accepted her destiny. The soldier by the tree protected her, gave her food and a special place to sleep, so that she could live as comfortably as was possible in these circumstances. However, if she tried to escape, he would have no recourse but to capture her and he would be forced to kill her. Knowing this, she accepted the situation and continued her healing work under these dreadful circumstances. I prayed over my daughter and blessed her.

As I left, the soldier by the tree approached me. He said, "Madam, I see you are the angel's mother. I am her protector; she is safe as long as I am here. She is an angel, you know. Go in peace, Mother, go in peace."

I can't describe the feeling. Words cannot fully and adequately describe this experience, but those of you who read this account, who have had similar experiences, will understand. I climbed upon my donkey, and we rode away. As we rode, I saw the eyes of that soldier and heard his words once again in my ears: "She is an angel, you know." This simple soldier knew my daughter for who she really was.

As I continued the journey, my heart began to feel lighter and lighter. I knew that Rachel would continue to transform all those around her with the beauty of her spirit, would lift the darkness and hatred, the ignorance, and the cruelty, with the help of the soldier who protected her. Truth shines luminescent, like my daughter, Rachel, like my son, Jesus, and like all of you who follow the inner light of God within you.

CHAPTER 31

Today I am standing on a hilltop with the sun beaming down upon me, overlooking the lands and the people below. There is a wind gently blowing and I can see the reflection of the sun dancing off the water in the stream. There are sheep grazing and the air smells clear and fresh.

I have come to you this day to escort Rachel back to her favorite and beloved spot, which is very near the hilltop where I am now standing. This was a special place of solace and peace for her where she spent so much of her time. Rachel sacrificed many personal aspects of her life out of her love and loyalty to our family and out of her concern to care and comfort me, and because of her dedication to the work of her brother.

Come now; let us walk down the hill. It is a rather steep hill and in fact we both have strong staffs in our hands to help us for it is rather slippery in places. Ahead we can see the tops of bushes and a few trees and as we walk toward them, we come to a little bower of trees that form almost a circle, and the trees are somewhat bent and almost form a roof where they have almost grown together. Up above and to one side is a brook, a stream that passes by these trees. In between the trees are foliage and bushes that snuggle between the trunks. It is a very quiet place to sit and think. The sound of the brook, the quiet nook between the trees, and the rustle of the leaves allowing sunlight to filter down between the trees add touches of warmth and beautiful light.

Now, Rachel would come here to sit and think alone and indeed spent many hours here. Sometimes I would accompany her, but more often than not she came here by herself.

I have asked Rachel to speak in her own words what this place meant to her. "I came to this place when it was too hard to bear so many things. There were so many people talking. People in the village spoke behind our backs, and many times I was afraid, because so many people seemed to dislike us. They would whisper things, I tried not to let Mother know these things and I tried to shield her from these people. Sometimes it was just too hard, and I would go down the hill as quickly as possible to my special place and I would think about the children that I had had, it was very hard.

"I would think about the hours I worked to make the banners that I flew for the people around there. At first my children helped me make those banners, but when they attracted so much attention, people misunderstood their purpose. They accused me of all sorts of terrible things, that I was bringing sickness and plague, pestilence, that I would infect the whole village with these terrible troubles, even that I would infect my own children and make them sick, that I had put them in danger. I would go to the rocks and take what food I had and divide it up among the desperate people lying there. I tried to make their lives happier, by putting up my special banners so that they had something to look at. As they lay there, they could look up and see my banners floating in the sky and that would distract them and help them forget the misery they were in.

"It got very hot on the rocks, so I would take water and splash it on the people to cool them and I would take a rag and wash their foreheads and faces. And to soothe them, I would hum and sing as I was doing this. But then people in the village thought that I would be infected with disease from touching and washing them. And so, when I went to the well to get water, they would not let me draw water and they would push me away and spit at me. It got worse and worse. Finally, my husband came and took my children away.

"I came home to find my house empty. My children were gone. Everything that belonged to them was gone. My husband's things were gone. I walked about in circles, not knowing what to do. I sat down on the floor and stared into space. I couldn't even cry. I felt numb. Nothing had prepared me for this. I couldn't understand why they had turned against me for helping people. Before he left, my husband berated me over and over again, telling me that I was jeopardizing the children and the whole family, that I was selfish. He said that I was crazy, and that hurt me very much. Many people thought I was crazy, they said only a crazy person would be the one who would go to the rocks and help the other people who were crazy.

"Then I was captured and taken to that horrible place, which my mother has told you about. My whole family were outcasts. In every way we were different. After Father died, it was much harder, because we didn't have him to protect us from the rest of the villagers. My Father was very respected by the other people in the Village. His presence provided an anchor to our family. But when Father died everything changed. The things that made us so different became much more apparent to the rest of the village. So, Mother and Jesus and I became even closer, for we really only had each other. Even though Jesus had the men who followed him, they came one by one, over a period of time, and there were many problems and conflicts with them as well.

"When I sat in my special place, I tried not to think about sad or frightening things. "Often, I felt anger toward my brother. I thought he was selfish, to take such risks, to put our family in constant danger. Sometimes I just wanted to cry out and tell him what I really thought, but I didn't feel that I could add to all our problems, so I kept it to myself. So, I would come here. Mother would try to talk to me, and I knew that she was concerned, but there was so much confusion. Sometimes we didn't know where Jesus was and sometimes even his disciples didn't know. They would come to our house looking for him and they would tell us rumors that were going around the countryside about him.

"One time when I returned from my special hiding place, I came home, and Jesus was sitting there. He asked me where I had been, and I told him that I had been walking and thinking. He asked me what I was thinking about, and I told him I was thinking about why we were so different from the rest of the village. Why we didn't seem to fit in.

He looked at me with a smile and laughed quietly. I asked him why he was laughing? And He said, 'Rachel, we are different. What is wrong with that?' I said, 'Different? What does that mean, Jesus?' And he said, 'Rachel, I don't mean that we are different in a better way, but we see something and we are trying to express what it is that we see. That is all that we are doing, Rachel. And, if that makes us different, then so be it.'

"Well, I couldn't exactly argue with what he said, so I was quiet for a few moments. Then, I said to him, 'Yes, but where will all this lead us? It seems so confusing, and we have so many enemies.' And he said, 'Rachel, one has enemies, if you call them enemies, but if you walk through this village and you see no enemies, then there will be no enemies. I do not see enemies, Rachel. I see people who have questions, doubts, and fears. Yes, they are confused; sometimes we are all confused. That is why I must go through the countryside and see the people and tell them what I know.'

"He always had the answers. And then, we would just laugh. Because somehow, even though I really didn't understand, somehow it made sense. And he would scoop me up and give me a big hug."

Rachel's voice and experience is vital for your world today. Indeed, Rachel was summoned in many ways to serve as a conduit, as a messenger, as a storyteller, as a linkage from the ancient to the present. Rachel, in her lifetime, was an artist, although we didn't give her that name. Rachel was a healer and she questioned everything and thought deeply. Rachel did not take the well-traveled path. Like her brother, she followed her inner spirit and we summoned Rachel to bring the news. Sometimes Rachel is shy and needs encouragement, but I have asked her to speak for our family and so she shall.

CHAPTER
32

When I left Rachel, I realized there was nothing I could do to change the circumstances of her situation. The soldiers were instructed to fulfill their duties and the tribunal who made their decision against my daughter was powerful and absolutely unwilling to review the case. I thanked God that Rachel was alive, even though it was clear that she was a prisoner and unable to escape. I knew that the difference between life and death for her resided in the belief of that soldier who thought she was an angel. I knew that his belief in her powers to heal others, to sing, tell stories, and show compassionate wisdom brought him to also believe that it was his duty to protect her. In the face of certain dangers to himself, he continued to guard and watch over her.

No mother is prepared for such a situation to come into the life of her child, and I became deeply and severely depressed after seeing her. I found that I could not eat or sleep, and I found my heart to be so heavy that I wondered if I could continue to live.

It was during a particularly black period that Jesus returned home. I was sitting under the olive tree in the courtyard, only this time I was not weaving a basket or preparing food as I normally would do. It was as if I were a shell, devoid of feeling and life force. Jesus found me in this bleak mood.

When he came into the courtyard, it seems unbelievable now that I tell this, but I did not even rise up to greet him. I was disheveled, my hair was unkempt. I had been spending hour after hour staring into space. I had found it physically impossible to pray or to read from the Torah or to take the walks that I once loved so much. Jesus came directly to me and knelt by my side. He said, "Mother, dear Mother, I can't bear to see you like this. I've heard what has happened to Rachel. I know your heart is broken. Oh, Mother, what can I do to help you, to bring you to life again? I cannot bear to see you like this, so unlike the mother I have known my whole life. Please, Mother, speak to me. Open your heart and tell me everything that you have kept inside. I know that if you can talk about all that troubles you that you will be able to live again. Mother, please, it is I, your son, Jesus, calling you to return to life."

When I heard the word "life," something about the way he said the word caused me to look at him directly and in so doing, it brought me back to the reality that I was working so hard to avoid. I burst into tears and wept and wept. Jesus stayed by my side, holding me, wiping the tears, and reassuring me that everything would be all right. This outpouring of emotion was the opening that I needed to see the reality before me; prior to that, I had been living in a state of blinding denial, virtually holding my breath against this terrible emotion that I felt over the loss of my daughter Rachel. By releasing this river of tears, I was able to face the true circumstances of her captivity.

I felt within me an incredible strength, deep within my soul; I found myself rising up from the bench where, only moments before, I had been as weak and compliant as a rag doll. Now I found myself filled with an all-consuming energy, driven by the fires of an anger so great, that the rage that now poured out of me had the strength of an army. I cried out, "How dare they lock up my daughter? And tear her from her children? And husband? No one has the right to do this! Who are these people, to tear my daughter from me? I will not stand by any longer and allow this madness to overrun my home. They can throw me into their prisons, but they will not keep my daughter any longer. Let them grab me, let them take me. Their wickedness is beyond redemption. I shall no longer be victim to the madness of those in power who respect the lives of no one. I'm going to rescue Rachel, and no one can stop me. I will free her, or I will die. I have a plan; it came to me in a dream. I must now make preparations to reach my daughter as soon as I can physically get there.

Don't try to stop me, Jesus. I stand before you now and declare that I will not sit by and allow this to go on any longer."

Jesus said, "Mother, I will help you. Tell me what to do, show me where to go and let us depart as quickly as possible, for I feel that Rachel needs us immediately."

We gathered up a few essential items and left within the hour. Neither of us could sleep. Under the cover of night, we might travel in safety. The moon was bright and lit our way and, as you remember, it was a lengthy journey made over a number of days. I was absolutely driven with the intent of getting to Rachel. I was determined that I would free her from bondage at any cost.

Jesus and I spoke very little during the journey; my concentration was rapt in determining every step of planning Rachel's escape. I played the scene over and over in my mind as we rode along, and I saw the events step by step. I wanted to be fully prepared for whatever needed to be done.

Several nights later, we finally came to the horrible place where my daughter had been banished and kept captive. I decided to dress as a sick beggar and to slip into the compound, find Rachel, and while the guards slept, slip out. Jesus would wait with the horses. We would ride through a familiar passage to the river below, where if necessary, we would take the horses across. If we were lucky, we would follow the river's bank for many miles until a safe haven was found. This was my plan.

It was two o'clock in the morning and there was a moon, however it was dim that night. Jesus was stationed with the horses at the agreed place. We did not exchange words, there were no hushed good-byes, and we never allowed ourselves to think that we would not be successful. We had work to do, a task to complete, and we entered this realm with all the strength we had.

There were soldiers spread around the compound, but they were all asleep. I slipped in past them and came to an area that looked like a stable carved out in the side of a hill. It was very dark and had an odor. Most of this place was bordered by fences, but as I got nearer, I saw that there were some broken places that had not been repaired. Probably, by this time, they did not think anyone would attempt to escape, much less enter.

I hurried through an opening. The only light was the moon and, as this compound was carved out underneath and within a rocky hill, it was not easy to see where I was going. I could hear people moaning, groaning, coughing, and combined with the sounds of animals. There were bats everywhere with their muddy excrement. I had one thought, only: to find my Rachel.

I stepped over people, some of whom stirred, and someone cried out, "Ohhhhhhhhhh, ohhhhh." I prayed that the soldiers would not hear their cries. Every direction I looked there was a foot, a leg, an arm, but nowhere did I see Rachel. I continued farther and deeper into this horrible compound. At last, I found her. There she was, lying on a rock, sleeping. She had managed to find the one dry spot above the muck of this hideous place.

For a moment, I marveled at her ability to survive in this deathbed. I realized then that it wasn't that she had purposefully taken the best place; no one else there had the strength to climb that rock, so, it became her bed and preaching post.

I slipped quietly toward her; I did not want to awaken and frighten her or startle her in any way. In my dream of saving her, I had sung her the lullaby I had sung when she was a child. I crept toward her and in the softest tones possible, I sang. She awoke immediately and grasped my arm. I whispered quickly, "It is your mother, follow me." Without hesitation we slithered down off a stone, each of us leading toward a pathway she knew that could take a quicker route than I had coming in. Again, we heard the awful sounds, the moans, and groans, and coughing.

Little by little, we inched our way. I had with me a cloak that I threw around us both, that would better hide us. At last, we came to the opening in the fence. There we were, about to flee, but suddenly we were met by the soldier, who had been somehow awakened. As we tried to climb through, his arms reached down and grabbed us both. He pulled us back in and into the light of the moon. We were immobile in his hands.

He held us fiercely but never said a word, all the while looking directly into our faces. Then, almost as if he had been shot, he hurled us with such force that we both went flying forward down the hill. It almost felt as if someone had picked us up and carried us through the air. We never gave it a thought; we saw the opportunity to escape and ran, hand in hand, through the tall grasses and reeds. We ran until I saw the horses and Jesus, waiting. We threw ourselves upon the animals and rode and rode, and rode. We did not look back, we did not stop, and the animals seemed to understand their purpose. We did not stop until we reached the river. As we reached the bank of the river, Jesus said, "It's dangerous to cross the river here, but there is no alternative but to ride straight ahead." Again, the horses seemed to know their purpose and they carried us safely to the other side. Even then we continued on, not wanting to take any chances. It was dawn before we allowed ourselves the luxury of stopping. We had reached a thicket with many trees, and we virtually fell off the horses and collapsed to the ground. We were so exhausted that we wrapped ourselves in each other's arms and slept.

In the morning, we awoke and for the first time, I could see my daughter's face and feel her arms around me. I held her close and sang to her and cradled her and kissed her and stroked her hair. I told her I would never let anyone harm her, ever again. Rachel looked up with the most beautiful smile. Indeed, she had the light of an angel around her. It was true what the soldier had said.

We prayed and gave thanks for our safety, and I made a special prayer of thanks for the soldier who had let us go. When he hurled us out of the compound, looking back on it, I realized by the force he used he had given us the head start we needed to get away before the other soldiers woke up.

Now it was just the three of us, bonded by adversity; outcasts, on the run, with no place to call home. We could not return to our village. That was impossible.

By this time in my life, the loss of another home or hearth had become a familiar circumstance in my life and I had found the strength to bear it. After all, I had my son and daughter who meant more to me than any home or hearth ever could. My other children were with their families. I only prayed that they would not suffer any retribution because of our actions.

We decided to travel farther; Jesus knew a place nearby where he and his disciples had been well received.

As we traveled, I noticed that Rachel's hand had begun to blister. I feared that she had contracted a disease from the encampment. I made a silent prayer in my heart that she would be healed; I couldn't bear to think that Rachel should suffer any additional misfortune. She had experienced enough.

I put this out of my mind temporarily until we came to the village. We were received by Jesus' friends who took us to where we could bathe, eat, and sleep. These comforts now seemed like luxuries more wonderful than any of us had words to express. We stayed with them for quite a long time. We were no longer just social outcasts but fugitives from the law.

For those of you, who have suffered atrocities in your life, be certain in the belief and knowledge that they are only passing images and that the Light, the true Light is soon to be seen and experienced. Never give up, hold fast, and believe.

CHAPTER
33

The first night, as we settled into our new home, the three of us sat together in loving unity; we had survived a dangerous and frightening episode, but I was worried about Rachel's hand. The blisters had developed into a terrible sore. When I pointed it out, Jesus said, "Mother, let me tend to this. I believe I know what to do." He took Rachel's hand in the palm of his left hand while lifting and waving his right hand over it. At the same time, he prayed deeply, giving praise and thanks for our safety. He asked God to come into our home, to bring forth the light, to bless and to protect us. Then he said, "Oh, Lord, my sister stands before you and she has suffered greatly. She has tended to those in need. Now, I call upon you, Holy Father, to heal my sister's hand, for she has much work to do. She needs the Spirit to shine upon her and to heal her, so that she may carry on the work that you have laid before her. I call upon you, Father, enter this room now and heal my sister. Our hearts are open to thee."

In that moment, the room was filled with a brilliant light, so brilliant that we fell to our knees, not out of fear, but out of adoration. A floating sensation came upon us, as if we were fully embraced, caressed, and held in loving arms. We could surrender, like babes in a mother's arms, to a love that entered this space, cleansing all the fears, terrors, and horrors we had experienced together. It seemed also that time was suspended. At last Jesus cried out, "Oh, Father, Holy Father, your blessings are magnificent." As we looked at Rachel's hand, miraculously it was healed.

Jesus lifted her hand to his heart and then raised her hand straight up to the sky and said, "Great is the power of the Lord." He threw his arms around Rachel, hugging and embracing her; I joined in, and we laughed and cried together. There we were, far from our home, cut off from the rest of our family, having escaped certain death, and through faith, Rachel had been healed.

This event marked a turning point in all of our lives. We knew, each one of us, that we were to fulfill a mission that was perhaps not completely of this world. The ordinary details of life as we had known it would never be the same again. Our strength lay in the certain knowledge that we had given our lives to the fulfillment of God's work, wherever it might take us.

Rachel loved her brother and she knelt and kissed his hands and wept, thanking him over and over for healing her. He lifted her face and brushed away her hair, wiping her tears, "My dear, beautiful Rachel, it was not I who healed you, I am only the messenger. Weep not, but rise up in strength, for we have much left to do to fulfill God's word."

Then we went to our beds and slept a long and peaceful sleep for the first time in many, many weeks. I was so relieved that Rachel's hand was healed, not only for the obvious reason of her suffering, but also, I did not want the villagers to say that she had brought a disease into their midst. My heart exalted with joy and thankfulness for this tremendous blessing that came to us through prayer. As I lay in my bed, I reviewed my life up to this point and I gave thanks for every moment of it, the struggles, and the joys. I was being asked to walk upon my path, one step at a time; that is all any of us can ever do. As we move forward, we go in God's grace carried forward with love, in and out of the darkness.

Though I did not know what tomorrow would bring, I no longer had illusions about what my life should be, could be, or would be. I lived now fully in the eyes of God. I gave over, that night, all that I had been to what I was being called to do. It was a new chapter in my life. I was in a sense, reborn.

From this point on, time seemed to quicken. Event after event tumbled upon itself as Jesus' ministry grew and word of him spread throughout the land. There was no stopping this, there was no stepping away from this, there was no changing the course of events, as things moved on in ways that seemed both foretold and unpredictable.

The task, a task, any task is simply a series of tiny steps along the way—whether it is building a large dwelling or walking across the room for a glass of water. Where you reach a closed door within yourself, dear ones, you may have a tendency to bog yourself down with the myriad details needing completion. You might jump to conclusions that throw you into a state of turmoil, confusion, or fear. Instead of maintaining a joyful trust that you can accomplish your task, you let the longing for security overwhelm you. All of this involves trust. To make something come to life: a painting, a piece of music, a building, or project, one must nurture feelings of hope, of joy, of lightness, of playfulness in imagining the fulfillment of it, as the process methodically unfolds day by day, slowly fulfilled through the necessary little steps. The key ingredient, my dear ones, is the spirit, the energy, the light, the vision of your God source within. It is a combination of completely giving over your faith to God's fulfillment of your vision. Even as you take on the daily work, you must never try to control or force, maneuver, or manipulate the outcome. It will never happen in that way.

Trust in yourself equals trust in the Lord and trust in the Lord equals trust in yourself. One affects the other as they mirror each other. You may pray, asking that trust to be strengthened in you. Everyone on this planet grapples with the challenges of the ego, the desire to force your will into the making. And this is the opposite of what needs to happen!

It is the self-defeating fear within ourselves that causes us to try to force things to happen as we would like them to be instead of how they naturally will be. Love cannot be forced, pressed, maneuvered, or manipulated. That is all that God is: Love. Pure, total, complete everlasting, love. It is not always easy for us to accept the everyday, ordinary obstacles that we face. But I assure you, as they are the very essence of your life, tend to them, fully and with love, and you will see enormous changes. You may have to pray over each step, to give you the trust that you need, but it is well worth tending to that part of your heart's garden.

Remember the process of seed planting and the transformation of a plant as it grows. This mirrors the progression you make to accomplish whatever goals you set. A seed planted in the earth does not become a tree in one fell swoop. There are many, many steps along the way but I can assure you that that tiny seed has within it the trust, the joy, the belief, and the lightheartedness to become a tree and to enjoy each and every stage of its growth. Think of yourself as a small seed and picture yourself as a plant at different stages of growth. Invite the spirit, to transform you; instead of, like so many, rushing to some unknown, undesired destination. Prayer will help you, just like water and soil for a seed. For love wishes all things to be brought into its light.

CHAPTER
34

As our lives had changed significantly from the time we had rescued Rachel, our days felt to be passing more quickly. Now we were together, the three of us, living mostly, you might call it in your time, underground. There were death threats issued for my son, Jesus. Although he chose not to live in fear of these threats, they were an ever-present reality for Rachel and me. His disciples were also concerned, not only for Jesus, but for themselves as well. This, of course, was a natural and human response to the situation; it was also the day-to-day reality for my son and his followers.

As I told you in the last chapter, something inside of me had changed significantly. I had become a true believer in the call that I had received from the time I was a very young girl. Now I was able to clearly see the true path for my mission. I realized I was no longer a legitimate part of my community. We had been involved in too much scandal and I no longer could live as a normal wife and mother. I accepted my new role of the fugitive. We lived hour to hour, week to week, by pulling together and reassuring one another that we could live our lives and continue to assist Jesus in his work.

Peter's strong personality, leadership, and sense of humor helped to smooth over small arguments or misunderstandings that occurred from time to time among the disciples. Peter had an ability to inject just the right amount of humor into a situation to cause those who were upset to let go of their tensions and often even to dissolve into laughter. He told exaggerated stories based on actual things that were happening at the time, turning the words in such a way that we could not help but laugh, and in the process, let go of our fears. Peter was a rosy-cheeked man whose capacity to lighten a situation helped hold together groups of people from various backgrounds who were traveling and living together while moving from place to place, and constantly being involved in dangerous, unpredictable situations. Peter's way of holding together the disciples was as a good-humored, steadying, father-brother figure. So, in my son's eyes, Peter was the rock of stability for the group, with this unique capacity for lightheartedness and the ability to deflect the fears and concerns of the men. Remember, that these young men were away from their families for the first time. They had made the choice to follow my son and to assist him in the work. And, yet like many young people, they had insecurities, personal problems, family relationship concerns, and disputes among each other. So, Peter was the wise, older leader, who was a highly dedicated person to my son's mission and therefore the other men respected and followed him. Peter made it possible for Jesus to have the necessary hours he needed to pray and meditate, for without that alone time, he would not have been able to arrive at the understanding and depth of knowledge that he achieved.

Jesus called Peter the "Rock" because he provided a steadying foundation for the rest of the disciples. When Jesus would leave the disciples, they would oftentimes become distressed, fearful, and in danger of losing sight of their purpose. Peter took over and held the reins tightly, with love and humor. I cannot emphasize enough to those of you who read my story that my son spent every waking moment of his life seeking the fullest realization and communication with the Holy Father. His unification with his heavenly father was his sole purpose and single-minded dedication and Peter helped make this possible.

As Jesus grew as a leader and clarified his purpose, he gained physical strength. He also was better able to use his charismatic ability to reach the minds and hearts of all those who came to hear him speak. I saw it with my own eyes many, many times. Disbelievers, doubters, hecklers, fortune hunters, skeptics, and all those with hardened hearts would be cleansed and become like children through the words and the manner in which my son spoke. It was as if he pulled forth a light from within them, as if he lifted these people away from the illusions that they held of themselves. He lifted them up simply, gently into his arms, leaving what was like a pile of ragged clothes behind them. Huge crowds of people would be transformed before my very eyes. He moved their hearts, lifted their spirits, and brought forth the light within them, so that they could see it, feel it, and experience it. When there were huge masses of people, it was as if there was an electrical thunderstorm sending down currents of utter joy that rained over the people. Never had any of us witnessed such a phenomenon before.

Those who experienced my son's love were forever changed. Sometimes I wept from the magnificence of what I saw. Beggars and lepers became whole and healed. There was a blind man, blinded as a child in an accident; my son healed him and restored his eyesight. I was there when this happened. No one could mistake his powers to heal and always Jesus praised the Heavenly Father for his magnificence and his miracles.

The more Jesus preached to and reached the hearts of thousands, the more dangerous it became for him and by association, the rest of us. When his sermon was over, we would all slip away as quietly and as quickly as we could; there were spies and soldiers who would infiltrate the ordinary crowds who came to hear my son. They were forever following, asking questions, intimidating those who wished to hear my son's words and generally creating a sense of chaos and fear among those who gathered at my son's feet. Little did they realize that the more they used these tactics, the more determined people became to get as close to my son as possible.

There was an underground network of messengers, who fanned out across the countryside, alerting the villagers of our whereabouts and where Jesus would preach next. These messages spread like wildfire throughout the land. There was no earthly power that could stamp out this energy, this enthusiasm, this extraordinary desire to receive the word.

It was within this context that a very sad and upsetting situation was developing within our family. My other children who lived in our old village, in order to protect themselves and maintain their position in the community, let it be known that their brother had taken leave of his senses. They thought he had influenced me and had driven Rachel mad. It broke my heart that my own family, my own children, could say such things, could even believe such things. However, I could also understand their fear. I understood their need to be accepted and to live normal lives among their tribe. I, even as their mother, could not expect them to give this up, but it pained me deeply to see my family divided. I felt a failure as a mother and tried to determine what Joseph would have done had he been alive. I knew that I had to take action; I could no longer stand by and watch my family remain torn apart in this way.

I sent word to my children in the village that I needed them by my side. They arrived on a feast day, when there would be much celebration and high spirits. Jesus and his disciples were traveling, so when they arrived, it was only Rachel and I who greeted them. They were cold and harsh to Rachel, blaming her for the initial trouble when I had to leave the village to rescue her. They called her self-centered and irresponsible. Gathered around her, they accused her of breaking up the family to help beggars and sick people, and as a result risking all of our lives.

I intervened on Rachel's behalf, as she would not defend herself against these accusations. Her innocence was so great that she had no words to use in defense. She only said simply, "Yes, it is true what you say, I did all of that." This only infuriated her brothers and sister more, because they could not possibly understand why anyone in their right mind would do the things that she had done. They turned upon me and told me that they could not understand how Jesus could go about the countryside, making a ridiculous spectacle of himself to teach things that also jeopardized our lives. How could he do this? What was the matter with him? How could I, their mother, allow him to do such things? They cried out that if I couldn't stop him, they would. They had talked about this and concluded that without a husband by my side, I surely must not have the strength to reach Jesus with common sense. Therefore, they were here to take the necessary measures. They were determined to find Jesus preaching in the nearby town, to go there and confront him, to call upon him to give up these foolish, foolish sermons.

I knew it was pointless to try to stop them; they had made up their minds. Rachel looked mystified, as she had absolutely no idea why her brothers and sister could be so infuriated. Rachel had the most incredible ability to remain pure in her vulnerability. Their harsh words and accusations could not penetrate her heart and she continued ministering to the sick and poor for the rest of her days. She was present at many of the healings that Jesus performed and even helped him. All this she did with a joyful spirit and a quiet demeanor, as she never sought to assume the center of attention, but very quietly and delicately fulfilled her calling.

My children left as quickly as they had arrived to go and find Jesus in the neighboring town. There were hundreds of people already gathered to hear his words. As the sermon was ending, his brothers and sister ran toward him and laid their hands upon him, beseeching him to come away with them. With worried countenances, they demanded that he put an end to his travels and come home to resume the life of a good son and to settle down. Jesus listened, silently. He allowed them to say everything that was on their minds. He did not interrupt them. They screamed, "Jesus, it is time that you return to your home and assume the life of the oldest son. It is time that you set an example for our family. Come with us now, Jesus."

There was silence, and Jesus replied, "My beloved brothers and sister, I love you with all my heart. I cherish you with all my heart and I am thankful for you, my family. You must understand that I must be about my Father's work. It is He who I follow every moment of every hour. It is He who lights the path upon which I walk, now and forevermore. Go in peace, my beloved family. Go safely to your home and know that my love for you is eternal. I bless you all."

They were stunned at the calmness and sweetness of those words. They looked at each other in amazement, until finally one replied; "Now we see. Now we know. You are surely mad. You are truly mad! All right then. Have it your way! Go ahead with your plans, but we will have no part in them. Mark our words; we do not see a good end to this, Jesus. You are risking all our lives and if you insist on so doing, then we must wash our hands of it."

My children cried and continued to try to change his mind. The more emotional they became the calmer and more loving Jesus grew.

Peter went among his brothers and sister, reassuring them that all was well, with words that occasionally brought a smile. No one wanted to leave with harsh words. Peter's influence made it so that there could still be an opening for later communication in the future. This was always Peter's contribution.

Before the children left, I went to them and reaffirmed my love for them. I promised that we would all be reunited someday, even though presently that seemed impossible. I told them that I was certain in my heart that our love for each other would shine through all of us, once again. I blessed all of my children and said prayers for my grandchildren as I sent them on their way home.

Those of you, who have experienced something similar to what I have described in your own lives, should be calm and rest in the certainty that a love truly honored in one's heart will always succeed, no matter how chaotic and distressful a situation may seem.

I know this is true because I lived it. Love conquers all adversity. This is God's promise to each and every one of us. I watched my children leave with heavy hearts, but also with knowing hearts. I knew that my duty was to fulfill God's plan for my life. There was no turning back from that plan, despite the pain of seeing my children suffer.

It was my destiny to stay with Jesus and Rachel; all three of us were bound together in a calling so demanding that we only could follow it with all of our hearts.

CHAPTER
35

Now, it was only a matter of time before the inevitable took place and my son's life was in grave danger. From the time my family came to visit on the feast day, until now at this time in my story, the political climate became extremely violent and chaotic. There were continual threats on my son's life and on the lives of the disciples. Even Peter, who normally was able to deflect a great deal of the fear and tension, was himself hard pressed to carry on.

In the darkest hours, many of the disciples began to doubt the validity of their worth. From time to time they consulted me for my opinion about what to do and how to proceed. While my life as a mother and wife within my tribe had long since ceased to exist, as I became a part of the underground network faithful to my son, I felt fulfilled in those roles once more.

One day I was visited by a Roman official, who came in disguise, but under official command. My sons were not with me. He wanted to speak with me alone. He wore a cloak that hid his face, a cloak that any ordinary traveler would wear. Rachel answered the door when he knocked. I was inside reading scriptures. At this time in my life, I spent many hours in prayer, reading the Torah. Rachel asked him to wait at the door, came over to me and whispered, "Mother, there is a man here to see you. He says it is very important that he speak with you immediately. I asked him who he was, and he said only that he has been sent to speak with you in an official capacity, and again asked to see you."

Upon hearing her words, as I lifted my head from my book, I could see his figure in the doorway. I sensed something close to fear, but what also seemed more like urgency in his demeanor. I could feel the tension within him. I had a very uneasy feeling inside my stomach. I really did not want to speak with this person, so, I took my time before telling Rachel to invite him in.

I rose from my chair as Rachel escorted him into the room. This man had very intense eyes and a slight stoop to his shoulders. I observed that his hand was shaking slightly.

He spoke to me first. "I have been sent as a special messenger to speak with you directly. I have traveled quite far in disguise so that I would not cause trouble for you, that is, any further trouble than you already have. I am here now to speak to you, to implore you to take immediate steps to put an end to your son's activities."

All of these words came out very swiftly, almost as if he had memorized this initial speech. To be honest, he was so nervous while speaking to me, that I found myself suppressing a smile. I said to him, "Won't you please sit down? You must be tired from your journey." He appeared to be very grateful and sat down without any hesitation. I motioned to Rachel to get something to drink and eat. As she placed food before him, and I nodded to encourage him to partake, he dove in with great relish, almost in spite of himself.

Shortly after gobbling down most of what we had offered, he began the second part of his seemingly prepared speech. "Thank you for your hospitality. I am grateful. I have been sent here with the best intentions for your family. My superiors want me to inform you of impending danger if your son does not desist from his revolutionary activities. I am here to tell you directly that his behavior will not be tolerated by the Roman government. Your son seems to have the impression that he is outside and beyond the law of the land. I have been sent to inform you by edict that this is not the case. Many high officials have discussed this case and we felt that it was only fair that we should contact you directly as his mother.

We expect your cooperation to take effect by sundown tomorrow. You have our promise that with your submission, you and your family will have a long and fulfilling life without disturbance. We are certain that you, a wise mother, who cares about her family, will be moved to take the necessary steps."

The soldier paused and took a long, deep drink of the wine we had provided him; smacking his lips with pleasure, he placed the empty goblet on the table and continued, and "I have a letter here for you to sign, in agreement that you will instruct Jesus to stop all travel and communication regarding his beliefs."

This man's audacity was an affront to me. He had entered my home, accepted my hospitality, and assumed that I would simply, and without thought, sign an edict written by someone threatening Jesus with harm.

I sat there in stunned silence for I could see the cleverness in their threatening, manipulative techniques. Rachel stood in the corner dumbfounded, waiting to see what I would do next.

I placed my hands on the table and did the only thing I knew to do: I prayed to God, in front of this man, a Roman with no belief in the God that I prayed to or understanding of the Hebrew words that I spoke. I made a long and passionate prayer. I even sang, for I wanted him to hear a song of pure praise.

He sat staring coldly, with those very intense black eyes. I saw him glance at the wine flask. He seemed to be continuously thirsty, and now more so. When I began the hymn of praise, Rachel, as always with a glad heart, immediately joined in and the two of us lifted our voices in song.

As we finished, the soldier looked at me and asked, nonchalantly, "May I have another glass of that wine? As I was saying, only your signature is needed." With a sly smile, he lifted the goblet and drank its contents in one gulp and set it down.

I followed his gaze to the open doorway, suddenly realizing, as he must have, that given the hour, Jesus and his disciples would all be returning very soon. Perhaps this had been his intention, I cannot say. He suddenly took a far stronger tone. Perhaps his own fear in combination with the wine brought out a strength in his voice that he had not had until now.

"You must sign this paper and sign it now, for your own peace of mind and for the well-being of your family. I implore you to sign this edict and make an end of this unfortunate business."

At that, I quietly stood up. I picked up the letter in my hand; I rolled it up and with a gracious smile, held it out to him, "Here is your edict. Take it and leave my house with my blessings."

He grasped it in his hand and shook his head. "With this gesture you have sealed your fate." He turned and strode out of our house.

I watched him as he walked down the path, knowing that he was quite correct. There is an agony and a relief from knowing that the inevitable will happen soon. I looked at Rachel, who had grown quite pale. She knew of edicts from experience. She whispered, "Oh, Mother, they are coming again with documents for us to sign. When will it end, Mother? When will it end?"

I answered her, "My child, I do not know. I can assure you of only one thing: I will not sell my son's soul on any piece of paper. Come, let us go. There is nothing we can do to stop whatever will be. I must find Jesus and tell him about what has happened. I feel we must plan for the worst. Our lives can never be the same."

I felt a cloud of blackness floating around me—a dark, black emptiness of unbelievable utter fear. There was no place to hide where we would not inevitably be found. I knew that nothing would stop Jesus from his work; there was nothing to do but continue living as best we could.

About two hours later, I found Jesus with the disciples. I did not want to deliver this news to the group as a whole, but Jesus implored me to come forth and to tell him what news I had. Of course, when he asked me that question, he did not expect what I was about to tell him. I felt compelled to warn them, now even more so as I saw where they were intending to travel unprotected.

Peter was the first disciple to speak. "Dear Mother," as he always called me, "I am saddened to hear of the Romans' actions and even more saddened that you and dear Rachel should have had to suffer this news by yourselves. We should have been there to speak for you. We must meet among ourselves and decide what to do."

As Peter was talking, Jesus rose and walked away from the rest of the group. The tension was palpable. Roman edicts delivered directly to the mother of a family were generally the last straw.

Peter continued, "Let us remember that his words are only those of a wine drinking, flat-footed messenger from Rome. Who is he, anyway? He probably won't be able to find his way back home, with all the wine he guzzled. He'll probably end up miles from his destination and come crawling back on his hands and knees for another big snort of that wine."

This was Peter trying his best to lighten the tension with an exaggerated image. In this case, however, he could not elicit one smile. The other disciples looked terrified, as they were quite aware of the imminent danger.

Now it was Jesus who spoke, "Dearly beloved ones, rest easy in your hearts; I must make this journey alone. I promise you deliverance at the darkest hour. You have nothing to fear. You can believe and trust me completely. It is I who will walk this path."

The disciples cried out, "No, no Jesus, we will never leave you. You can trust in us, we will take your place!" Jesus smiled, and I remember looking at him, for I was puzzled at the quality of the smile on his face. I still remember that moment without understanding the meaning of it.

Rachel saw this smile as well and she impulsively threw her arms around her brother and hugged him. He set her aside, and he kissed her hands, speaking softly "Dear Rachel," he said, "I must go now into the garden to pray. I would appreciate it if you would come with my disciples and pray with me. I need you by my side during these hours. Thank you, dear Mother; your courage is an example to us all. What a fortunate person I am to have such a strong and courageous mother. Now, I must leave as I have much to think about and contemplate. I know that you understand this."

He left and it was a long while before his disciples joined him. They needed to speak amongst themselves about what had happened.

Peter accompanied me back to our home. As he bid me goodnight, he said, "Mother Mary, fear not, your son lives so brightly that no edict can ever extinguish that light. We must believe in him more than ever before; we have all made the conscious decision to walk in that light. We must band together and carry through to the ultimate conclusion, whatever that may be. He will show us the way. Jesus will know what to do. We shall remain steadfast to whatever is to be."

I replied, "You are right, Peter. Your words have the ring of truth and the knowledge of the light. Now we must all pray, deeply, as we have never prayed before. I feel the final hour approaching."

I went to my bed, with a quiet and heavy heart. It was a long time before I fell asleep.

It rained all the next day and the following night, yet no amount of pleading could bring Jesus indoors. Rachel and I continued to pray unceasingly, as the insistent rains poured down.

CHAPTER
36

The rain finally subsided, and Jesus came into the house, intent upon continuing his travel to the village, as he and the disciples had discussed. I pulled him aside, "My son, my heart is with you in every word and deed as you go from village to village to spread the word of God and heal those in need. My heart is with you every moment. Yet as your mother I have the concerns and fears of any mother. Jesus, you well remember our visitor from Rome and their demands, their threats. It is not up to me to sign such a letter. Dear Son, you and I know what people in authority can do; we have all suffered as a result, all of our lives even though we have managed to circumvent their authority for the most part. In my heart, something tells me that this cannot go on forever. I feel a tightening pressure surrounding our lives. They know where we live. They have spies who watch our comings and goings and from time to time I almost feel that they have infiltrated even the disciples. Although I have no proof, my eyes and ears and certain things that I have observed have left me worried that their latest tactic is to persuade one of the disciples to their way of thinking. As your mother, I must speak out and warn you of what I sense. I hope that you will not be angry with me for saying this. Oh, Jesus, I love you so, dear son, and I see all that you are."

At this, I began to cry. Jesus took my hands, gently, and kissed them. He lifted my face to his and looking into my eyes as the tears rolled down, he replied, "Gentle Mother, it is because of you that I have come so safely through this world. Every day as I step forth into my work, I know that I am fully protected by the depth of your love. Never does a moment go by that I don't think of and hold dear to my heart, the beauty of your face and eyes and the love that you have surrounded me within my life. I carry this with me every moment, all during my teaching, throughout my prayers, and in the quiet hours of my meditation. I understand the fears and concerns you have for my well-being. Indeed, you are right, mother, they are looking for ways to stop my work. I do not understand why; it is not for me to understand their thinking.

"Mother, I have come so far in this work that I can only continue. I am far past the time of turning back or changing courses. I must follow this fully and in whatever way my Holy Father asks. I know that you know this, Mother. Honestly from my heart, I am able to face whatever lies ahead of me because I know that you truly believe in what I am doing. With your belief in me, and your love that protects me day and night I am able to continue with the strength that I would not have otherwise. Oh, Mother, I do not understand many things. My heart cries out when I see the faces, the eyes of all those in need. If I have something to offer them, I cannot withhold it for fear of those who do not understand. I must fulfill what it is that I must do for the love of all living creatures."

We embraced and as we did so the room filled with brilliant light, light so pure and so clear that it embraced us both and surrounded us. We fell to our knees in reverence, for the light was a gift to us and a sign of that great love that awaits all of us. This same love is present, ever-present, and never-ending.

I wept with joy, for I had borne a son, who walked in the purest love that I had ever known. In the face of that love, I was inspired to embrace it fully.

Jesus rose and he embraced me again. "Dear mother, I have heard your words and I have taken them into my heart, I must go now I am called to do so."

He looked at me for a long time before taking a few steps toward the door. He paused then came back closer and knelt down in front of my feet, taking my hand, and placing my palm against his forehead. I knelt down toward him and embraced him. Why did I have the feeling that this would be the last time that I would hold him like this? We both wept because we knew that the final hours were upon us.

Then, it was time. We were fulfilled. At this point, words were no longer necessary. It was time for him to depart. I accompanied him to the door and watched him as he walked the familiar pathway toward the homes of the disciples who were to accompany him.

I watched until he disappeared out of sight. His familiar steps and the way that he walked: I took note of every aspect until once again I was overcome with emotion. I couldn't go back inside. I would have felt too confined. I had to walk.

I headed toward the countryside, toward the mountains. I had taken a moment to bring a basket with me, thinking it a wise idea to pick some figs along the way.

I walked quite a way and came to a hilly area. I seemed to have an unusual energy and strength. I began the climb. In retrospect, I realized that I had hurried to the top in the hope that I might catch a glimpse of Jesus and the disciples as they made their way. He was my son ... Why did he have to jeopardize his life like this? I suddenly felt a kind of anger, rage even, at the unfairness of his having to give so much, to sacrifice so much, while never asking anything in return.

Suddenly, I had lost sight of the purpose, the point of it all, and why it had to be this way. All of these feelings I stamped down into the ground as I climbed higher and higher. I abandoned the basket needing both hands to climb. I hiked up my skirts and climbed harder and faster. I felt as though somehow the effort I was making would help Jesus on his journey.

I came to level ground where some goats grazed on the nearby grass. They looked at me with lazy, sleepy eyes and continued chewing the tasty grass that was there to nourish them. I quickly moved to the side, where I thought I had the best chance of seeing Jesus and the disciples as they passed below. Sure enough, I could see them gathered together walking, and a crowd gathered around them as they went. At first it was only one or two people, then three or four and then little by little, a much larger crowd formed. It was amazing to watch, it was as if they were a magnet. I moved to a higher point and was able to follow them for quite a while, but at long last they disappeared.

I sat down on a rock, took my shoes off, and rubbed my toes in the grass. I realized that I had walked a long distance and had been using my feet and toes to balance on the rocky surface as I leaned this way or that way to catch a better glimpse. I sat there and rested. There was a gentle wind rustling the leaves and the grasses. I could hear some of the goats chewing and moving around. Otherwise, everything was quiet. Then I lay down on the rock. It was warm in the sun and so peaceful there. I dozed off, I don't know for how long, for maybe half an hour or so. I woke up and put my shoes back on. I saw a flower and it seemed to call out to me. It was a small flower, with pink petals; it just seemed like such a happy flower. It was bobbing in the breeze. I went closer to look at it and something about that flower put a smile on my face. It lifted my heart.

I began to climb back down. It was much easier going down than it had been climbing up, but it was steep, and I needed to be careful. I took my time. The image of the little flower stayed in my mind. I saw my basket where I had left it. I picked it up and kept going. When I reached the bottom, I saw a fig tree that I had never noticed before. I filled the basket.

Slowly, I returned home, enjoying the walk, breathing in the air, and seeing the little pink face of the flower. How could one little flower give me so much strength? Somehow, it did. When I returned home, Rachel greeted me. She had met with her brother at a friend's home and had spent time with him before he left.

Rachel had made dinner and set it out before me. Never had any food tasted as good as this. Each morsel was a delight. Rachel looked at me, having noticed that I was unusually quiet. "Mother," she said, "Jesus has left us. He is going far away now. It will be quiet here without him; he always makes me laugh. He told me the silliest story before he left, just like when we were children." She bit her lip and began to cry.

I patted her head. "Now, now Rachel, it will be all right, don't worry."

"I told him that I didn't want him to go, Mother. I told them not to go. They all laughed and teased and said, 'We'll see you soon, Rachel. Don't forget us, now. We'll be back before you know it.' Jesus hugged me, lifted me up off the ground and he twirled me around two times and said, 'Little Sister, you lift up my heart and always will.' Then, away he went. I saw lots of people joining them, to walk with them. When I turned around, I saw a man who looked like a beggar. When I got closer, he looked at me with such hatred. I thought that he was going to grab me, and I quickly ran away from him before he could do anything and hurried home. I turned back once and saw the man still staring at me. I did not like his face, Mother. He had a cruel and angry look about him."

"Rachel, let's try to sleep now. Try to put these people out of our heads. We must pray and ask that their hearts be moved. We must pray, dear Rachel, for Jesus and the disciples, that they will be protected from any harm."

We prayed together and we blew the candles out. We went to our beds and slept.

CHAPTER
37

The day after Jesus left, while I sat indoors at my table, a vision came to me. I saw my son surrounded by heavily armed Roman soldiers. I heard the cries of women and children in the background; nowhere in this vision did any of the disciples appear.

I felt this was proof of my fear that my son would be deserted by his followers. I don't say this in anger or rage toward his disciples; living at the time in which we lived, under the severe political strictures that were enforced during those times, it took an unusual person to stand up to tyranny. For those of you who live in countries where human rights are something taken for granted, it may be difficult to imagine a time in which individual people had absolutely no rights. My son had to be very strong to face the authorities of his day.

Let me assure you, my dearest beloved ones, that our Holy Father, who created us all, embodies the pure spirit of deep and abiding love, a love that emanates from the heart with gentleness, all knowing of the magnificence of each person. The love of the Holy Father reaches and teaches through this gentle love, never by violent tyranny. No matter what person in authority says differently, they are wrong. They do not know. They have not sufficiently opened their hearts to embrace the pure knowledge of the Holy Father. This, my son did. This is why he lives in the hearts and minds of so many people all over the world. He opened his heart and mind fully; he committed his soul and life to the absolute and total fulfillment and understanding of the Holy

Father. This is why he could face terror, violence, and cruelty, a total lack of understanding, and eventually, his own destiny.

You see, my beloved ones, my son walked in the purity of the love of God, showing us all that we too can bring this miracle to our lives and to our families. Remember that my son was just like you and me. He came from my flesh; he was human and vulnerable, just like you and me. I held him as a tiny babe in my arms; I heard his cries and watched him grow. I was there to answer his questions, to hold him close when he was confused or distressed by those things that happen to all of us in life. I knew he was special from the time he was a tiny child because he asked questions, thought, and felt deeply about everything, every person, and every living creature. It was as if he were more spirit than living body. I don't mean to suggest that he was not fully human, because he was, but he exhibited an ability to be a part of every living thing. He was not separate; he was a part. What that really means is that he fully embraced the power and love that God had given him.

Now, as I sat at my table, thinking about Jesus' possible betrayal, I wondered what I was to do. Was I to sit here helplessly or, was I to follow after him and the disciples? I bowed my head in quiet prayer, praying to the Holy Father to lead and guide me, so that I would know what course to take. Time seemed to stand still, and I heard my son, in a clear voice, saying to me, "Mother, I will live forever. I am with you forever, know this, dear mother."

I lifted my head from prayer, knowing that I must follow my son to the city, Jerusalem, even though it was quite far from where I was at the time. I knew that I must be with him and that it was my place to be with him. I felt him calling me to be there. I also knew that it was going to be very dangerous, but calmness surrounded me that came from a source of energy that I believe to be the tenderness, the tender heart, of God. During the events that were about to unfold, the violence, the treachery, the horror, I could always feel a greater calmness surrounding me.

The spirit and the body both belong to God, but within the world in which we were living tyrannical authorities laid claim to the body. When the people subscribed to this belief, they became heir to, victim to, that belief—-that their bodies were controlled by higher governmental authorities. That left the Spirit, which became the domain of the Holy Father, and so we have developed through the centuries a concept of the Spirit and the Body and the Material World. My beloved friends, know for certain in your hearts that everything that we are, body and spirit, lives in the tender heart of God. Jesus, through his diligent fulfillment of his own story, brought together the body and the spirit, and gave the world an image of magnificent unity with God.

The image of the risen Christ, amazingly, is so quickly forgotten. The significance of this event has not fully penetrated the hearts and minds of many. It must be understood that there are many, many lessons to be learned from the story of Jesus. Through the centuries, there have been many minds and hearts who have sought to interpret and communicate the story and the meaning of the life of my son. There have been wars and violent conflicts as a result of confusion about the nature of God's love. There are philosophical differences from one religion to another, and many times these philosophical differences have aligned themselves with governmental forces advocating conflict, separation, and artificial belief systems once again separating the body and the spirit.

I speak now to my beloved ones who have suffered under modern day tyranny in countries around this world. I speak to each one of you: mother, father, grandmother, grandfather, son, and daughter. I promise you that the Light, the fulfillment of unity of the body and spirit and the tender heart of God shall be brought to you, your families, and your countries and even to those who oppress you. I know what you have suffered, for I lived it in my human life. The love of God will be fulfilled—know this.

I rose from my little table in my house and with a clear head and a very full heart. I gathered things together that I would need on the journey. I knew that Rachel would come with me, that it was right for her to be with us all. I had no doubts about what I was doing.

As I finished packing, Rachel walked in and said to me, "Yes, Mother, I know it is time. I too had a vision of Jesus and I know that it is time for us to join him. Let me be your strength, dear Mother. I will carry our belongings. I want you to rest as much as possible and know that I will take care of the day-to-day matters of this trip. Now, let us get a good night's sleep and in the morning, we will depart early for Jerusalem."

Rachel embraced me and held me tightly. It was true that I felt a strength that I could not have had without her. Looking back on this episode in our lives, I would never have made it to Jerusalem without her and it became very clear to me, later on, that she had dedicated her life to me and through me, to her brother. Never once did she ask anything for herself. That was never her way. Rachel was the type of person who did whatever needed to be done, very simply, forthrightly, and with a beautiful spirit. The things that Rachel did throughout her life in caring for the sick, the needy, the mentally disturbed, she did easily; for many people, the things that Rachel did so easily would have been impossible. Rachel understood the power of the Spirit and how spiritual power affected and infused the body. This was a gift; she became like a sculptor, molding the spirit that then became personified in the body.

CHAPTER
38

Just as Rachel and I were falling asleep, there came a knock at the door. At first, I was afraid, I crept quietly to the door and with a fearful voice, said, "Yes, who is it?" And immediately came a voice, "It is I, James, your son's faithful disciple, please let me in."

I recognized his voice and opened the door. "Thank you, mother, I am glad to see you well."

"Come," I said, "sit down. You have had a long journey and it is quite late. Let me get you something to eat and drink; I know you must be hungry and thirsty from your travels."

He thanked me. "You are right. I am glad to be here safely, I have been sent by Peter to fetch you to come to Jerusalem. Jesus does not know that I have been sent here. He has been deep in meditation preparing for what he calls the final hours. We are all worried and afraid. We are unsure what is to come in these next days. Peter implored me to travel here to bring you this news and to request that you come with me. Peter said that he would understand if you chose not to come, but he felt that the seriousness of the situation was such that he must, in all good conscience, convey this to you directly. I am sorry to bring this news so late at night. We are in a rather chaotic state now, for Jesus spends much of his days in prayer and we are left alone with rumors swirling around and the constant threats from the authorities. Peter has stepped forward to lead us while Jesus is in prayer, but to be honest, Peter cannot assuage our fears or even daily concerns. Peter felt that if you were there with us, you might help to hold us all together and keep a firm foothold through whatever is to take place. Dear Mother, we need you with us very, very much. I don't think that any of us has the strength to step forward as leader in the same way that you would."

I looked into James' eyes and saw a very frightened young man. He looked so vulnerable, so fragile, and so very young. As he drank and ate, he shivered, and his slender body bent over with a heavy burden of cares. I realized the serious nature of this situation, for unless it was very serious indeed, Peter would never have called me to join them. I was glad that by providence, Rachel and I had already prepared to leave.

James was like a son to me because he lived close to Jesus and our family. He was one of the first disciples to follow Jesus and to help him in the very early days.

I showed James to a place where he could sleep. As he laid his head on the pillow, I watched over him and prayed silently for the strength to make this journey and to be guided by the Holy Father. I knew that these young men were terrified. I sensed that they were on the brink of losing their faith, their hope, their belief in all the work that they had done. I knew that Peter too was in need. I prayed to be shown what to do. I asked to be an instrument of the Lord. I vowed that I was ready to do whatever was asked of me.

As I lifted my head from prayer, I saw an angel stand before me. I knelt down. The angel spoke, saying, "Mary, do not be afraid, you will be protected in every way. Your son calls you to him in his heart and he will need you by his side, for the final days are near. We will be with you and your son every moment. Do not be afraid." The Angel smiled, very delicately and faded from sight. I rose and returned to bed.

For the way of the Lord is to assist you and all others. For as you give to yourself, the things that enrich your spirit, then through that spiritual enrichment you will happily give back to others. This is the way. I love you so very much; my love for you goes beyond words. I want you to feel this love, every moment of your lives, I want you to drink it in and feel it wash over you, like a gentle waterfall or like a very soft spring rain or like a beautiful warm light, filtered through leaves or like a soft, cooling breeze. I want you to feel my love every single moment. I want you to ask for what it is you need, to know that we, your Mother and Father, want you to ask for our help. We want you to come to us for everything; nothing is too insignificant for our hearts. Now, my dear children, it pleases me greatly when you call upon me, for I have been waiting for this and when you open the door and invite me in, I can respond in a greater way. My dear ones, the most difficult thing for you is to ask: first, for the things you need and want; and second, for the help and assistance you need to get them. This holds true in your relationship to us in the spirit realm, with your Holy Father and Mother, as well as in the material realm with your friends and colleagues. If there is one element missing it is in asking for what you want. This can be very frightening, even impossible for you. You have many defense mechanisms that you build up around this area. Now, much growth can occur for you, but you are still not certain what to do to have the things you want.

Now, I shall give you a step-by-step plan that you may follow and I guarantee that if you follow this plan, everything that you desire will come to you, easily and without effort.

Step One:

Every single day you are to set aside a time when you talk with your loved ones about the things you really want. This talk is to be gentle and loving. Allow the Spirit to interact with this conversation. This is something that must happen every day. At the end of this gentle talk, you shall take hands and shall pray together.

Step Two:

Each one of you has special talents and gifts. Now is the time to luxuriate in each other's gifts. I can assure you that if you ask for the help that each of you can give, the other person will be so happy to be asked, that they will pour forth in a happy and helpful manner, all the things that they know and will assist you in accomplishing all the tasks that need to be done. In the past, there has been a competitive spirit rather than a cooperative spirit. That has held you back. Part of that has been an outgrowth of the fact that you carry the same fear of asking for what you want, and because of your fears of asking for what you want you have not been able to harness the best gifts that each of you has. Step Two then involves time spent quietly helping the other person with letters, phone calls, forms, applications, whatever it is they need. Do the actions, let go of the results, but work together, gently and easily. There is no shame in asking for what you want, dear friends. You win no badge of honor by denying the deepest parts of yourself.

Step Three:

When you receive the gifts and blessings that come as a result of this approach, immediately give thanks to the source out of which these gifts have come. You will recognize immediately the fruits of your efforts. Acknowledge yourself and each other; give thanks and praise that the spirit and love in your heart brought these gifts to you. By doing so, you will live in supreme happiness and balance and will spread the sunshine to countless others. Follow these three steps diligently and without interruption and you will see absolute miracles in your life.

You have the ability to unlock and release the deepest fears within you. I wish to tell you directly that God wants you to express what you want, for that is the fullest expression of God and all that he is. If you deny yourself, you deny God and he becomes sad, lonely, and isolated. As we are the mirror of God, then the same thing happens to you. Because of certain realities in your past, you have somehow accepted the premise that it is either not right to have what you want, or selfish to have what you want, or that you do not deserve to have what you want. But I, Mary, am here to tell you that God, who is the source of all things, truly wants you to ask for all things; so, put aside your old beliefs and follow the three steps that I have outlined for you. Put aside your pride and old images of yourself; be like children again. Allow your innocence to come forth. What I have given to you in these Three Steps will completely change your life, I assure you. Open yourselves to the fullest realization of the light, for it stands before you. You have asked and you shall receive. For that is God's way and He asks only to be asked, with the fullness of your heart.

Do you understand? I give you the keys to turn your life around, please take these keys and unlock the doors that have held you back. Do it today. For we need you to live in the fullest happiness and energetic state that you possibly can. For by doing so, you will be fulfilling the greater work of the Holy Lord.

Remember to hold those three steps lightly, as if holding a butterfly, a beautiful fragile exquisite butterfly, hold that butterfly lightly, easily, and gently and the three steps will be a joy-filled time. It should never feel as if it is a task. If it begins to feel that way, then simply stop and recall the butterfly image and let it go for the time being. You see, my dear friends, what happens between you is, asking and receiving; it is the simplest, most direct communication in the universe. It is the very basis of how God works. Man has confused this beautiful method with fears and emotions that twist and turn and have confused and destroyed this beautiful mechanism. Many times, you have spent hours on end in pointless emotional torments because you have run away and turned your back on God's method. There is probably also the fear of actually receiving what you ask for, because if you don't feel good about yourself, then why should you receive? But all of these thoughts, dear friends, are man-made ego thoughts that have nothing whatsoever with how God thinks at all. God only thinks in love and light and magnificence. Erase from your mind and consciousness these other thoughts. By holding onto them, by continuing to hurl your emotions into a chaotic, unhappy state of mind, your path, your process will just take you longer. God waits for you in happy, quiet, gentle, eternal lovingness. He awaits you and comes as soon as you beckon him. He has only to be asked. Give over your pride and walk into the open arms of the greatest love you can ever possibly know. It is your choice to make.

CHAPTER
39

When the cock crowed, I hesitated for a moment before awakening James; he looked so peaceful and comfortable as he lay there sleeping. I watched him and memories of my own son began to fill my mind. I began to think about what lay ahead for us, what experiences we would encounter, but I could not afford to think very long about these things, for we had a great distance to travel. Rachel was already up, and she wanted to get started as soon as possible. I reached down and touched James' shoulder. "James," I said, "it is time now. Everything is prepared. Please take your time and when you are ready, we shall go."

He touched my hand, squeezed it and as he sat up, he said, "Mother, bless you, for I know now we are in safe hands. Everyone will rejoice and be glad of heart. I'll be with you shortly."

Rachel and I went outside to put some baskets of food and water onto the backs of the donkeys. It was important to take enough water and food for the entire journey. The air was chilly, but I sensed that before long it would warm up. For the moment, the chill in the air was a welcome feeling and gave us a bracing vitality for what we had to do.

At last James came out, looking refreshed and with a smile, said to us, "If you will allow me, I will lead the way, as I am now very familiar with this route."

Rachel answered, "Yes, James, we will follow directly behind you."

We rode steadily for several hours and at last James signaled for us to stop at a place where travelers could fetch water for their animals. By now the sun had fully risen and it was quite pleasant. We got off our donkeys and James tended to their needs while Rachel unpacked some food for all of us. We sat quietly for some moments, listening to the animals as they drank and ate and lightly stomped their feet. There were no other sounds except for a faint breeze rustling through the grasses.

I took Rachel's and James' hands and said to them, "Let us take a moment to pray, oh, Lord, grant us a safe journey. May we soon be with our loved ones. Protect all of us, guide and watch over us, for we are now, each and every one of us, a family dedicated to your work, oh, Lord, watch over us as we gather together in love and unity. Thank you oh Father, for all of your blessings. Amen."

With that, we climbed back onto our donkeys and continued on our way. We rode for three more days, stopping to sleep at night, sometimes in places where other travelers would stop and sometimes by ourselves underneath the stars. We were fortunate to have good weather. Each night we gave thanks for the success of our journey and prayed that we would soon see our loved one in Jerusalem.

Finally, at about 5:00 in the afternoon we approached the outskirts of the city and James, knowing the route, escorted us along a less-traveled pathway to the place where Jesus and the disciples were staying. They were not exactly in hiding, simply tucked away in a place that was not easily accessible to the townspeople.

Simon was the first one to see us. He cried out in a loud voice, "Look, they are here! It's James and Mother Mary and yes, Rachel, too. Come quickly."

Then I saw Peter coming forth and most of the other disciples following him. Peter arrived first, with the others close behind. He had a broad smile on his face, and he reached out his arms and cried out, "Thank you, oh Lord, thank you! Welcome, welcome, dear friends. James, you have brought them safely here. Come now; let us welcome you with food and drink, then you must come inside and rest."

They escorted us into the main room where they ate. While others took the animals, some brought basins of fresh water in which we could wash ourselves. There was a flurry of activity. They laid out bread and cheese and wine and carried in our baskets and bags. I cannot express the relief to finally be among the men who spent their lives with my son.

Peter came to me immediately and took my hands in his. He bowed to me and said, "Mother, it is with a glad heart that I receive you here. I speak on behalf of all of the disciples when I say that we are grateful, deeply grateful, that you have joined us at this time. Jesus is in the mountains now, in deep prayer and meditation. I did not tell him that you were coming because I was not certain what decision you would make, although, in my heart, I believed that you would come. I beg your pardon that your son is not here to greet you upon your arrival. I know the joy that he will feel upon seeing you and Rachel. He asked all of us to have supper with him tonight and so while he has been praying, we have been preparing this evening's meal. Thank you, Mary. Your presence lifts our hearts and our spirits."

"Peter, bless you, for nothing could have kept me from being here with you. Thank you for sending James to bring me here."

Someone came with some goblets of fresh water. We were thirsty from traveling. We sat and relaxed and drank the cold liquid; and ate the figs, olives, and nuts that were passed. They were fresh and tasted so good. As I sat there looking around the room, I saw the men each had a different task and they seemed well organized and carried out their duties in good spirit. Peter noticed me watching them and came to sit by my side.

"Mother," he said, "as you can see, we have been quite busy here. We have taken a short respite before entering Jerusalem. Jesus has been in uninterrupted prayer and meditation; he has told me there are important preparations to be made. We don't know what lies ahead, Mother. I don't want to frighten you, but there have been all sorts of rumors and we have received some threats. I do not want to keep anything from you, as you have always asked me to be direct and honest. I am greatly relieved that you are here. There have been some days when I have been worried that we might lose our faith. Of course, this could never happen. Now that you are here, your strength and wisdom will help to guide us and set an example for us."

"Peter, thank you for your kind words. I have felt that you especially have carried a heavy burden. I am here now with you to assist in carrying that burden. Now, if you don't mind, I think I will take a short rest. Please wake me before dinner, or as soon as my son arrives."

"Yes, Mother, please let me escort you. We have laid out a place for you and Rachel, for your very own."

Time passed, and just as I was waking from my nap, I heard sounds of singing. At first, it was very faint, but it grew stronger. I now heard drums and the sound of timbrels. For a moment, I didn't know where I was. I looked about the room; I lifted my head from the pillow, listened, and recognized Rachel's voice. It was she who was singing and playing the timbrels. The disciples joined in the chorus and played some drums and a harp. I laid there for a moment. It felt so unreal, I was in a strange place with familiar voices, and had that tired, yet excited feeling that comes after a long journey. The anticipation of seeing my son conflicted with the awful, nagging fear of what was to come when we entered Jerusalem. The singing became louder, and I could hear dancing and clapping. Rachel had known that these men were tense and had needed the release of celebration and song.

Others had joined. Mary Magdalene was there with a few other women who were faithful followers. They assisted the disciples in many of the preparations needed to minister to the large groups of people wherever Jesus spoke. There were a number of such women who were dedicated, loyal, committed believers and followers. They had joined in the festivities which Rachel was leading. I noticed Peter leaning against the wall, quietly watching.

I wandered outside and began to make my way up the hill in the hopes that I might have some moments alone with my son. It was not yet dark, only twilight. I walked up the path for quite some distance. I saw a smooth rock and decided to sit for a moment to catch my breath. It was then that I looked up and saw Jesus coming toward me. He saw me right away and his face broke into a smile of utter joy.

"Mother," he cried. "Mother!" He ran toward me. I stood up and I felt his strong arms around me. He embraced me and cried out once again, "Oh, Mother, Mother! You are an answer to my prayer. I can't believe you are here. I wanted to see you so much, but I didn't think it was possible. Perhaps, I am dreaming. Are you really here, Mother?"

"Yes, my son, it is I. Rachel is here, too. I felt you call, in my heart, but it was Peter who sent James to bring us here safely."

"Oh, Mother, thank heavens you are here. I'll tell you honestly; these days have not been easy. My friends are fearful, and it has been hard for Peter to hold them together. I have been in the mountains, where my Father has shown me what is to come and what I am to do. Sometimes, Mother, even I am afraid and unsure."

"My son, whatever is to be is God's will. We must trust and believe and follow what is put before us. I will never leave you. I will be by your side, every moment. I want you to rest easy in this knowledge, so that you may be free to fulfill your destiny, so that you are free to fulfill God's plan for you."

"Oh, Mother, you are the answer to my prayer. You have said exactly what I need to hear."

"Come, my son, let us go now. Your sister and all your disciples, friends, and followers await your arrival. You must lead and inspire them, for Peter tells me that it is time to enter Jerusalem. This night of togetherness will prepare all of us. My son, I love you so, with all my heart. Remember, I will be with you every moment."

"Yes, Mother, I know this."

Arm in arm, we walked down the hill. As we reached the awaiting crowd, someone shouted, "The Master is here! He is here! Mary walks with him."

With great cries of rejoicing, they gathered around us, singing, and praising God in loud voices, some fell to their knees in prayer. Rachel ran to her brother, and he scooped her up and cried out, "My beloved sister, my beloved friends, my cherished disciples, come, let us eat, let us rest together, for tomorrow we ride to Jerusalem to sing the praises and the glory of the Holiest Father. It is time, my friends and loved ones, to reach the hearts of those who live within the confines of this great city. It is time to reach their hearts and fill them with the love of God."

As he said that, the group answered, with a call and response, singing praises and hosannas.

"Come now, let us give thanks and praise for this magnificent feast that nourishes us and makes it possible to perform our work. Blessings on this food that we each shall partake!"

He picked up a loaf of bread and broke it, saying "Break this bread in remembrance of me; this is my body. Drink this wine in remembrance of me; this is my blood given for thee. Remember this week, oh, loved ones, for this night we are one family in the eyes of God, our Father. We are all one family, now and forevermore." My son broke bread and drank wine with these symbolic words many times during this period. This was the supper shared by all on this final evening before entering the heart of Jerusalem.

A great cry went up and we began breaking the bread, serving the rest of the food, drinking the wine, and continuing to celebrate. Jesus walked among us, talking with each person individually. He touched us and said special words to each person, something significant to each and every one.

At one point, Rachel ran to her brother and stayed by his side with her arm around his waist, as if never to let him go. He was tender and loving to her. He never showed any signs of irritability with any of his followers. He was gentle, tender, and solicitous, with each and every person. At long last, one by one, they began to settle into a restful, quiet state. Jesus came forth once again to give a final prayer. Peter was by his side this time. He raised his right hand in blessing. "May the Lord bless you and keep you. May the light shine on you and around you, for all the days of your life. We shall all live in our Father's house forever."

Peter broke into a hymn of praise, and everyone joined in its beautiful melody. At the end of the song, we kissed each other good night and everyone dispersed.

Jesus came and put his arms around me and Rachel and said, "My mother, my sister, you have made me so happy this day. I thank you with all my heart for coming here to be with me."

We snuggled up against him. He walked us to our beds, knelt by our sides, kissed our foreheads, cheeks, and hands. "Sleep now, rest. Bless you, Mother, and bless you, Rachel. Until the morning."

He rose and went to his bed, and I murmured a prayer of thanksgiving. I breathed the cool air and turned my head, looking at the sky and the stars, and felt at peace. As I turned my head back, I heard Rachel say, "Mother, I am so happy. I am so happy." Those were the last words I heard as I fell asleep.

CHAPTER
40

It was 5:00 in the morning when I arose; others had been up even earlier. Everyone was assigned a particular task to perform in anticipation for the departure to Jerusalem. The disciples and other followers, who had traveled together and preached for quite some time, had developed an organized method for going from place to place. This morning, Rachel was particularly excited, and she went from person to person offering to help in any way she possibly could. As long as she was busy, she felt useful, and she needed an outlet for her enthusiasm. It was rather chilly, and we all gathered around a fire, eating warm figs and bread. Some people had hot, scorched goat milk with honey stirred in it. We knew the importance of eating something hot before we began our departure.

At last, our caravan was ready. There was much excitement, as well as trepidation entering the city of Jerusalem. Remember that we were simple village folk, none of us were experienced in getting around a large city. We were all aware of the political climate and tried not to think too deeply about the potential dangers. Before we climbed onto our donkeys, Jesus asked us to come together in a circle around the dying embers of the fire. He asked us to take each other's hands in united friendship and love. He led us in a prayer: "Most Holy Father, we stand before you in a love united. Our hearts are united. Our souls are united through everlasting love. We call upon you with joyous hearts as we, as one body, enter the city of Jerusalem to bring your love and your word, oh Lord, to the people there who hunger and thirst for knowledge. Oh, Father, be with us. Help us to reach each heart. Let us sing your praises and carry your word, which is love eternal and everlasting, to each woman, man, and child that we meet. Let us not turn our back to anyone. For your love, oh Lord, is so great that each of us standing in this circle can embrace all those in need. We praise you, oh Father, and ask you to grant us safe passage as we carry out our mission. Bless each of my family members, my mother, and my sister. Oh Lord, bless my dearest and most faithful and loving disciples. Bless my followers, all of whom make it possible to carry your Word to the people. My heart is aflame with loving passion for each and every person who stands with me in this circle of love. Father, we bow our heads before You, in humble reverence and ask that we may perform the work that lies ahead of us. We rejoice in Your name: Creator, Father, the living word, life everlasting. Amen."

As Jesus said "Amen," everyone in the crowd cried out "Amen, Hosanna in the highest!" Immediately the circle broke, and the members went to their donkeys, mounted, and the procession began.

You could feel the excitement in the air. There were twenty-five or thirty of us. Rachel had made a banner. Mary Magdalene and some of the other women admired it and Rachel helped them to make one also. The younger disciples were at the head of the caravan. Peter and Jesus rode side-by-side. John and Samuel were closest to me. Rachel and Mary Magdalene and Johanna rode together. James and a few others rode in front as well, for they were familiar with the route into Jerusalem. We were approximately fifteen to twenty miles outside of the city and we departed at 6:30. Everyone was in high spirits. There was a cool, gentle wind and very clear skies. I remember that I was very aware of these details, as perhaps I did not share the exuberant enthusiasm of the others. I had a gnawing feeling of uneasiness within me.

The only other person who I felt shared my uneasiness was John. John was a gentle, quiet, steady, and loving disciple of Jesus. John never spoke out of turn or lightly. He always contemplated his thoughts fully before sharing them. He was a loyal and wise man. I felt particularly close to John. I could sit next to him for long hours and say nothing and yet feel a deep communion with him. This morning, as we were departing, we exchanged knowing glances that there was much more that lay ahead.

Up ahead, Peter was his jovial self, filled with laughter and humorous observations. We rode for quite some time and eventually stopped to give the animals a rest and to feed them. James announced that we were within an hour's time of the heart of the city. Again, as we climbed upon our animals, a great cry went up and by this time people began to gather around the caravan, accompanying us.

At last, we reached the gates of Jerusalem and by now a huge crowd had gathered. We craned our necks and could see hundreds of people, waving and shouting. Rachel, Mary Magdalene, and Johanna raised the banners even higher. At this, the people shouted, "Jesu, Jesu, Hosanna, Hosanna." We proceeded through the city gates to loud acclaim, shouts. People in the crowd were waving palm leaves. Children ran ahead laying palm leaves on the ground. There was a sea of people reaching up to touch us, crying out. There were young people, old people, beggars, rich people, farmers, pregnant women and children, hundreds upon hundreds upon hundreds.

At one point the crowds became so thick, that we had to stop, because they surrounded us and cried out for Jesus to bless them. He sang a prayer in Hebrew, a prayer with a beautiful melody. The crowds cried out even louder. Finally, they began to part so that we could continue, and at last, we came to the steps of the great temple. Many of the people ran up to the steps for a better view. The temple loomed over the heart of the city, dwarfing the people below. We continued on through the city, picking up more and more people as we went. It was as though we were swimming in the sea, making waves as we rode.

To the northeast of us stood a regiment of Roman soldiers, fanned out amongst the people to keep them in control. Their shields and armor gleamed in the sun and their headgear was a brilliant hue, unmistakable in contrast to the common people. Some of them jeered and laughed. A few spat at us as we came by, but they did not stop us or prevent us from passing. They looked at us as if we were farm animals passing through the streets. Their disdain was all too evident to me. I lowered my head and pulled my veil closer around me as I did not want their eyes pouring into mine, nor did I want to acknowledge their looks of derision as we passed.

We continued and came to the other side of the city, where the terrain became more mountainous. We had already made provisions to set up camp on the outskirts of the city. There was much to do to set up camp. Jesus, Peter, John, James, and Samuel had broken off to meet with a group of men who were leaders from various regions. They had brought their people to Jerusalem and were making plans for Jesus to speak in an open forum. Many of the people that these leaders had brought with them were aged and sick, in need of healing. The rest of the group set about preparing the campsite.

I looked around and did not see Rachel, Johanna, or Mary Magdalene. We soon learned that they were meeting with the wives of these leaders. The women were caring for the aged, sick, and desperate people, and were also in charge of food and water for their entire group.

I was tired and decided to go with the followers to establish the campsite and to leave the younger people to do the work at hand. This kind of tension and travel was hard on me, as I was not used to big cities or large crowds. And more than anything, the Roman Soldiers frightened me. I thought it best if I stayed in the tents to help with food preparation and preparing the beds for the night.

By evening, everyone returned to the camp, and I observed an animated discussion between Peter and James, who then drew Jesus into their conversation. John came over and asked me how I was doing. I appreciated the distraction of our conversation. Now, Peter, James, and Jesus were nowhere to be seen, but I sensed an excitement among the other disciples, as if an important message was circulating. I was glad not to be involved. Once again, the dancing and singing began, the timbrels began to play, and everyone celebrated and marveled at the incredible reception we had in the great city of Jerusalem.

The singing and dancing went on into the night, but I turned in early and before doing so, stole a few moments with Jesus. His face was burned by the sun and his eyes were fiery bright. "At last, we have arrived in Jerusalem, the day we all have waited for. What a great day this is, Mother! Now I can reach the hearts of so many more. Leaders from all the regions have brought their faithful and their needy to be healed. It is a great day for rejoicing, dear Mother. I am so glad that you were here with me to share it."

He kissed my hands and forehead. "Now, Mother, please rest. I worry about you. I have asked Rachel to take special care and I have noticed that you and John have become good friends. I know that you are safe with him and for that I am grateful because I may have to be away from you more than I would like, but I know you will understand that I am fulfilling my work and that I will return to you as quickly as I can."

"My son, my love goes with you and my heart is with you every moment. Go; tend to your work and your mission. I am here and well taken care of. I do not want you to worry about me." I hugged him tightly, kissed his brow, and said to him, "You are my beloved son and I cherish you with all my heart. Go now, I will sleep well tonight."

He walked with me to my tent and Rachel came to attend me. She kissed her brother. Just then a few of the disciples rushed over to Jesus and said they had something important to speak to him about.

As I lay on my bed, in the tent, I made a silent prayer that we would all live through this, for I had a very dark feeling that I could not shake off, try as I might. Still worrying, I fell into a deep sleep.

CHAPTER
41

It was a terrible time, with days and nights filled with fear and anguish. The disciples had become frightened to their inner core and ran in different directions in a state of terrible confusion. Jesus had gone into the upper hills to pray and had asked some of his disciples to accompany him there, which they did with some reluctance, for they had the idea that they needed to keep guard of the encampment, fearing that the Roman soldiers might come and take everyone to prison. All the work that seemed to hold everyone together now seemed to have fallen to pieces. I tried to speak to the followers, to allay their fears, but they just shook their heads in pity and told me that I needed to be very careful, for the soldiers would come after me as well.

Some people offered to take me back to my village, for they said that it would only get worse. I sought out Peter and implored him to take the situation in hand. I was surprised by his words.

He said, "Mother, Mary, I feel as if I am a weak man, unable to lead us out of this situation, I myself do not know which way to turn. I don't have the strength to lead this expedition and the men have not followed me through times of great strife. They feel lost and leaderless, and it is difficult for me to hold them together; they see Jesus' long hours of prayer as a sign of weakness. They feel he is retreating, hiding, walking away, and that frightens them. They are losing faith in all that they once believed in so fervently. Mother, you must see that I have no power in this situation. Even I am afraid, for I too feel that none of us are safe. Our very lives are at stake and the tides have changed radically. We must prepare to save ourselves. My advice to you is to take Rachel and leave within the hour, for the worst is yet to come and I cannot hold back the inevitable. I feel weaker and more afraid than I have ever felt in all my life. I feel the earth rumbling beneath me in terror. Go, Mother, take Rachel and leave this place, for there is nothing that you can do but stay alive and to tell what you have seen here. I know that Jesus is preparing as best that he can, but we are so weak, we cannot possibly hold back what is to come."

Then he looked at me, helplessly, wordlessly, and I placed my hand upon his arm and looked him straight in the eyes. I said, "Peter, I am not leaving. I am staying here. I am not taking one step away from this place. No matter what happens, I shall remain here every moment, until whatever happens, happens. Nothing, Peter, nothing will cause me to turn my back, ever. My strength is great, Peter, I have the strength of a hundred men. I shall stand steadfast, in this plain. Go, Peter, go wherever you need to go, do whatever you need to do, I cannot hold you to your commitment. That is for your own heart to decide, but know that should you choose to stay, I am here and will welcome your presence by my side. I feel the call of the Holy Father, I feel His presence, He is here all around us and nothing can shake my confidence."

A wind began to stir along the open plains. We were in a somewhat protected, though barren, area and as the wind began to blow, dust was swirling through the air. The sky darkened and an eerie feeling swept through the encampment, as if to foreshadow the events to come. It seemed almost as if even Nature needed to provide the secrecy of fog or misty night—for the cruel work that was to take place in the light of day.

Jesus had been praying in the Mount of Olives for hours and hours and he called upon some of his closest disciples to stay near him, to pray with him and as much as they tried to concentrate, one by one, they returned to the encampment. They huddled together in a group, talking and whispering.

I watched them from a distance, puzzled, for in many ways they seemed so unlike themselves that I could hardly recognize them. Suddenly, someone suggested that they should prepare the food for the evening. I suggested that we should prepare a table that all of us could gather around together. I felt that this night would have everlasting significance, as surely, we would never forget it.

Everyone set about their tasks, working efficiently and quietly. There was eeriness in the air, otherworldliness, a density, a thickness in the air of dust and heat. It was an unnatural feeling. We all felt it. At long last, John announced that Jesus was coming. We prepared a special place for him and some of the disciples brought water to wash his hands and feet.

When he entered, the disciples quietly motioned for Him to come to the table.

At last, gathered around the table, everyone found their place and there came a long silence where not a word was spoken. Then Jesus said, "My beloved ones, this meal together shall be our last but we shall be together eternally in our Father's House. My beloved ones, I am with you always. Although strange events will occur, know that I am with you, now and forevermore. Take this bread, break it, eat it in remembrance of me and take this wine, drink it in remembrance of my blood, which shall be shed for you. My beloved ones, I bless each and every one of you, for my heart is entwined with your hearts. You may sleep peacefully this night, for I give you my assurance that no harm shall come to any of you, for I have been promised by my Father in Heaven, whose name is hallowed above all, that you shall be safe in his bosom, protected from all harm. Now my faithful, beloved friends and family, I must leave you, for I am called back to the Mount where I must pray and keep a vigil with my Holy Father. If some of you wish to escort me there, I would be grateful for your fellowship and your company."

He rose from the table, bowing his head to his followers. He came up to me, took my hands in his, and knelt in front of me. "Gracious Mother, I commend my spirit to you, now and forevermore." He kissed my hands, lifted his head, and looked into my eyes. I embraced him and Rachel came forward to embrace him. We spoke no more, and he went out into the night to make his way back to the Mount of Olives.

Some of the disciples followed and went with him. Others began to clean up. Again, there was a strange silence in the air. An eerie coldness came as the hours passed. People began to go to their beds.

In the distance came the sound of horses, a large number of horses. At first, we could not tell what the sound was, but in time this rumble became louder and louder and closer, until an entire regiment of Roman Soldiers arrived on horseback and surrounded the camp. They carried torches and there were shouts. Our people, when they saw the soldiers, ran in every direction trying to hide. Rachel turned to me in terror. "Mother, what is this? What are they doing? Have they come for Jesus? I must run and warn him." With that she bolted from the tent. I hurried to the entrance of the tent and saw Rachel running toward where Jesus had departed, until two of the men stopped her, grabbing her roughly. She was fighting them. I ran to Rachel and pleaded with the soldiers that she was just a child, a young woman, to let her go.

They looked at us with disdain, as if we were the lowest of low animals and they threw her off, into my arms. We both fell to the ground. The horses were rearing up, someone threw some rocks, and I grabbed Rachel and pulled her away. Rachel screamed for me to let her go. She wanted to find Jesus and warn him before it was too late.

Together we ran to the outskirts of the encampment, away from the fights and horses to find a route back up through the rocks desperately hoping to warn Jesus. I could not keep up with Rachel, but I kept her in my sight and moved as quickly as I possibly could. By the time we got there, Jesus was already surrounded by the soldiers. Many of the disciples were standing just where they had risen up from their prayers. I had caught up with Rachel and I grabbed her arm and held her back out of sight. I would not lose both my children to these horrible soldiers. Rachel was virtually foaming at the mouth. She was quivering, but I knew that if I let her go and she ran into the middle of this scene, it would be her certain death.

With all my strength, I held her fast even as we saw Judas walk toward Jesus, kiss him on each cheek, and thereupon the soldiers surrounded Jesus and dragged him off into the night. It happened so quickly, in the flash of an eye. Jesus' hands were bound, and he was dragged away to the lower part of the mountain, where they threw him across a horse.

I saw the bag of gold in Judas' hands and in my shock, I let go of Rachel, who ran screaming, headlong into Judas, where she knocked the gold out of his hands and beat him with her fists, kicking him, screaming. The gold pieces went flying and several people pulled her away from him. Judas threw himself to the ground to gather up his bounty, and like a snake, slithered off into the night, scratched and bruised from Rachel's attack. Rachel wept uncontrollably, howling like an animal. Her cries frightened the men, and they ran from us as if we were lepers.

Now we were alone. I feared that Rachel would never come to her senses. We laid there for a long time, clinging to one another. At last, I heard a small voice say to me, "I will never leave you, Mother. I will be by your side, always. I hate them, Mother! I hate them. I despise them."

I looked at my little Rachel who, in all her years of terrible struggle and misfortune, had never uttered the word hate. I could see that she was consumed by it now. Her little face that had once looked so innocent, in a matter of moments she had seen too much.

I did not try to change her mind, but put my arm around her and held her close by my side. Then, through the darkness, with only the light of the moon and stars to guide our way back down to the camp, with Rachel limping and I feeling weak and faint, we made our way back. As we got closer, we saw that everything had been destroyed. The tents ripped, everything that we had, strewn, broken, stomped over by the horses. Nothing was left. Everyone had scattered to the hills, and Rachel and I stood quivering in this desolate place.

There was now, again, a breeze over the plain, and in the distance, I saw something stirred by the wind. I led Rachel toward it seeing that it was a remnant of a blanket. I picked it up, "Come, Rachel, let us sleep by this rock. Let me put this blanket around us. We need to rest. Lay your head against me." As she did so, I found myself rocking her gently and singing a lullaby I used to sing to her as a child, that my mother sang to me and her mother to her. At last, we fell into the arms of sleep, a deep, tortured sleep.

CHAPTER
42

Rachel and I fled into hiding to remove ourselves from the hysteria that had consumed everyone around us, so that we could muster our strength and determine a course of action. Rachel wanted to go directly to the authorities and plead for her brother. We talked about the wisdom of doing this, but we both knew that this time it was far past our ability as mother and sister to convince those in power to release him. Imagine us sitting among the rocks with nothing but the clothes on our backs and the blanket that we had found, trying to plan a way to help Jesus. Rachel began to cry, and she looked so small and desperate sitting there.

I determined in that moment that I would not give in; rather I would confront the situation directly without fear. I knew that we could not stay in this place, cowering like frightened animals. My son had done nothing except preach ideas of love. I would not accept the verdict of those who could not see or hear the truth of my son's words. I would not slink away into the night with fear for my life or for my daughter's life, but rather we would go forward as innocent people who had unwillingly been brought into a state of desperation and chaos. With my veil, I dried Rachel's tears and took her face in my hands. "Dearest Rachel, it is you and I who must find the strength to pick up the pieces of our lives for the sake of Jesus. We know the true meaning of his life. No matter what happens, no matter what they do, we will stay together.

"I am no longer afraid of these people in authority. They can never have what resides in my heart, they can never rob me of the deep and abiding love which lives within me; these are gifts from the Holy Father.

Now, my Rachel, I ask you this day to trust in everything you know to be true, for you and I together will carry to fulfillment whatever plan God has in store for us. Let us make our way into the city with our heads held high, for Jesus is a Son of God and His light pours forth and around us and we shall bask in that light no matter what they do or say. The real test is nigh upon us. I was told in the night by an Angel that we would be protected and cared for. We have no time to fall into the trap of overwhelming self-pity and emotions; we must carry on for Jesus. He needs us now more than at any other time in his life."

Rachel put her hand on my face and said simply, "Yes, Mother, we must find Jesus, come let us go before it is too late."

With that, we gathered ourselves together and began the walk into the city. It was a clear day and we walked hand in hand silently for several hours. Up ahead we could see storm clouds in the sky swirling, dark, foreboding. I told Rachel, "Let us continue on in the hope of finding some shelter before the sky breaks with rain."

We quickened our steps and soon saw a rocky cliff like area before us, just as the clouds burst and it began to rain. There was an area under the rocks, and we climbed in beneath it. Suddenly, we heard a voice. We turned and saw an old woman, who had a home inside this cave-like part of the cliff. She motioned to us to come in further, "Come on, come on in, don't be afraid. It is cold and wet out there, you can stay here. Come, come, come."

We drew closer and she pulled out a tattered, thick blanket and spread it out for us to sit on. "Here, rest yourselves on this now. Ha, ha, ha, ha, ha, ha. Doesn't that feel good? Ha, ha, ha, ha," she laughed and laughed. She seemed so pleased to have visitors. "I have lived here forever, you know. I was born right here and have never left this spot. No better spot around, won't find a better spot than this. Here, have something to eat. You look hungry."

She offered us some greasy stew and some very thick, hard bread. We ate it with relish. "That's it now, eat it all up, eat every bite now. Ha, ha, ha."

She laughed and laughed. "Here, you still look hungry. Take some of this. It's honey, mixed with some nuts." She got up and went deeper into the cave and brought out some more cloth to wrap around our shoulders. "Here you are, put this on. You are shivering all over. Here, girl, put this on. Wrap it tight now. That's it."

She shuffled back into her spot, which was quite elaborately set up with pillows, rugs, blankets: a throne inside this cave. "Well, well, well, well, well, well." Then she just stopped and stared into space, almost as if she was in some sort of a trance. By this time, we were both so tired and the rain was still pouring down, we just curled up and fell asleep almost immediately.

Hours passed. This was the first real sleep that we had had since Jesus' capture. During this sleep, I had a dream. I saw Jesus sitting on a cloud and he was floating over the Mount of Olives, as if peaceably watching over us. In my dream, I called out to him. But the cloud and Jesus kept on floating, back and forth. At one point, I was running after the cloud, chasing it almost, but I could never bring it down to earth, it just kept floating. I woke up, sweating and shaking, from the stress of running after the cloud in my dream.

Rachel was already awake, and she and the old woman were talking. "Here, girl, take this. This will protect you; it wards off evil spirits and those who would do you harm. I am giving it to you, girl, because you are going to need it. Here's one for your mother, too. Take my word: you are going to need it. Don't ever take it off. Wear it night and day."

We thanked the old woman and told her it was time for us to be on our way. "Remember, I keep my eye out on things. Don't think I don't know what goes on. The whole pack of them out there, running around like mad dogs . . . chasing after nothing . . . they'll find out . . . mark my words on that . . . oh, yes, they'll find out. Well, there it is now, there's the sun. Better get going. I have my eye on you, mark my words."

We thanked her profusely, for her great kindnesses to us and she just cackled and cackled with laughter. The more we thanked her, the more she cackled. We had to laugh in spite of it. "Get going now, ha, ha, ha, ha." As we left, we still heard her cackle. Even far away we heard it. She gave us just what we needed: the spirit to go on, the strength to believe that we could go on. Also, we knew that if we needed to, we could come back and stay with her.

Rachel wrote a little song about her. "In a cave, rests an old woman, night and day, rests she there, in a cave lives an old woman, watching, watching, watching over us."

We put our arms around each other. By now it felt as though we were in some strange fairy tale, our existence a kind of dream. We walked and walked and at last in the far distance we could see the portals of the city gates. We decided that we would simply enter the city, drape our veils tightly around us, so as not to be recognized, try to be inconspicuous, and listen for gossip or information that would prove useful in our search for Jesus.

We entered the part of the city where there was a market. People were buying and selling goods, there was a great deal of activity, and it was very crowded. We moved along with the crowd, clinging tightly to each other, so that we would not be separated or lost.

Before long, I grew tired. So, Rachel took me over to the side, where I was able to sit. There was a woman selling beads. Rachel asked if it was all right for me to sit by her wagon. She nodded her head yes. Then I grew faint. The bead-selling woman saw I was in distress and said to Rachel, "Here, let her stretch out this way, let me get her water, she does not look well."

She hurried to the other end of the wagon, and brought a cloth dipped in water and placed it on my head. She went back, got another cloth dipped in water and wrapped them on my wrists. Then she motioned to Rachel, "Help me get her feet up."

After a little while, I was able to sit up and the blood began to come back into my face. The woman offered me some water mixed with honey to drink. Then she offered us both some bread. We thanked her profusely.

Then she said, "Have you heard what they have done to Jesus?" We just stared at her. "They have taken him to the Sanhedrin. They are going to put him on trial. Many people around here are wondering what is going to happen. Did you ever hear him preach? He converted my son, you know. And made a good man out of him. I thank him from the bottom of my heart for that. Don't know what is going to happen."

We were both speechless. Because we didn't say anything, she looked at us more closely and said, "Guess you haven't heard much about this man, Jesus. You must not be from around here. You look like country people." We nodded our heads yes.

"Well," she went on, "it is a shame," she said, "He seemed to be such a good man, but now he is in a lot of trouble. We will just have to see what happens."

By now, I was able to get up after resting. We thanked the woman once again for her kindness and continued on our way. For now, we knew that Jesus was being interrogated by the highest Jewish officials. We began to walk toward the temple.

As we drew closer, we saw a crowd of people gathered outside the temple, people were shouting and shoving and pushing. We could hardly see anything. Then we heard someone yell, "Jesus, king of the Jews, kill him, Jesus, king of the Jews." Rachel grabbed my arm and we tried to get into a better position where we could see, but it was very difficult. Someone yelled, "There he is, there he is. It is the Jew King. Look at him now."

We caught just a glimpse of soldiers surrounding Jesus. His hands were tied, and they seemed to be dragging him from the temple to another place. By this time the crowds were thick, and people were yelling all sorts of things. Some people were throwing stones and shaking their fists. Rachel maneuvered me onto the outskirts of the crowd and tried to place me so that I could see where they were taking Jesus. At one point, I heard somebody say, "Look, the Roman soldiers have him now, they have him. He is going to pay now, with his life."

And the crowds again surged forward. I noticed some women weeping and Rachel took me toward them. As we got closer, we saw that it was Mary Magdalene and two of her friends. They recognized us. The five of us gathered together, crying. The others gathered around Rachel and me and saw the state that we were in and said, "Quickly, come with us, it is very dangerous." They swooped us quickly away from the crowd and Mary Magdalene told us that they were taking Jesus to Pontius Pilate. "God, alone, knows what will happen to him now," they said. "Come with us, to our house, you shall be protected with us." We set off immediately for Mary Magdalene's house on the outskirts of the city.

It was a relief to be there, and they immediately made a bed for me to lie down on. Later, we realized the reason that I was so weak was that some of the food that I had eaten had made me ill. We had eaten mainly fruits, vegetables, and grains but the greasy stew that the old woman had given us had made me quite ill.

Mary Magdalene was a very beautiful woman, and her house reflected her beauty. Everything in it was soothing and soft and comforting. She immediately began to tend to me. She laid me on a very clean, soft, and beautiful cloth. She began to wash me and tend to my needs. It was my first opportunity to really study Mary Magdalene, for I could see why my son loved her so. I thought she was breathtakingly beautiful, and her eyes were so deep and dark and wise and sparkling. Rachel told me that Jesus had spoken of Mary Magdalene only once. He told her, "Rachel, I have a friend, her name is Mary, like our mother and her other name is Magdalene. She soothes my spirit when I am near her; I feel the ecstasy of joy. Her words are melodious, and her mind is keen. She is my dear, dear friend." Rachel said that is all he ever said about Mary Magdalene, but now that she was in her home and could observe her, she understood her brother's feelings. In Rachel's mind, Mary was a kind of princess; there was something magical about her. There was a glow around her. She was very gentle and delicate and loving in all of her dealings with people.

When she had made me comfortable, she turned to Rachel and said, "Rachel, I would like for you to take my bed this night, for I want you both to rest comfortably and I had just prepared it and I am so honored to have you in my house."

Rachel bowed to her and took her hands and thanked her, for her great kindness. She said, "Won't you rest here quietly with your mother? I'll leave you for a few moments to attend to some things and in short order I shall return. My dear friend Esther will stay here with you while I am gone. So, please, rest now and know that you are safe in my home."

CHAPTER
43

Now the days were dark and there was much heaviness in the air. Those who loved my son most feared for their lives and many of them had to reach into the deepest parts of themselves to find the strength and the courage to remain loyal and faithful during these times of extreme terror. Rachel and I were embraced and taken care of by Mary Magdalene and her circle of friends. As we were all women, we were better able to move about freely and in many ways were better protected than the male disciples of Jesus.

Our lives were in danger as well, but the authorities were not as concerned that we would start uprisings among the people. Instead, they openly feared that Jesus and his disciples would carry out mass uprisings. Each of the disciples dealt with these realities in his own way and through his own personality. My son had warned them of an impending disloyalty. I had been there when he spoke to them directly. They, of course, did not believe him and they tried in every way possible to reassure him that nothing of the sort could ever happen.

In these terrible days, the disciples dispersed and split apart from each other, many were in hiding. My own feelings during this time were that I had nothing to lose and that I would be by my son's side every moment when it was possible. I had an inner strength that I had no way of explaining, except by God's grace. Rachel worried about my health and my ability to withstand the terror of the events that were unfolding.

In the morning, when Rachel and I arose from sleep at Mary Magdalene's house, there was a great commotion outside the door. A woman came running down the street, bringing news that Jesus had been taken to Pontius Pilate for interrogation. The women—and this is not known, for it has not been written about—had established quite an elaborate and sophisticated underground messenger service. It was a network of women spread throughout the city of Jerusalem with means to relay messages into the villages throughout the region. These messengers were all women and they worked carefully and efficiently to communicate important news.

Mary Magdalene led this group. Indeed, she was very important among Jesus' followers. Because she was so careful, and knew the importance of what she was doing, her contributions are not generally known. Throughout the years of Jesus' teachings, Mary Magdalene's messenger abilities made it possible for him and the disciples to go more safely and more efficiently into the villages and countryside to teach and to reach the hearts of the people. Had the men attempted these intricate communication systems themselves, they would have been discovered very quickly by the official surveillance apparatus and would have been destroyed. But the women, under the guidance, and leadership of Mary Magdalene, were able to employ unusual and unsuspected techniques that garnered no suspicion.

I had a great love for Mary Magdalene, which increased as I observed her quiet dedication to the work of my son. She was loyal to him, and she never showed fear for her own life. She had the qualities of wisdom, maturity, extreme intelligence, and a very open and generous spiritual understanding. I believe that had my son not given his life fully and completely to his work, that he and Mary Magdalene would have loved each other their whole life through, but she was a wise and experienced woman, and her love was so great that she gave everything in the service of Jesus' mission instead.

Many people do not have full understanding of the strong participation on a daily basis of the women who were followers and members of Mary Magdalene's messengers. They were the ones behind the scenes who carried information and messages, who alerted the village officials, and who helped establish the schedule for safe passage of Jesus and the disciples to go about their teaching. It could not have been done without the help of these women, who in addition, provided food and places to live and carried the word throughout the region.

The commotion outside the door of Mary's house had caused a stir among the passers-by, for the woman who brought this message had been mortally wounded by a Roman soldier who had discovered that she was a spy for the followers of Jesus. Though she was near death, through the fervor of her belief she had managed to find her way to Mary Magdalene's house. She collapsed a few feet away from the neighbor's house and some of the passers-by went to her assistance, but in a state of hysteria, thrashing about, crawling frantically toward Mary's house, the woman refused the assistance offered by those who realized the seriousness of her injuries. Mary, immediately, along with two other women, gathered her up and brought her inside. They closed the door and barred it. Some rocks and sticks were thrown at the door, because by now, in fear, people were choosing sides, for and against Jesus.

Mary laid the woman down and two other women took basins of water and began to wipe her face and tend to her wounds. She had been stabbed by some sort of long dagger, and it had gone right through her. How she made it to Mary's house, we never knew. She had lost so much blood; she was feverish and utterly exhausted. She did not have long to live. Mary Magdalene placed her hand on her forehead to comfort her and to assure her. She was very young, which was probably why she had had the strength to come this far, with such a wound. She murmured, slowly, and very softly. "Jesus is in great danger. They have beaten him and tortured him. They want him to confess that he believes himself to be the King of the Jews. They will kill him surely, and I had to come here to tell you of his plight." At that, she took a huge gasp for air and died before our eyes. The room fell silent; all you could hear was the sound of each of us breathing. Very slowly, very quietly, Mary Magdalene closed the young girl's eyes and laid a beautiful white cloth over her. I sang a lamentation prayer, in Hebrew. Other women joined me.

Suddenly we heard shouts, a commotion, people yelling and again the sound of some stones and rocks being thrown at the door. Mary had constructed a house with thick, wooden shutters that were barred from inside. So, there we were a band of women, in a small fortress, in the outer part of this huge city, Jerusalem.

Mary Magdalene, our leader, said solemnly, "We have lost a brave and courageous friend, who gave her life to bring us this news of our beloved Jesus. We know that her soul rests with the Holy Father and with our prayers and our hymns; her soul takes flight and will remain in eternity forever. Under cover of night, we shall take her to the tomb, but now we must prepare for the events to come."

"As soon as night falls, we will spread the word throughout Jerusalem and the villages, so that by morning, it will be known of Jesus' condition. I think the only thing we can hope for now, is that enough people will gather outside the palace of Pontius Pilate, to rally and stand up for Jesus. I cannot possibly imagine what these Roman officials will do to him, if they will kill a mere girl that they feel is a threat to their power. We must stand firm in our resolve, to do everything that we can to summon our strength in numbers, so that these officials see the power and the strength of the people whom Jesus has touched."

"Dear Mary, your son has shed the light of the Holy Father upon all of us and we will never let him down, never. We will be by his side, through whatever comes. We are not afraid of these men, we are not afraid. We know what they can do, we know what they are capable of, but I tell you from my heart that we know the greater power of love and we have seen this love and experienced this love through the words and actions of Jesus, whose very life is a living testimony to love."

"Therefore, we must draw upon this wellspring of love, so that it may carry us into the streets and houses of those who must know what is happening. We must draw strength; for we women can go to places the men cannot go. We will and we must. Leila, who lies here having given her life, we must go for her."

Mary Magdalene rose up, came to me, and embraced me and embraced and kissed Rachel. Some of the other women lifted Leila and began to place candles around her and to wash and prepare her body for burial. Mary said, "I must go and make certain preparations. I shall be back. Please stay here inside, where it is safe. I shall have further news when I return. Please try to rest as best you can." She placed a veil over her head and slipped out a very small door unbeknownst to us in the back of her house, leading to an underground tunnel that allowed her to travel a substantial distance without anyone being aware of what she was doing.

Rachel came to my side and laid her head in my lap. I stroked her hair and brushed the tears from her eyes. It was very quiet in the room. The other women were sitting by the body of Leila and the air was heavy. Rachel turned to me and said, "Oh, Mother, I want to leave this place and go to the palace and beg for my brother's life. What good is it for us to stay here hidden behind these doors? Perhaps, if I go there, they will feel sorry and release him, once I have told them how much my Brother has done for his family and for so many people. Surely, their hearts will be moved, and they will let him go."

I looked into Rachel's eyes and brushed her hair away from her face. I shook my head, "My dearest Rachel, their hearts are as cold as stone and fear controls their lives, they will not be moved by your words, my child. Do you see what they have done to this young girl? I will not let this happen to you. No, my daughter, you cannot go, for they will only torture you. I will not have that. We must trust in Mary Magdalene's experience and wait for her return, come nightfall. We must stay strong in every way possible, for we are and shall be the voice of Jesus. We must live in order that he may live." Rachel buried her head in my lap and sobbed. She felt so helpless; he had saved her from that terrible prison so long ago, and now she wanted to do the same for him.

I leaned my head against the wall of the house and sleep began to overtake me. As I was drifting off, I saw Jesus' face before me. He reached out and touched my cheek. "Mother," He said, "I love you. It is all right."

I fell asleep but was awakened a few hours later: Mary Magdalene had returned. She spoke first to the other women, telling them it was safe to take the body of Leila to the tomb, which they did. She then came to me and Rachel and said, "Mother, I have news of Jesus. Come morning, Pontius Pilate will make his decision and announce Jesus' fate. Pilate has ordered his men not to harm Jesus any further and to leave him alone until tomorrow.

"We have sent word to all of the villages and to all of those who live in Jerusalem who would show their support, publicly. The Romans are gathering their people, for they wish to make a fervent public display against Jesus. They want to demonstrate to the populace that there are more people against him than for him. They are sending armed forces into the villages to terrify and intimidate the followers of Jesus, so that they will not be there to demonstrate in his behalf. The heartiest, most courageous followers will be present when Jesus is brought out and you and I and Rachel and all the women will be there.

"I have been told by someone very close to Pontius Pilate that he, himself, has been moved by your son. He stands in fear of this fateful decision. Something exchanged between him and Jesus made Pontius Pilate aware that this is not an ordinary situation. This is all the information that I could gather at this time. If I leave during the night, do not worry about me, for I have other means to gather additional news. In the morning, I will be here and will lead us to the place where we must go to demonstrate on Jesus' behalf. I have also been told that the officials are searching for the disciples, one by one, to frighten them and to prevent them from leading large groups of people to demonstrate on Jesus' behalf. Though you may not feel like it, please try to eat and drink something, for we will all need our strength. Rest quietly and sleep if you can, for tomorrow will come quickly."

"Thank you, dear Mary Magdalene, you are a brave woman. A brave and fearless woman and I thank you with all my heart that we are here with you. If only things could be different, but they are not, and we must trust in the plans of the Holy Father for us all. Good night and please, Mary, be safe. Do not take unnecessary chances."

"I assure you I won't. Now, please rest here."

Reluctantly we laid our heads on the soft pillows Mary Magdalene provided for us. I felt sick to my stomach. I wanted to weep, but I could not. My daughter and the others looked to me for strength and whichever way my emotions took me, they would follow. Something told me that this man, Pilate, from the words of Mary Magdalene, would allow Jesus to rest quietly that night.

For a moment, I remembered when I held him as a babe in the pasture, when the people in the village had gathered around us, and they had looked at us with love and delight. It was so pure and so simple and so utterly magnificent. How could something so beautiful have come to this? How could words of love cause so much anger, violence, and aggression in people? I prayed for my son. Indeed, I prayed the whole night through. I held him in my arms, I stroked his hair, I whispered to him that everything would be all right, I washed his bruises and his wounds, I stayed by his side, praying all the while. I believed that if I concentrated and prayed with all of my inner resources, that he would be able to feel this as he lay in his prison cell.

I know that many women and mothers who read this story will know these feelings; for they have seen their loved ones suffer the violence and aggression that hatred and fear bring to us all. We, the women and the mothers of the world have stood steadfast in the deepest knowledge that love shall prevail. I assure you, women of the world, that the day is coming, for the day is already here in the hearts of those who walk in the light. I assure you that the power of love will manifest fully, and that the world shall know and experience this. That thought burned in my heart that night, for even in this dark hour the faces of the simple shepherds and village people who had surrounded us at Jesus' birth gave me the strength, the hope, and the promise. For especially in the darkest hours, we must remember the simplicity, the majesty and the all-embracing power of love.

Although I did not sleep that night, when Mary Magdalene came to us, I was ready. I was prepared to step forward into the sunlight, to take a stand, and to cry out for my son, for Jesus, for his teachings, for his life.

We prepared ourselves and took with us the necessary food and water, and when we were ready, we followed Mary Magdalene and the other women to the palace gates. We made our way through crowds of people; there were hundreds, even thousands of people. There were heavily armed Roman soldiers on horseback who were riding through the crowds, stirring them up.

Rachel clung to my arm. People were running every which way, but Mary Magdalene led us directly through the crowds, to a place very near the palace. Many of the true believers from the villages had gathered there, and they surrounded us while still others fanned out through the crowds.

People began shouting, "Bring out the King of the Jews. Let us see him. Let us see this king with no crown." Roman soldiers on horseback were jeering and laughing; it was clear there were hecklers planted throughout the crowd. It seemed unreal; there was something very false even in the gathering of the crowds. There were very few women.

Suddenly, a great cry went up. "There he is! There he is! King of the Jews. King of the Jews. Crucify him. Crucify him. Crucify him. Kill him. Kill him. Kill him."

Others cried out, "Save him. Save him. He is holy. Save him." But their voices were drowned out by those crying, "Crucify him" in opposition. A small band of people ran through the crowds crying, "Save him" and the Roman soldiers grabbed them, crushing them and trampling them.

Pontius Pilate stood somewhat behind Jesus, overlooking this crowd. Jesus stood in quiet dignity. Rachel was screaming, and we had to hold her back once again. At last, the hand of Pontius Pilate went up, the crowd fell silent and through a large horn-like device the words came forth, "Shall this man live, or shall this man die? You be the judge."

Again, a great cry went forth, simultaneous shouting, "Crucify him, kill him, crucify him, kill him, King of the Jews, destroy him, crucify him." Pontius Pilate brought his arm down and cried out, "You have spoken. I wash my hands of this decision. It is yours, made this day, by you the people."

Two guards grabbed Jesus by either side and roughly took him inside. It suddenly became very dark. Clouds covered the sun, and it began to pour rain, violent rain, which dispersed the people. The women surrounded Rachel and me and took us quickly back to Mary Magdalene's house using a back route, away from the hysterical crowds and the Roman soldiers. We were drenched from the rain and practically faint from exhaustion. Rachel and I were in a state of disbelief. None of this seemed real to us. The women undressed us and bathed us, putting fresh, clean clothes upon us. They fed us and one woman sang a very soothing melody, trying to give us some peace and comfort.

Rachel became ill and I was practically paralyzed. Though I had feared the very worst, in experiencing this madness I had totally lost my ability to cry out, either in anger or sadness; I was bereft of words. The women once again gathered around us, holding us, rocking us, tending to our every need, singing melodies of comfort and peace. They stayed with us the whole night through. Outside we could hear the rain still pouring down. Mary Magdalene had not returned home and when I asked about her, one of the women said to me, "Do not fear, Mary can take care of herself. She will return, I am certain."

At long last, even in this dark hour of grief, sleep overtook us. I felt my prayers had reached my son's ears, for again, in sleep, I placed myself beside him in my mind's eye and promised him that I would be by his side always.

CHAPTER
44

Now the days were very hard, and the women and I grew even closer together; the male disciples had dispersed to far corners. Although Jesus had warned of these events, I don't think that anyone at the time fully understood their meaning. When we women were together, we reviewed some of the things that Jesus had said on the night that he was captured. I remember sitting in Mary Magdalene's house, while outside terrible riots raged. The Roman soldiers were hunting down any follower of Jesus, hoping to make an example of them before the others. They rode through the streets, chasing down people with spears and swords. There were many people who fought against them, throwing stones or whatever they could. The city of Jerusalem and all the surrounding countryside was in a state of chaos, and it was definitely not safe to be outdoors. Rachel tried to sneak out several times. She had it in her mind that if she could reach the palace and beg for her brother's life that she could save him. Mary Magdalene and the other women knew that this was a foolhardy, dangerous, and hopeless endeavor. They attempted to reason with Rachel, but she would not listen. She had made up her mind.

Eventually it was necessary for one of the women to act as a guard to ensure that Rachel did not leave. This was almost too much for me to bear, as I understood her desire and wanted to do the same thing. Knowing the hopelessness of the situation, we sat together for many hours and talked. Mary Magdalene and two of her closest messengers were devising a plan. Within the palace there was a person who Mary Magdalene knew had been converted by Jesus, but still worked in a highly regarded position within the Roman government. Mary Magdalene knew him well and she hoped to send a message to Jesus, some words that would comfort him, while perhaps gaining some information about his condition.

They determined that one of the three women would go, and they drew lots to decide who it would be. Mary Magdalene had wanted to be the one to go, but the other two women said no, that it was too risky for anyone to volunteer. As they prepared to choose, Rachel cried out that she could no longer stand by and watch her brother die at the hands of the Romans. They drew their lots and Judith, who was the right hand of Mary Magdalene, was selected. Mary said, "Judith, please allow me to go in your place. It was my idea, and I can find my way easily to the palace." Judith was firm, saying, "No, Mary, it is I who is to complete this task. I know what to do."

Without further discussion, Judith made ready to leave. We each went to her and whispered special things to relay to Jesus, if somehow she were able to speak with him. We still carried hope in our hearts that Judith would be able to free Jesus from this terrible imprisonment. Once more, before she left, Rachel begged the women to let her go with Judith. Mary Magdalene took Rachel in her arms and looked her fully in the face. Mary said, "My dearest Rachel, you cannot leave this house. It will mean certain death and you will not be able to save your brother. Your mother needs you, Rachel. She needs you to be her strength and to stand by her; in the hours and days to come we will all need each other. Judith is experienced; through her efforts we may be able to receive word of Jesus' condition. Through her, we may be able to send a message to him from all of us who love him."

Mary, herself, was trembling to hold back tears. Rachel threw her arms around Mary Magdalene, and they held each other very tightly. Then, Rachel came to me and embraced me. Mary and Judith had some last words together. All of us gathered around her to bless her as she departed. Then, quickly, she turned and left.

Outside, I heard continual shouting, people running and throwing things, the sounds of horses' hooves. As the horses passed, we huddled together, waiting for news from Judith, and as we waited, we gathered together in a circle. We held each other's hands and we prayed without stopping. We praised the Holy Father, we cried out for him to save Jesus' life. We prayed for Judith's safety. We prayed that Jesus would not suffer. We sang hymns of praise. After many hours we heard footsteps. It was Judith. She was exhausted and threw herself down upon the floor.

"My friends, I bring you news. Within the hour they will begin the climb to where Jesus will be crucified, there is no turning back. Jesus has been wounded by one of the guards. They plan to walk him through the streets at dawn; so that all may see this heretic they call the King of the Jews. I reached our friend in the palace and he told me that Pontius Pilate is sick with agony over his decision. If he had the means to set aside this decision, he would do so, but even he cannot call off this death sentence. The Roman government is using Jesus as an example to all others, of any sort, who dare convince the masses to go against them. The only thing Pilate has been able to do is to see that Jesus is not harmed any further by the guards during the few hours that remain. Our friend in the palace promised me that he would do everything in his power to send our words of love to Jesus tonight. He told me that unless he himself was able to do it, unfortunately, there is no other person trustworthy enough to deliver our messages."

Judith went on to tell us that there had been numerous people injured and killed in the riots. The disciples, she heard, were slowly, one by one, finding each other again and reuniting as best they could. Judith told us that once Jesus walked through the streets, there would be an end to the violence. The Romans wanted the focus to be upon Jesus alone; they wanted the people to see what happened when such a peasant proclaimed himself a king.

Judith turned to Mary Magdalene and Rachel, "I know that you each wished to go in my place, but it is better that I bring you this news. Our friend in the palace said that even the guards have been touched by Jesus' calmness, loving spirit, and humility. Mother Mary, our friend in the palace also said that Jesus' prison cell is filled with a glowing light of love and that all who pass there cannot help but to see it."

Hearing her words, we gathered together closely, holding each other, knowing that Jesus was protected by the holy light of love eternal. We knew that Jesus' love was so great that no person or thing could have ever extinguished that light. In those moments, we felt Jesus' arms around us. We felt his presence in the room and a great calm came over us, a strength came into us, and we were no longer afraid.

That the fear left our bodies was a miracle. None of us was afraid. We stayed with our own thoughts, quietly contemplating and praying, each within ourselves. At last, Mary Magdalene spoke, "I think it is time now. Let us gather our things together and I will show you the way."

It was dawn and thousands of people were already stretched out for miles and miles around the crucifixion site. Many were yelling. Mary Magdalene took us to a place where we could be protected behind some rocky areas if we needed to escape. A cry went up from the crowd, "There he is, King of the Jews, look at him now. See him torn and beaten!"

We could not see anything; we could only hear the shouts and the taunts. Suddenly, I became ill; I could not catch my breath and I fainted. Rachel and Mary came to my aid. All of the tension had finally overwhelmed me. It was as if I could feel my son's heart beating in my own chest. The pain was excruciating. I could barely breathe. The women gathered around me and began to loosen my clothes. Still there was the terrible pounding in my chest. Someone ran to get water; this pounding wouldn't stop. They lifted me up and shouted, "Make way there is a sick woman! Make way!" They were trying desperately to get me out of the crowd. They took me to a grassy area and laid me down.

There was no color in my face, and I was hardly breathing. Rachel was at my side, and she had her hands around my wrists, stroking them. I heard her pleading, "Mother, Mother, come back. Mother, don't leave us, Mother, come back. Please come back, Mother."

Suddenly, my eyes opened, and I looked at Rachel, full in the face. She moaned, "Mother, you must live, you must live. We must go to Jesus now. Come back Mother, come back." I felt my strength come back to me and I sat up. The women were around me; they urged, "Rest, Mary, don't move quickly." Feeling better, I insisted, "No, I must get up. I must go to my son, get me up. Get me up!" I rose up with the help of the women and I said with a replenished conviction, "Come and follow me. I am going to my son."

Where I got this strength, I'll never know. I ran across the grassy plain and I continued to run, the women following behind me. Though it was I running, something else was leading me. As I pushed through the crowds, I saw Jesus getting to the top of the hill. I continued to run. There were soldiers surrounding the area. They rebuked me, "Stay back, woman. Go no further." Up above, they had laid Jesus down and stretched his hands across the length of the cross. There were three men, one at each hand and one at his feet. They took nails and hammered them through his hands and into his feet. We saw and heard it all.

I screamed at the guard, "That is my son! You will let me pass, you will let me pass!" At that moment, they lifted up the cross and drove it into the ground. The guard stepped aside, and I ran past him. I threw myself down at Jesus' feet. He looked down to me, and said, "Mother don't weep; they know not what they do."

I touched his feet. By this time the guards had stepped far away from us. Rachel growled at them, baring her teeth, and they turned away. They wouldn't even look at us. I gazed up at Jesus' face and at the crown of thorns on his head. His side was deeply wounded. Even so cruelly injured, he kept a soft smile on his face. He was too weak to speak, but I stayed with him and touched his feet to let him know that I was still there. The sun bore down hot. Jesus cried out for water, and they brushed a rag dipped in vinegar across his lips. As they did this, Rachel screamed, and she tore at the guards. They grabbed her by the hair and threw her violently to the ground, kicking her.

As I watched these soldiers terrorizing my beloved children, it was as if I were floating outside my body. Watching myself convulsing in agony, I couldn't hear their screams or my own wailing. In that silence I heard Jesus speak . . . "Mother, I am with God, love is everywhere." The sun went out of the sky, and he was gone. His soul had left his body. I felt the life go out of him. I prayed the Prayer of the Dead. Rachel crawled over to me and together we knelt there and prayed. It was growing dark. The guards had again retreated, and it seemed that the crowds were leaving.

I don't know, I wasn't paying attention to them. I stayed still there, on the ground, as it grew darker, until I felt a hand upon my back. It was Mary Magdalene. She had just placed her hand on me, and kept it there, without speaking. Once the sky had gone black, beautiful stars emerged. We stayed there through the night. At the first sign of light, the soldiers returned.

There we were a little band of loved ones. Mary Magdalene went to the guard and told him that we wanted to prepare Jesus' body for burial. For some reason, they allowed it. The soldiers took the cross and laid it flat on the ground. We attended to Jesus' body; we washed him, prepared him with oils, and lovingly wrapped him in a clean shroud that Mary Magdalene had brought. When we were finished, the guards came and carried him to the tomb. We followed: me, Rachel, Mary Magdalene, Judith, and a few other women. We went to the tomb and watched them place Jesus inside. They rolled a huge stone in front of the door and the guards assumed their posts there.

There was one guard, with a kindly face, who saw that I did not want to leave. He quietly said to me, "It is all right, I promise you. I will take care of him." I looked at this guard with wonder and amazement, for they had all been so cruel. I bowed my head and thanked him for his kindness. He replied, quieter still, "Go in peace." I thought of what Judith had told us after her visit to the palace and wondered if this guard had been with my son during those final days.

We gathered ourselves together and slowly made our way back to Mary Magdalene's house. There, we waited—for what, we did not know.

CHAPTER
45

In the days following the burial, I did not wish to be indoors. I wanted to go to the countryside. I needed to speak to the Lord. All that had passed was such a great mystery to me and nothing about the events, for the moment, seemed real.

The women understood that I wished to be alone. Mary Magdalene stayed by Rachel's side. Rachel was still crying, but very weak and exhausted with anger. She willingly stayed home with Mary Magdalene. One afternoon, I followed a small pathway that led to an isolated spot high above the city of Jerusalem.

As I reached the top, I found a rock to sit upon and for a while I stayed there, allowing the breezes of the air and the sounds of nature to comfort me. So many times in my life, I found myself alone, with only the sounds of the wind and the air around me. I gave myself over to this feeling. I released my thoughts and let go of my expectations. If I could have at that moment, I would have happily melted into the air or gladly disintegrated into the ethers to join my son. I had faith that he was now in the arms of the most Holy Spirit and walking in the light of purest love. I myself would have joined him fully prepared.

I sat for hours like this. In some ways I felt invisible, an open vessel. I could no longer feel my own body. It was as if it had disappeared and only my spirit was hovering over the stone that I was sitting upon. I had accepted that my son was with his Father at last, yet, I had not accepted his leaving me in such a way.

Time passed. I noticed a gentle breeze blowing softly, caressing my face and hair. It was so warm and comforting. Then, I heard these words, "Mary, it is Joseph here with you. I've come to be here with you, my wife. I cannot bear to see you alone." I felt his arms around me. I laid my head against his shoulder, and it felt so good to have him there.

He continued, "Mary, I bring you a message of hope. You shall know and you shall see all things for your heart is pure. You will walk among the living and carry to them news. Joy is everywhere and life is a magnificent love affair with all things, you know this in your heart. You will carry this vision into the world. Mary, I love you. I am still with you, don't be afraid. There is no fear, there is no fear. This is the promise."

I felt him kiss me, I felt his arms around me, and I was overcome with a love so great. He said, "Mary, come now, I will walk with you to Mary Magdalene's house. They have wonderful news for you. I will be by your side, my dear wife."

We walked, happily. When we reached Mary Magdalene's house, there were many people gathered there. She was addressing them all. When she saw me, she called out, "Mother" and ran toward me, putting her arms around me, and "Mother, Mother, I have seen Jesus! He is alive, walking among us. He is not dead! He is alive. I went to the tomb, to pray and the stone was gone. I entered the tomb and Jesus was not there. At first, I thought that the guards had removed his body. I was crazed with anger and sickness in my heart. I cried out and tore my clothes in agony, thinking how they could have done this to him. Wasn't it enough, what they had done? I ran out to find the guards; I was prepared to kill them and myself as well. I came upon that guard, who had been kind to us, and I threw myself at him screaming, 'What have you done with our Lord? What have you done with him?' This man looked at me in astonishment and said, 'He is alive, I saw him with my own eyes, He rose up, pushed open the tomb and walked outside. He touched my head and blessed me, telling me that my life was now and forever changed. Then, he smiled and disappeared. I do not know where he went, but I assure you that he is alive. I saw him with my own eyes. I looked at the face of this guard, deep into his eyes, and I knew that he was telling the truth. He went on, 'I cannot leave this tomb, it is my task to guard it. I do not know what to say. These are strange times and I do not understand what I have seen; however, I saw him with my own eyes.' Then, he sat down in a daze."

"While I walked away from him in a state of total confusion and uncertainty, I felt drawn to walk in a certain direction. So, I followed a pathway which led to a quieter area with many trees and bushes. As I drew closer to this garden, and it was a garden, a beautiful garden, the scent of the trees and the leaves and the flowering bushes was delicious. The earth under my feet was soft and warm. As I stood there, breathing in the atmosphere of this place, I heard these words, 'Mary Magdalene, it is I.' I turned, and there stood Jesus. He came to me and placed his hands upon my face, touching my forehead and cheeks. He drew me into his arms, held me close, and he kissed me. I looked up at his face and he said, 'Now you know the promise, Mary. Now you know, for certain, the promise of life eternal. I am here with you. You can feel my body. I have held you close to me, and you have felt my arms around you. You know that my love for you is fully alive. Mary Magdalene, I loved you fully in my life and I love you fully now. Carry this love to all others, for that is the deepest wish of my Father. I place this love in your hands, Mary Magdalene, I place it in your hands, and you know the meaning of that love.' Once again, he held me closely in his arms and he kissed me, many times. Then, we slowly walked together down the path, and he turned and said, 'Mary, you carry the promise with you. You know now. Spread the word to everyone, that I am alive. Go now, hurry.' I ran the rest of the way back to the village. Mother Mary, Jesus is alive, and we must spread the news, for it is the truth."

Crowds began to gather around us and very quickly, like a wildfire, the word spread through the countryside and all through the villages. There were not enough Roman soldiers to stifle these words. All sorts of miracles began to happen in these hours: sick people rose up, sad and forlorn people were filled with joy and light, old people began to dance as if they were young. A metamorphosis occurred among those who heard and those who knew the truth.

It was during these hours that I found Peter. "Mother," he said, "I have seen that Jesus has risen. I have spoken with him and so have John and Thomas. I am certain that many others have seen him. It is crystal clear now, what it has all been about. Jesus has forgiven us for our weaknesses, our human frailties of fear and greed, all has been forgiven. He asks only that we carry forth the promise of life everlasting through pure love. He asks us to go everywhere without fear and proclaim that love is God."

Peter knelt down and placed his head against my hand. "Mother, I ask your forgiveness for my own weakness of spirit which made a coward out of me. I fled in fear and was not able to face the consequences of my own beliefs. I ask your forgiveness for deserting you and Rachel. I will understand if you cannot forgive this act of cowardice, but I have learned a great lesson, a lesson that I never thought to know: when one walks in the light of love there is nothing to fear, absolutely nothing, and now I know."

"Rise up, Peter, you are a man this day and my love for you is boundless. Today we both know, with love there are no boundaries, no borders. I forgive you, Peter. I embrace you as a son. This is a happy day, for my son is alive and walks among us."

Peter went on his way. As I walked back, pondering all that had happened so quickly, I felt within me a lightness of spirit that I had not felt since I was a very young girl. I walked toward a place with a stream flowing over rocks. I walked along this stream, watching the water flow, and sensing inside of me the calming effect of this flowing stream of water. I felt full and young and strong. I looked up and I saw him, there he was, my son. I hugged him and hugged him and touched him, looked at his hands and his feet. He was perfectly well.

I said, "My son, it is a miracle. How did this happen? What has happened? It is like a dream. Is it a dream? Am I dreaming? Tell me, I want to know. Tell me, so that I may know more than I know now."

He said, "Mother, it is not a dream. What you see now is the promise, the hope. Indeed, Mother, it is reality. Everything else, Mother, is the dream. We have awakened from that dream, Mother. Now, we stand here fully aware, fully awake, and fully alive. This is what my life has been about. I was meant to show others the way to awake from the dream and to live fully alive. Mother, you are so beautiful and having a mother like you has made it possible for me to awaken. I ask you to walk in my footsteps, proclaiming the magnificence of all that you have seen and know. I love you so. Let us find Rachel. I have not seen her yet and I long to."

He led me toward an open field, where Rachel was walking through very tall grasses, wandering aimlessly, in a state of confusion. Jesus said, "Wait here, Mother. Let me go to her first."

Rachel was walking in circles.

Jesus called out, "Rachel, Rachel" but she did nothing. She continued to walk in large circles. Jesus ran toward her, right up to her and scooped her up, just as he had done years before. "Rachel, it is your brother. I'm here." He twirled her around in the grass until she began to laugh and laugh and laugh. He took her hand, and they began to run through the grass, playing tag and acting the way they did as children, whooping and hollering. I stood there watching them with utter joy. After some time, they ran toward me. Rachel was flushed with excitement; she threw her arms around me, and we all threw our arms around each other. Then we took hands, all three of us, and walked to the end of the field. There was a young lamb, a little baby lamb there. Jesus lifted it up and he gave it to Rachel saying, "Sister, I give you this baby lamb. Remember this moment together. Care for this lamb and more shall grow from her. Tell everyone what you know, in your own way, from your hearts. Go, now to Mary Magdalene and the disciples, they have prepared a celebration feast. Hurry now, they are looking for you."

CHAPTER
46

The land was alive with excitement, as word spread from person to person that Jesus was alive and walking through the villages where he had once preached. Although not everyone saw him with their own eyes, the word had spread so rapidly and with such fervor, that even those who had disbelieved before, had their hearts opened. They accepted the message that my son had put forth before.

Word of Jesus' renewed life had also spread throughout the Roman Empire and caused shock, fear, and anger among the authorities. They had been so certain that they would wipe out not only Jesus and his cause, but also any memory of him by simply destroying him physically. The reactions of the people who saw and heard that Jesus was alive and walking among them, made the Roman authorities shiver in fear. Their pagan beliefs were called into question; could the ghost of Jesus enter their domain and gain control over them?

Through Mary Magdalene, we heard that the highest Roman officials were nearly in a panic with fear. They had received enough first-hand witness accounts of Jesus' renewed life that they knew that his missing body was no hoax. Word came to us that Pontius Pilate himself was so terrorized that he had sought out a follower of Jesus and asked him how he could receive peace of mind for his part in my son's death. Roman officials were consumed by their own nightmarish fears, self-doubts, and panicked confusion. There was part of each and every one of them which simultaneously believed and disbelieved that what had transpired was possible. For the first time it seemed that they recognized the true power of Jesus' work. Amazingly, many Romans converted and sought out the followers of Jesus. Something in their hearts had been moved, and despite having been driven by fear and guilt, they truly wished to repent for a deed they then realized had been absolutely wrong.

At the same time that these things were happening, there developed another violent faction of Roman officials, whose fear became so great that they became even more violent and destructive. They set up militias to stamp out the followers of Jesus. They would stop at nothing to kill anyone who had any dealings whatsoever with his work.

These were chaotic times. No one was certain of who they could believe or trust. At any time during the night or day, a regiment of Roman soldiers could appear on horseback and drag people away to be publicly slaughtered. Entire villages were fleeing to the mountains, on foot and horseback, as quickly as they could go. People were looking for any place that they could hide.

It was not safe for us to gather together in one place. Now, even I, who was looked upon as just a harmless, misguided mother, before, now became a threat. My life was in danger. We did not have much time to draw up plans. We had to act spontaneously. When the Roman officials imagined that the ghost of Jesus would haunt them for the rest of their lives, they took violent measures.

John came to Mary Magdalene's house; he had hidden some documents that he had been keeping about the work of Jesus in her safekeeping. He feared that if he were ever captured, that they would ransack his home and destroy his work. As a messenger, many people entrusted written documents to her care. John arrived at Mary Magdalene's house, planning to take his writings and escape over the mountains to a distant territory. Everyone was preparing to depart and many people who had entrusted their work to Mary Magdalene were also coming to collect their documents.

Rachel and I did not know in which direction to travel. Mary Magdalene felt it was not safe for the women to be together any longer. The messenger network had been discovered. Roman officials announced to their regiments that all women who had followed Jesus were to be killed along with the men. Terrible things happened to the women, cruel and violent tactics beyond death were used by the Roman soldiers. We were preparing to run for our lives when John appeared to collect his writings. Mary Magdalene suggested that the three of us depart immediately.

I was happy and relieved to do so; I had always liked and trusted him. I believed that he had enjoyed my company as well. We only gathered a few things; it was no time to be burdened down with heavy objects. We needed to make haste and leave Jerusalem as quickly as possible.

The Roman soldiers were on the major roadways, so we had to take alternative and more treacherous routes through mountain passes. Rachel was very helpful in leading us through the rocky terrain. Her years of helping the outcasts had taught her how to traverse with ease through the rocky regions that we now had to pass through. Fortunately, over the years, Mary Magdalene's network of messengers had established safe havens with contacts familiar with Jesus' work. Although we had to travel many of the rocky passageways through the mountains by foot, after a certain point there were people who met us with horses to help us make the longer journey into a completely different territory. They had a relay system; people went by horseback to a safe territory and upon arriving signaled a second team to head out for the next set of passengers. It went like this, until as many people as possible were safely transported out of the violent Romans' reach.

Many people believed that the Jewish scribes, lawmakers, and rabbinical teachers were a part of Jesus' destruction. However, this was not the case. Jesus, although he was a rebel in the eyes of the official Jewish scholars, was still seen as a man of the Jewish faith who should, therefore, not be harmed. It was the Roman government who set upon the followers of Jesus. Their personal beliefs were such that they feared repercussions from not only the living followers of Jesus but also from dark forces that they thought had come to haunt them. Even some of the most influential Jewish rabbis and teachers feared for their lives, simply because they were Jewish, just as Jesus was Jewish, just as my family and father's family and his father before him and his father before him and on and on, had been Jewish.

Make no mistake, my son, Jesus, was a Jewish man and learned all of the laws and the teachings of the Jewish faith. Make no mistake, my son also walked in the path of pure and utter love. His heart was filled with such light and joy. He embraced all people and drew them to him with such compassionate understanding of all that they were, that he transformed everyone that he touched.

You see, my beloved friends, the light of the Living God is brilliant with love, with love for all people, each and every one of you. God's light sees only the magnificence and the breathtaking beauty of pure love and that, my dear beloved friends, is what my Son revealed.

Rachel, John, and I arrived in a place called Ephesus and there we stayed for some time. Mary Magdalene, with other members of her messenger network, were organizing safe passage for hundreds of people into this out-of-the-way part of the country. Mary Magdalene had close friends and loved ones among these people, and she felt called to work in this particular area.

It was a relief to come to this resting place. By this time in my life, it was not so easy for me to travel and adjust to new surroundings. It was always difficult for me. I always found it hard to leave the places that I had grown to love, that were familiar to me. I was never an adventurous type of person. I would have been happy living in one house, in one small village in the countryside, having never seen a city. That would have been just fine with me.

It was wonderful to arrive in Ephesus. The people there were gracious. They had kind eyes and they helped us settle into a home. They were quiet and unassuming. They did not ply us with questions but allowed us to adjust in our own time. I think that I slept for nearly a week, rarely even rising from my bed. I was so grateful and thankful that I could, at last, sleep at night without fear and trepidation.

Rachel was completely attentive to me, feeding me and watching over me. I could see that she was feeling more like herself again. I think we both were so happy to be far away from the land that had betrayed and destroyed our beloved Jesus.

As I lay in my comfortable bed, many scenes from my life flashed before my eyes. I thought about my other children who were now very, very far away from me. I missed them so. It was very painful to have our family broken in pieces. I wondered if we would ever be able to reunite and if my other sons would ever come to truly understand the work of their brother.

Rachel brought me a cup of warm, honey-flavored tea and sat by my side. She seemed to be reading my mind. She leaned my head against her shoulder, just as I had done with her so many times before. Now, she was my mother. She sang sweetly, gently, and lovingly, until I fell into a deep sleep.

CHAPTER 47

Time passed, the days grew long and sometimes I felt that it was very difficult growing old in a place so far away from my home and the rest of my family. I longed for my other children; I wanted to make peace and come to a resolution with the things that had happened within our family.

Rachel knew of my distress. During these days I spent many hours contemplating, thinking about all of the things that had happened in my life. I found that many unresolved areas lay heavily on my heart.

Rachel, as always, was by my side. We were both outcasts living in a strange land. We had no family near us and in these days, family members guided and protected each other from the dangers so prevalent during this time. Rachel and I only had each other. John was very busy with his work, but we saw him often and he was still very much a part of our lives. But inside of me were questions, memories, longings, and confused emotions. I very much wanted to return and see my children.

Rachel, too, was overcome at times with sorrow and grief over the loss of her family and her children. It was impossible to even get word of them because of all of the upheaval and political unrest.

I did not want to burden Rachel with my troubles, but being so sensitive, she always knew when my heart was heavy. One day, she came and invited me to take a walk with her. She thought it would help me. I knew that she was right about this, but it seemed easier and easier just to stay inside.

When she invited me to go for a walk, I was happy to do so. She put her arm around my waist, and we began to stroll. At first, we walked along quietly, not saying too much to each other. Finally, Rachel said, "Dear Mother, I see in your face and in your eyes that you are not happy. I see that you spend much time indoors by yourself, and this is so unlike you. Oh, Mother, I want to lift your spirits and see you happy again. I find it difficult to sleep at night because I worry so for you. If only I could take us back home, so that we could reunite with our family. Perhaps, then, your spirit would be lifted. I spoke to John about doing this, but he said that the dangers are still too great. The Roman soldiers are stationed all over the countryside and they would recognize us, since now we are known throughout the land. He said that we might be able to get a message through to the village, but we could not tell them where we are. They would not be able to reply to us. I know how hard this is on you, Mother. I, myself, would like to know about my children and my brothers. It seems impossible, but I am sure, Mother, that there will be a way, for God has always watched over us and he has helped us when everything seemed impossible."

I hugged Rachel tightly and murmured to her that she was right, that God had always watched over us, protected us, and guided us. I knew that we had to trust in that knowledge.

We walked further along the path, arm in arm, looking at the trees and the grass, both of us lost in our own thoughts. Rachel broke the silence, saying, "Mother, I have an idea. It has just come to me. I could go to our village. There must be a way that I could conceal my identity and using the safe havens that we know about. I believe that I can do it, Mother. I am not afraid to try. If we plan it out, I will be fully prepared and can overcome any obstacles or dangers. Mother, what do you think?"

"Oh, Rachel, I don't know. I don't think that you should even dare attempt such a journey. You heard what John said. The Roman soldiers are everywhere. Oh, no Rachel, it is surely an impossible idea. No, no, child, I cannot allow you to do such a thing. Put this idea out of your mind. Let us return home now. I know your desire to do this thing, but I could not bear to lose you, Rachel. I do not want you to sacrifice your life in service to my needs. Let's return home now and put this aside and into the hands of God."

That night, I sat alone in my room and gazed out the window. It was a beautiful, clear night. I began to think about what Rachel had proposed. I began to ponder the possibility of making such a journey. Could another long journey through dangerous terrain be done? I imagined seeing the faces of my children, the places in our old village and standing on familiar ground. I imagined ways for us to get there. I realized that I would never allow Rachel to go by herself. If I went with her, at least it would be the two of us together. We would have each other. The more I looked at the sky and the stars and felt the night air blowing through the window, the more I felt the deep desire to make this journey.

By morning, when I awoke, I had decided that Rachel and I were going home. It was time. I decided to go directly to John and talk to him about my decision. I knew that he would try to dissuade me, but I also knew that once he understood that my mind was made up, he would do everything in his power to assist us.

I sought him out first thing in the morning. I wanted to create a plan of action as soon as possible. At first, when I told him my idea, he was shocked and dismayed. He tried in every way to change my mind. When he saw that I had made the decision, just as I had predicted, he said that he would help in any way that he could. He begged me not to take one step forward until every part of our plan had been calculated carefully and minutely. He told me very directly that our lives would be in extreme danger and that he could not possibly predict the outcome of such a dangerous journey. He said to me, "Mother Mary, I only hope that you will change your mind."

I took his hand and thanked him graciously for his support. I knew that Rachel and I would be relying on the support of many people in order to make this journey.

Through our network, we set about finding the safe havens along the route and how to get to them. Getting this information took approximately three months. By then we were able to compile an itinerary taking us through the mountains using less traveled and sometimes circuitous roadways. Eventually we would reach our village.

Rachel was determined and spent night and day making maps and charts and calculating the distance from one point to another and planning how we could arrive there safely.

John was not satisfied that our plans were complete enough; he felt that we did not have adequate information about the safe havens for the latter part of our journey. They were very far away, and it was difficult to communicate directly with those camps. He did not want to trust people who spoke on behalf of others. He did not trust that they had the latest information as to their safety.

The Romans, during this time, would search out and destroy these small camps in their quest to destroy the growing influence of Jesus' teachings. They continued in their attempts to identify our enclaves and destroyed them with fires and pillaging. John was worried that we might be able to get very far into our journey, but at the end, when we were so near, the safe havens would have been destroyed. He persuaded us not to set out until we received more information.

Rachel became more and more determined and impatient; she was driven by an energy that I had not seen in her for a long time. She continued to spend hours with her maps, charts, and list of contacts. It was important for her to memorize all of this information, for if we were caught, we could not have these names with us. Rachel studied and worked to have all our plans etched in her mind.

At long last, John heard directly from the safe haven closest to my home village. They encouraged us and showed that it was possible to reach our village through an obscure route that hardly anyone knew about.

John knew the man who headed up this safe haven personally and John felt that he was a leader. If there were anyone who could protect us, it was him. This was the missing piece of information that we had needed. Now John became more confident that we could get there safely. Still, he begged me to reconsider and to think again about the dangers that surely lay ahead. I promised him that I would, but in fact it was very clear to me that we were going to make this trip no matter what. Rachel and I, as we realized again in planning this trip, had never turned our back on danger. We both had been through too much in our lives. We both also believed that with the help of God, we would make this trip safely.

We packed our things, made all the necessary preparations, and set out upon our journey. The plan was to travel only at night. If we stayed on schedule, we would arrive at a safe haven by morning and then stay there until we had enough strength to make the next leg of the journey. We were disguised in men's clothing. A young man, whom John knew, volunteered to take us to the first safe haven, after which someone else would go with us to the next one and someone else from there would go with us to the next in a relay.

Under cover of night, we rode upon horseback, arriving at the first stop without any problem. Our escort dropped us off and within a few hours prepared himself to go back to Ephesus. People in this enclave were happy to receive news from the outside; they had been in hiding here for some time and did not often venture out of their very small community. They plied Rachel and me with questions. They were amazed that Jesus was my son and Rachel's brother.

Before long it was time to go onto the next stop. A very experienced and physically strong man was to be our escort. He knew the route that we would have to take very well. Again, we left under cover of night, only this time the distance was so far that we had planned to stop in several rocky areas with caves where we could hide until night fell again.

The journey was rough; there was no pathway. We had to make our own path through the rocks and winding, rough terrain. We managed to find a hidden place where we could tie up the horses and sleep. It was critically important that we were able to sleep. During this journey, very little was said between Rachel and me or between us and our escort. We had to galvanize all of our energies to stay alert, to navigate our horses, and to follow the route.

As night fell, we loaded up our horses and began once again, this time moving toward a more trafficked, and therefore more dangerous part of the countryside. We reached our second safe haven without incident. As we climbed off our horses, we were greeted by a husband and wife, the leaders of this community. They were a very strong and loving couple. They had lost two sons to the Roman soldiers. When they embraced us both, there was an immediate warmth and understanding between us that was very special and tender. They had made a special dinner for us. The wife laid out a beautiful supper that she had prepared mostly by gathering roots and berries. She had grown some of her own vegetables and had put this meal together with an ingenuity that was miraculous. They had a small fire burning and the glow of the embers against our skin was soothing and warm. We felt protected and loved in their presence; they understood our reasons for making this journey. They understood what was in our hearts and it meant a great deal to me that they believed in what Rachel and I were doing. The husband had been converted by my son. Before he met Jesus, he did not believe in any god. He told me that upon hearing Jesus speak, his heart had been so opened that he had broken down in tears and had wept for days. He hadn't even known why he wept, only that the words had so moved him that it was as if years of sorrow poured out of him. He told me that when the tears stopped, he was like a new man. He could breathe the air in a way that he had never done before. He felt lifted up and was moved to share what he knew with others in his village. He began to speak the words that Jesus had taught him and to carry these words to many others. His whole family became a part of this preaching. When Jesus was crucified, his two sons had gone into Jerusalem to defend Jesus. In so doing, they had been murdered by the Roman soldiers. We sat there, all of us together, having lost three sons, but remaining strong in our beliefs. They placed their hands in mine and Rachel's and said that they would pray without stopping for our safe arrival in our home village. Their tenderness and sweetness, in the face of their loss, touched me deeply. I will never forget their kind eyes and warm embraces.

The next night, we climbed upon our horses to begin the third leg of our journey. This phase of the journey required us to go through more mountains. We had to climb some steep pathways, strewn with rocks, with only the moonlight to shine its light on our path. Rachel's horse slipped and fell down the side of an embankment. She managed to stay on the horse; fortunately, it was not injured, and she was able to get back up. It made us realize, though, just how treacherous the terrain had become. We had to move very, very slowly. As such, we did not make it as far as we needed to before daylight. Our escort was agitated; he did not wish to be caught in this part of the territory in daylight. He wanted to make an alternative plan. Either we should return to where we came from or take our chances hiding somewhere in these rocky areas. He hoped there would be a cave where we could hide.

We looked for somewhere to go. By now the sun was coming up. We could see in the distance what appeared to be a group of horses. Our escort became more agitated, saying that he was sure that these were Roman soldiers and if we did not find a place to hide, that we would surely be killed. He informed us coldly that the current policy was to kill strangers first and to ask questions later, and that these orders came from Rome.

I could tell that he regretted coming this far with us; although he was a physically strong man, he was also very aware of real danger. Rachel intervened, distracting him. She was able to engage him in conversation long enough to release his fears. He identified a place where we could go and hide until nightfall, probably just in time.

Later, as night approached, he told us to remain hidden while he ventured out to see what lay ahead. It was not completely safe to ride at night, it was only safer. Roman soldiers could be out at night as well. He promised to return in a short time, not more than an hour at most. He never came back. We waited for almost three hours and there was no sign of him. We were completely on our own; we could only suspect the worst as to what had happened to him unless he had decided to desert us. We decided to stay hidden. So much time had expired in the night, and he was the one who knew the intricate pathways through this terrain. We would have to figure it out on our own.

It was at this point that the reality of what we had undertaken hit us both, fully and completely. Up to this point, it had been a kind of adventure, perhaps even a bit of a fairy tale. A harsh reality had set in. Alone and not knowing what had happened to our escort, we did not know if there would be soldiers surrounding us immediately. We did not know if he had deserted us. His horse could have fallen down a cliff and taken him with it. We simply did not know what was ahead. We did not have much food or water with us, because we needed to travel lightly. We had planned to renew our supplies when we arrived at each new safe haven.

We did not know what to do. Rachel offered to ride ahead and when she determined it was safe, to come back for me. I told her no, that we were to stick together and that whatever happened, would happen. So, once again, as night fell, we made our way forward. We were not absolutely certain of the path, but we kept moving. Our horses seemed to know the way somehow, for they managed to climb and circle and climb and go down pathways that we would never have imagined horses finding.

We continued through the night, hoping that we could make it to the next haven before daylight broke. At one point Rachel's horse took off, galloping out of control, leaving me very far behind. I saw Rachel struggle with this horse, trying in every way to stop it. It kept galloping, farther and farther ahead until I could not even see them. I was, at that moment, completely alone. We had been warned that this leg of the trip was dangerous and that soldiers could really be anywhere. I prayed and just concentrated on keeping my horse going forward. I think I shut my eyes and turned my faith over to my horse and to the Holy Father. Before too long I opened my eyes and saw Rachel far ahead, waving something. I sped up on my horse and caught up with her. As I came close enough to see her face, she gestured that the safe haven was just across the next hill. She kicked her horse's side and was off again. I paused before following her and looked back. A regiment of Roman soldiers was close behind us. Again, Rachel shouted for me to hurry. I kicked my horse and we rode as fast as the horses could take us. We rode for what seemed hours, but, of course, it wasn't that long. Rachel seemed to know where she was going; we made a sharp turn behind some rocks and trees that led into an overhang obscuring the hill. It must have appeared as if we were swallowed up by the mountainside.

All at once, we were inside a large cave and heard voices. Some people rushed toward us with weapons, thinking that we were the enemy. We called out announcing who we were and there was much rejoicing and greeting. They took us even further into the cave, where they had food and blankets. We fell happily onto these blankets; we were exhausted.

We fell asleep almost immediately and did not wake up until many hours later. We were told when we awoke that very few people had ever made it through this stretch. We asked about our escort, had they seen him? No one had been through there in months; it was truly a miracle that we had gotten this far.

We told them that the soldiers had probably seen us from the top of the hill. We were fearful that we might have placed them in danger. They did not seem greatly concerned; they felt that their caves and their hideaways were not known by the soldiers. Although they had seen us from the top of the hill, we would have disappeared out of sight for some time before they reached the next vantage point.

Our hosts told us to rest and complimented our bravery. They gave us food and drink and told us that they wanted to talk to us more, but felt we needed to sleep to regain our strength. Gladly, we went to sleep, feeling safe in the hands of these people.

We awoke hours later. As we opened our eyes a man was sitting by our side, a very thin old man with many wrinkles. Much to our surprise, he quickly began to ask us a series of questions. "Dear ones," he said, "Why do you make this journey? Why do you place yourselves in this danger? Why do you test yourselves in this way? What do you hope to gain from this? Don't you know the danger you are putting yourselves in? And, for that matter, the danger you are creating for many others? I ask you, once again, why do you make this journey? What do you hope to gain from it?"

We were shocked to hear this man speak to us in this way. "Well," he said, "What are your answers? Speak up, now."

I answered first, saying, "My dear man, I am going home to see my children, nothing will stop me from that. No danger, nor your questions, can deter me from my plan. My daughter, Rachel, comes with me. Together, we are going home."

The man looked at me and replied, "Then I shall come with you, all the way and see that you arrive home safely. I can see that you need someone to be with you. I see that your determination is genuine and therefore I feel compelled to be your escort and protector."

I questioned, "Do you feel strong enough to make this journey?"

He laughed, "You will soon see the power of my strength. I may look old and feeble, but I will get you home safely. Mary, Rachel—I am Haifsis."

CHAPTER
48

Rachel woke me up only a short time later. She said prayers of safekeeping before we ate. The distance we were to travel tonight went through the most heavily populated area we had yet passed through. As our last companion had said, the Romans were known to cut down travelers before asking who they were. There was no way to avoid this route.

I watched Rachel as she made preparations. I knew that she had studied and memorized so much information before we left on this trip. I could tell that she was reviewing some of these things in her mind. She felt that it would be her place to be the leader, to act as spokesperson in the event that something did happen. By this point in the journey, I had made my peace with destiny and was completely prepared to meet whatever situation was to come our way. I was not afraid for myself. I did worry though, for Rachel. She had lived such a difficult life and she had been so loyal to me and to her brother, giving up many possibilities for her own happiness. It lay heavy on my heart to see her once again, work so diligently to bring me peace and happiness. I knew that Rachel embarked on this journey as a gift to me. I also knew that she desired to see her own children again, but it was above all else because of her love for me that she risked everything to return. Rachel's tenderness as a daughter can never be fully described, but many mothers who read this book will recognize similar qualities in their own daughters.

As I continued to watch Rachel making the final preparation, I could not help but begin to think that these could be our final hours. I did not want to dwell upon these thoughts. After what we had both been through getting here, I struggled with the guilt of having allowed Rachel to put herself in such danger. We had come this far safely, thanks to the Holy Father. I thought for a moment, that I could not go any further forward with this trip in good conscience; I was jeopardizing my only daughter's life. How could I as a mother, take advantage of her love for me? I watched as she said good-bye to each person we had met. She was so self-assured and deeply loving, always spending a few moments with each person individually, to say something special to them. I thought to myself, no, I cannot go forward. I cannot jeopardize my daughter's life. How can I put her safety and the safety of my other children in conflict with each other? It seemed to be either Rachel or the other children. Yes, I loved them and carried them in my heart, but it was Rachel who had devoted her life to her brother's teachings, and to tending to our welfare. All through the years, never once had she asked for anything for herself. Now, she was prepared to make the supreme sacrifice to reunite our family.

I heard Rachel's footsteps behind me. She put her arms around me, pulling my scarf closer, tucking it in around my neck and gently hugging me, said, "Mother, it is time for us to depart. Everything is ready. Haifsis will lead us. I know we will be safe, Mother. God spoke to me in a dream and promised that we would arrive safely in our village. I see in your eyes, Mother, that you have been thinking regretful thoughts about this journey. I assure you, I know that we will arrive safely and that we are doing the right thing. We must find our family and bind ourselves together with them. We won't be able to live with ourselves unless we do this. We know this, Mother. I am not afraid. I have received God's promise and I have the strength for both of us. I can carry us through to safety, I know it. Besides, Haifsis knows the habits of the soldiers. Should they find us, he feels certain that he can talk his way out of any possible situation. I do not know what to expect, but I am certain that we are on the path that we are meant to follow. Come now, Mother, let me help you on your horse. It is time for us to begin."

I climbed upon my horse with Rachel's help. I took hold of the reins and made my way forward. It was completely dark, and the air was cold against our faces. The horses seemed to enjoy the movement and so we rode for quite a while in silence, the three of us. In some ways, it felt like a dream. We had come far enough that the terrain was beginning to look familiar. I could recognize the shapes of trees and plants from my childhood. We rode through an open plains area where we were not protected by any foliage; and we needed to hurry because there were no safe havens during this stretch. By dawn we would be back in the hills where we could stay somewhat hidden among the trees and rocky areas. We managed to get to the hills while it was still dark. We needed to rest the horses and luckily found a secluded spot.

I was extremely nervous and irritated with myself, for I felt that my faith was being put to the test. (Any mother, who reads this book, the world over, will know the feelings that I describe. When you or your children are in dangerous places and at the mercy of soldiers or other powerful people, who can rob you of breath of life, the inability to protect them is maddening).

As we approached camp, I started to have flashbacks of that terrible night when the soldiers surrounded us, when they grabbed Jesus and took him away. Suddenly I could hear the pounding of the nails as they ripped through his flesh. I heard them nailing the cross, as they slammed it into the earth. I could see him hanging there in agony. My heart began to pound so fast just as it had that day; I slumped over my horse's saddle.

Rachel was ahead some distance. Our escort saw and galloped toward me. He grabbed me before I fell and held me, but he was not strong. Rachel had turned and managed to catch me as I slid off the horse and fell to the ground. She immediately put something under my head and called for Haifsis to unpack some water. He did so and poured the water over my lips and onto my forehead. I was breathing very heavily, and my heart was racing.

Rachel whispered to me, "Mother, Mother you must breathe slowly and deeply. Breathe with me, Mother, feel my breath, breathe with me. It is all right; you will be all right. Breathe deeply, Mother. That's it."

She squeezed my hand and placed her other palm on my forehead. She continued to breathe very slowly and deeply, asking me to breathe with her. I found myself relaxing and my heart stopped racing. Rachel instructed me to continue lying there as long as I needed. She stayed by my side, stroking my brow, while Haifsis finished feeding the horses.

After a time, I was able to sit up and I told Rachel that I did not know what came over me. I did not want to be a burden to her; I was sorry to have collapsed and caused any problem for her. Rachel looked at me and said, "Oh, Mother, dear little Mother, you could never, ever, ever, be a problem or a burden to me. Now, can you stand up, Mother? Can you climb on the horse, again? Shall I ride with you on your horse? Let me do that for a while, until you have regained more strength."

She climbed behind me on my horse and held onto me. I was leaning against her for stability, I was not pretending to be strong, but I was determined to remain as strong as I could be. We continued on our way.

Miraculously, we reached the place we had planned to sleep without incident. We knew about this place geographically; it was high in the hills and there was a place that had been described to us in detail. It was not exactly a cave, but a kind of indented area underneath a cliff. It was large enough that we could also bring the horses under the overhang. Rachel lifted me down from the horse while Haifsis made a bed for me. I slept, while Rachel and Haifsis discussed the route for the next portion of our trip. A short time later, they heard a noise. The horses heard it first. Haifsis looked at Rachel and said, "Let us move quickly, as far into the cavern as possible."

Rachel gently woke me, and we scrambled far up into the rocky area where we took cover, awaiting our fate. There was no place to move the horses in such a short time. We heard men shouting below, "Over here! This way! I heard animals. Quickly. This way! Aha! Look, just as I thought—there are hoof prints of several horses."

The horses' hooves and the animals' snorts filled the air as the men pulled them aside to come in. I thought only of the angel who had come to me in my dream. I called upon that angel now, whispering, "Help us. Help us, Lord. Save us."

There were shouts and footsteps of perhaps eight or ten men. Suddenly, Haifsis threw himself into the middle of these men and began to wail and cry out that he was just an old man, lost and forlorn, who never harmed anybody. He cried out that he lived among these rocks.

He made all sorts of wailing sounds and made pathetic gestures. I realized immediately that he was distracting the men from our hiding place, moving them further away from us. The men followed. He made a great show, waving his arms and laughing hysterically. One of the men said, "Look at this crazy old man. He is a lunatic. Where did he come from? Where did he get these horses? Hey, old man, where did you get these horses?" At this, Haifsis began to kick his feet and whinny like a horse himself. One of the soldiers slapped him and cried out, "Shut up, old man. Shut up."

When they had knocked Haifsis down, he shouted, "These horses came from nowhere. They galloped up to my place; I don't know where they came from. I never saw them before. You can have them, but I think that they are cursed. There is evil in those horses. I saw a headless rider upon them as they came toward me. They have a curse on them and any man who rides them will surely die. I saw it with my own eyes. They are cursed, cursed, and cursed."

Haifsis took advantage of the superstitious fears of these men. Once he saw that he had them in his power, he ran even further away from where we were hidden, into the open, continuing to make a great display and calling upon the Roman Gods. From our hiding place, we could hear his voice as he made invocations in Latin. He asked them to save and preserve these poor soldiers, who had fallen upon cursed animals. At last, a soldier said to the others, "Let's get out of here. This man is insane. He is mad. Leave him and his horses; what harm can he do us?"

To our amazement, they left. We all stayed very still. After what felt like a long time, Haifsis came to us and said, "It is all right. It is safe now. They are gone. We must give thanks for they have left the horses here with us. God is surely with us this day." We all knelt to the ground and gave thanks for our lives and gave thanks for Haifsis, whose quick thinking and bravery saved us.

That night, Haifsis ventured out of the cave to make sure that the men were not nearby. He returned convinced that it was safe for us to go.

Once again, we climbed onto our horses. According to our calculations, we would be at the next safe haven before daybreak. After only a few hours, we saw ahead the landmark that told us we had arrived.

The village welcomed us. They were all amazed that we had arrived alive. They brought us blankets and pillows, food, and drink. People tended to us, washed us, and fed us. We were so tired, but we managed to tell a little about what had happened to us. Haifsis became an instant celebrity, and grateful prayers were given in thanks for his part in our safe arrival.

CHAPTER
49

After we had rested for a while, people started to gather around us. They were anxious to hear news of our journey from Ephesus and wanted to help us so that we could arrive home safely. We were still exhausted, but as we shared our stories with them, we felt so content and proud of ourselves for reaching this destination. The villagers wanted to hear more about Haifsis and the Roman soldiers and to find out the extent of their numbers. They told us that it was a miracle that we had arrived unscathed, as it had been virtually impossible for travelers to make their way safely through this treacherous territory until now.

They also asked us many questions about Jesus and his life. Specifically, they wanted to know how it was that He had risen from the dead. Word of this miracle had spread throughout the towns and villages to all those who had truly loved and been moved by Jesus' teachings. They marveled at the unbelievable nature of this miracle. The people of this tribe, hidden as they were in their mountainside, asked us how we understood the significance of His miraculous resurrection. I think that this was the first time that either Rachel or I had ever spoken to such a large gathering of people. We had always remained observers, primarily. We looked at each other and without any prompting, we began to tell them about our memories of Jesus and what our experience had meant to us.

Rachel spoke first. She sat by a small fire and the soft light from the embers glowed beautifully on her face. Here is what she said:

"My beloved friends, and all you faithful believers in my brother's work, I give thanks that I am here with you to share the joy and the significance and the meaning of my brother's life. My brother walked this earth with a pure and compassionate heart. Every day of His life He thought only of the poor, the feeble, the sick, and those whose spirits were sad, broken, desperate, and lonely. He was a scholar and knew the Jewish laws. He embraced everything our beliefs and religion stand for. He was a man of the people, and He felt their needs and saw the fear and sadness in their eyes. His heart cried out to help them. He looked and looked for answers in the teachings of the Torah. Not satisfied, He searched for answers within His own heart, which He opened fully to receive knowledge from His heavenly Father. My brother spent hours, days, weeks, and months in prayer and contemplation. He went into the mountains, leaving His family, to find His way to God. I believe that my brother found a doorway; I believe that He saw the Holy Kingdom and that He walked through that doorway, so that He could bring this knowledge to all of us who walk here today. He was never afraid and many times I was amazed, amazed at His gentleness, His joyfulness, and His ability to perform simple, ordinary tasks filled with so much compassion and love. I do not understand why my brother was tortured and humiliated; all He ever did was touch people's hearts and bring good to those around Him.

"After He died, I was in a field with my mother and He appeared, standing there. I ran to Him, and He caught me in His arms the way He had always done. I can tell you that my brother is alive. I felt Him, I saw Him, and I heard His voice. He told me, Rachel, this is the promise, this is the hope, and this is the reality. Everything shall come to pass for the love of God is all there is. Love is everywhere, sometimes it cannot be seen, and appears to be invisible, but dear Rachel, know that what you have seen this day, is the promise.

"Then He held me close, and I felt His strong arms. When I opened my eyes, He was gone. But, inside of me and all around me I felt a love so great that I knew even though I could not see Him, that He was there with me. He had given me a vision of hope, a promise, and now I pass that vision of hope, that promise onto each and every one of you, my friends. I bless you all, for I believe in this promise, and I hold it closely within my own heart. I ask that each and every one of you think about my words and allow their meaning to live inside your heart. Remember that my brother had no fear, for He once told me that He had experienced the penetrating light of God. He had seen the eyes of God. The love that poured from those eyes, took His breath away, and filled him with joy and laughter. Fear was a thing of the past."

Then Rachel began to sing, for this was the most that she had ever spoken publicly. "Hail, hall, alll, alll, uuuuu, oooohohoh, wowowowow, heyuwat, eyouwah, eeeeeuuuuuuuuu, eeeeeeuuuuuuuuuuu."

Rachel walked among the people, singing, and a holy mist came over all of us and silence came over the people. Through her singing, she lifted their hearts and minds, carrying them into a special unseen place, helping them arrive to that place.

Wordlessly, silently, the people went to their sleeping places, and we retired for the night and slept deeply and soundly. Indeed, Rachel, Haifsis, and I slept for two days. Those in the village understood our need. We had traveled far on this journey and in our lives.

Gradually, with renewed strength, we began to make preparations for the final leg of our journey. This time we were to be accompanied by one of the strongest and most experienced guides, who could protect us and who could lead us directly to our village. He had been a fierce fighter in battle, before being deeply affected by Jesus. He had given up fighting and killing. He had turned his considerable strength to helping those in need. Because he knew the routes and terrain, he was highly sought after as a guide to move people and goods through this perilous territory. Once again, we prepared to leave at night, under the cover of darkness. Haifsis had completed his journey with us, and we bid him a tearful good-bye. He had saved our lives and managed to bring us here unharmed.

The villagers gathered around us, embracing us, blessing us, and praying over us. It was time to go. We climbed on our horses. With a wave of our hands, we set out, for we had many hours ahead of us.

Although once again it was night, the moon above lit a path across the plains and we moved with alacrity, as this was open territory. We wanted to move through this part as quickly as possible. We came to a plateau with some trees and foliage and climbing through this, our horses needed to be sure of foot. We had to ride carefully as there were loose rocks and dangerous drops to the ravine below. By this time, we were used to this kind of riding, and we found that we were able to concentrate in such a way that we moved efficiently along the twisting path.

It was exciting to know that we were as close to our home village as we had been in many, many years. As the sun rose and we set up our hiding place, I thought about my grown children and prayed that I would be able to reunite our family completely. Rachel and I joined hands and made a prayer that our loved ones would receive us with open hearts, that all of us could share the love that we had for each other and allow the past to remain in the past. We really did not know how our family would receive us, but never did we entertain the idea that the trip might have been made in vain. We both knew that it was a part of our destinies to come full circle, to reunite with our family.

Night fell once again, and we climbed onto our horses. A light rain began to fall shortly after we set forth, but it was a refreshing rain, a gentle caressing rain. Something about the wetness made time pass more quickly. We rode and rode all through the night, coming at last to one more resting place, where we fed our horses and laid out our blankets to rest ourselves.

We were very close to our home, with one mountain to cross. When we reached the other side, we would be in our village. We did not talk much, needing our strength and our rest; we fell into a deep sleep with our guide watching over us.

As soon as the sun set, we ventured toward the mountain pass. At about one hundred yards, I heard a noise behind my horse. I turned around and saw two Roman soldiers directly behind us. I froze with fright. They wore those metal helmets, like the ones they had on when they came for Jesus. They yelled for us to stop. We already had no choice but to slow down, as they had circled around us. "Where do you think you are going? Who gave you permission to pass through this valley at night? Speak."

Rachel and I said nothing. Our guide replied, "I'm taking my mother and sister to see our grandfather who lies on his deathbed in the village on the other side of the mountain. He awaits our arrival that we may bless him and bid him goodbye. We travel at night because he has only a matter of hours to live. We must make haste before it is too late."

The soldiers looked at us and I could feel them sizing us up, deciding whether or not to believe what our guide had told them. One of the soldiers said to the other, "Oh, let them pass. We have work to do. Let them go."

The other soldier was not convinced and rode ahead to stop our guide from moving forward. "No," he said, "we must take these three to the authorities. I don't believe their story. They look like followers of Jesus to me, slinking through the mountains. Let's take them in."

His partner was either too tired or uninterested, we never understood which, but he argued with him saying, "Oh, let them pass. The ride is so long. What use is it? It is more trouble than it is worth. Look at them, they are nothing."

With bated breath, we waited, and he continued, "I know a place that's much more interesting, we will go there. I know some women, who will receive us. We have done enough, already. There is no reward in dragging these people in. Here, take some of this." He offered the man a flask of wine to drink, which the man readily took and began gulping down. Finally, they agreed. "Come on, let's go," the other man said. "Get along, get going and if we see you again in these parts your lives are over."

They slapped our horses and rode around us, shouting and making a lot of noise and then they took off, leaving us in a cloud of dust. Without a word, we rode forward and at dawn entered our village.

CHAPTER
50

Rachel and I were finally home. As we entered our village, tears of joy streamed down our faces, and I was overwhelmed with emotion. I stood there, looking around. Seeing familiar sights, floods of memories came over me. Rachel put her arms around me as I wept and wept.

We did not receive a welcoming reception, for we had not sent word ahead. We had been advised not to do this for our own safety's sake. As we entered the center of the village, we blended in with the other people and no one recognized us. Rachel led me to the well, where I had to sit down for a moment to collect myself. I suddenly felt very old and very tired. I was so overwhelmed that I thought that it was not possible for me to seek out my house or my children. Rachel tended to me. She drew water from the well and wet a cloth to wipe my brow as she whispered comforting words to me. She sat there with her arm around my waist and held me tightly, stroking my hand. Rachel knew me so well. She always knew what to do.

After a few minutes I looked at her and said, "Rachel, it is time to find our children and to make our peace with them."

Rachel nodded sweetly and said, "Yes, Mother, let us look for them together."

With Rachel's help, I stood up and we began walking toward where I remembered my son's house to be.

When we arrived at the door, a strange woman opened it. We did not recognize her. She peered out, "Yes, and who are you?" I asked her where the family was who had lived in this house. Suddenly there was a light of recognition in her eyes. "Oh, it's you. You are Mary, the mother of Jesus." She opened the door further, "I, I cannot believe what I am seeing. Oh, oh, oh. This is not possible. Oh, oh dear, I don't want to be the one . . ." And she began to cry.

We stood there, paralyzed, unsure of what to say. At last, she said, "Oh, please, come inside. You must be tired from your journey. Sit down here."

We sat and I took Rachel's hand as we waited and waited. The woman did not say a word while she prepared us something to eat. She returned to the table, placing two plates in front of us. She sat down, folding her hands on the table, and bowing her head.

Once again, she spoke. "These times have been very dangerous. This village was ransacked by the Roman soldiers. They found out where the members of Jesus' family were living and they came here one night in a surprise attack, without warning. They had torches and they set fire to many houses. People ran screaming from their homes, not knowing the nature of the attack."

"When the soldiers heard that your son had risen from the dead, they went wild with fear and anger. The word of this miracle spread very quickly and everyone in all the villages knew that Jesus walked among the living. That night they searched the village until they found your family and they took them and murdered them in cold blood right in front of the rest of us." Her words stopped as she began to weep.

We all cried, until there were no more tears and Rachel asked, "Is everyone gone? My family, as well?"

She answered, "My dear, I don't know for certain. Some of your people did try to escape and perhaps some of them managed. All I can tell you is that all of your brothers, their children, and their wives are gone from this place. This, I know for certain."

Minutes passed and she added, "It is a miracle that you have arrived here; there are still soldiers everywhere. This may be the safest place for you now. They are certain that they have done their horrifying work. I never, ever thought that I would live to tell this story to you both. Oh, what will you do now?"

I looked into this woman's eyes. I remember they were very, very pale blue. Like magnets, I was drawn to them. I think if it had not been for her eyes, my spirit would have left my body. As I locked my eyes with hers, she held me there, kept my spirit inside my body. I continued to look at her as I pondered her question. She seemed to sense the importance of this moment between us, and she held her gaze steady, never taking her eyes from mine.

At last, I had found my strength. I cannot possibly say from where this strength had come. I rose from the table and said calmly, "I want to visit my home, where I lived with Joseph. Do you know if it still exists?" I described it to her. She nodded her head, that yes by some miracle they had not burned it. It was there and that a young couple lived in it now, devout followers of Jesus who would gladly receive us.

She hesitated, "Don't you want to lie down and rest? I can take you there in the morning."

"No," I replied, "I wish to go soon, now. I thank you, though. Perhaps, if you don't mind, my daughter and I will take a short walk to collect ourselves and then we will visit this young couple."

She took my hands and again gazed into my eyes, filling me with strength and said, "Please, take all the time that you need, I will be here when you return, and we will go together. Should you need anything, you need only to ask. It is my greatest honor to be of service to you and your daughter."

"Bless you," I replied. Without another word, Rachel and I wrapped our scarves about our heads and walked into the familiar countryside. We put our arms around each other's waist and walked.

We walked to the place where Rachel had tended to the sick. It was a rocky path, where still very few people would walk on their own. When we arrived there, Rachel turned to me and said, "Mother, I would like to stay a moment in this place. I spent so much time here and it holds many memories for me."

Before she could say anything else, I said to her, "Go my child, enter the place where you brought light and love to those who needed it. Go there now and see if there is anyone to receive your blessings. I will wait here by the side of the road; I do not wish to disturb your remembrances. I would like to sit here quietly, myself."

And so, Rachel ventured onto the rocky pathway that led to the desperate and the desolate.

She walked quietly, noticing each familiar rock and twist of the pathway, overcome with memories. She felt happy there, in this place where all those with no other place to go had come. This place was her real home. She had tended to each and every person living there. The rocks that they had slept on were beautiful and comforting beds. As Rachel walked along, she could hear their voices. She could see them, and although the rocks were now empty, she could feel the presence of those whom she had loved. She felt great comfort there, knowing that those people had suffered terrible agonies, unspeakable pain and yet the love that they had poured back was so great that it remained palpable as once again she stood there alone.

Rachel walked on a little further imagining them singing one of the songs that she had taught them. Sitting for a moment, deluged with emotion, and listening to their song, my daughter heard footsteps.

There stood Jesus. He called out to her, "Rachel." She looked at Him, first almost without recognition. Then, in an instant, a horrible emotion spread over her, and Rachel screamed at him, "Look what you have done! Our whole family is gone. Hundreds and hundreds of people have been killed in your name. Our mother is devastated with grief. Why? Why?" She continued, "Why? Why? Why?" It was as though she were mad. She got up from the rock and paced, crying out, cursing, picking up handfuls of rocks and throwing them. They smashed so hard against the other rocks that they created sparks. Rachel cried out, "Was your work worth it, Brother? Was it? Our family ripped apart, our lives destroyed, for what, my brother, for what?" Rachel had never spoken such words in her entire life, never uttered such curses, such anger, and never questioned her brother's work. She became very ill and bent over, retching and heaving.

In a daze, she saw something moving in the grass. Sick and dizzy, and thinking it was an animal, she still moved forward to look closer. Stepping out to a treacherous ledge for a better view, Rachel realized that it was a baby, a deformed baby. It was a weak, little thing and something was terribly wrong with it. It was so weak that it couldn't even make a sound. Unbelievably, this little baby was just lying there on that ledge. She bent down and lifted it up, taking her scarf and wrapping it comfortingly around the child. Rachel held the baby close, rocking and comforting this tiny little creature that had been thrown away, who had been left here to die alone on the rocks. She began to pray and beg for the life of this little baby, who had never harmed anyone, who had been cast aside unloved because it wasn't perfect. She prayed as hard as she had ever prayed, determined that it would live.

When Rachel opened her eyes, Jesus had sat down next to her. He laid His hand on the baby's head and said, "Rachel, this baby will live to bring you joy and comfort in your old age. This baby will help you; this baby is a gift. There is a purpose, Rachel. There is Light, Rachel."

In a flash He was gone, and she lifted up the child to carefully make her way back to me.

I was waiting there, with open arms, already knowing what had happened, "Look, Mother, look what I found." Rachel exclaimed. "This baby was nearly dead, but Jesus came and healed him. There is something wrong with his leg and arm."

I replied, "I know, my child, I saw Jesus, too. We will care for this baby together. Jesus asked me to do this with you. Come now let us visit our old home, together."

Rachel carried the little, helpless baby in her arms. With each step, she was feeling happier and happier. He smiled weakly at us as she held him close.

When the kind woman saw the baby, she let out a shocked cry. Her heart opened to the baby, also. We fed the baby. We cleaned him and wrapped him in beautiful clothes, which the woman gave us, saying she had wondered where these things would go now that her children were grown. She asked us if we were ready to meet the young couple and we told her that we were.

We made our way to the home where we had lived for so long and there the couple was waiting for us. Earlier, the kind woman had gone ahead and told them that we would be arriving. They invited us in and in a very loving way, communicated that we were welcome in the house and the garden on our own. They stepped outside. They understood that we needed time by ourselves, and they left us.

My friends, my story concludes here as we have returned home. Rachel sat down with the baby, and I walked into the garden where I had spent hours preparing food for my family, eating with them, thinking and praying. It was just as beautiful and as peaceful as I remembered it. In fact, there were flowers growing that I had not seen before. The young woman who lived in the house now had tended to the plants in the yard and it flourished under her gentle hands.

We end here in this home, also because here we would stay for many years to come. The young couple invited us to live with them. They were loving and deeply devoted to carrying out the deepest and wisest teachings of Jesus. Together, we created another kind of family, a family who opened its hearts to each other. We were not related by blood, but we were united in purpose, in trust, and in a desire to live.

The baby grew and brought such love and joy to every person who saw him. He was a solace, comfort, and an absolute joy for Rachel. As we grew older, the young couple cared for us with tenderness and good humor. That this had become a part of our lives was like receiving a gift each and every day.

Rachel struggled with her anger and in time came to understand it.

Magnificent ones, I ask each of you to listen to your heart, open your heart, and see in the eyes of every living being, the miracle that is God, the miracle that is life. This miracle is light: pure, breathtaking light. For every heart that opens and unites with all other hearts, the truth of life everlasting is illuminated. The only living, breathing heart is another living, breathing heart. Allow illumination to burn brightly in this world, beloved ones. It is here, see it. It is everywhere. In the presence of that light all illusions, hatred, violence, cruelty, sickness, desolation, horror, and madness, disappear. That is the dream, my friends. The Light is the truth and the only truth. Amen.

POSTSCRIPT

Beloved children, upon the earth, magnificence shall grow, like a beautiful, flowering tree. Everywhere will be harmony, beauty, and grace. Those who have suffered will be touched by the arms of love, those who have caused suffering will become the arms of love and light. Miracles will take place, one after the other, in a way that has never been seen before. The earth will be returned to its original beauty and the creativity of every living creature will be manifest. How will this happen? Each person who reads these words carries the answer within their own heart, and as you read these words, already the vision comes alive. You are blessed, my children.

I have placed my heart into each of your hands. You hold my heart. I give it to you. Each thought, word, and deed that you make from this moment on, is imbued with my life's blood, with the meaning and fulfillment of my heart, which I have given to each one of you this day. Once you have taken my heart in your hands, you are forever changed, for your heart and mine have become as one, and so each of you who read these words are as one, with me and all others. This is the fulfillment of the Book, which is the love and the light of the great and magnificent Creator, whose heart lives in each and every one of you. I, the Mother, have come now simply to bring my arms of love to all of you who have been sad at heart, sick, and crying, who have given up hope, who have run away ashamed, who have lain in the darkest nights, shivering from fear and disgust, who have known deep, deep within, that the very light of God shines forth within you. I, Mary, your Mother, have given you my heart freely. My arms embrace each one of you. I hold you tenderly and unconditionally, pouring out my love for you. I ask each one of you to take care of my heart, to hold it tenderly. As you do this, you will enter this day into the promise of joy. You have arrived beloved ones, look around and see the world that you have made, for blessed are those who see and know.

When you look into the eyes of another person, you will see the whole world and at the center of that world, is the light within your own heart, which is the light of God. Beloved children, you are love, and love is all there is. See it, know it, and live it. This is my gift to you.

ABOUT THE AUTHOR

NANCY RHODES, international stage director, author, and educator, has directed operas and musicals all over the world, from Sweden, Finland, and Norway to Albania, Turkey, and the Netherlands. As Founding Artistic Director of Encompass New Opera Theatre in New York City, she has staged American operas by Virgil Thomson/Gertrude Stein, Benjamin Britten, Marc Blitzstein, Aaron Copland, and Langston Hughes/Ricky Ian Gordon, among many other composers and writers.

She is currently the commissioned librettist of *The Theory of Everything*, with composer John David Earnest, a new opera inspired by physics' superstring theory of multiple dimensions and alternate universes, recipient of two prestigious National Endowment for the Arts grants.

Her opera libretto *Ocean Dream* is published in *Facing Forward* by Broadway Play Publishing and was performed in Estonia.

Her opera premiere of Anna Christie, based on the play by Eugene O'Neill, music by Edward Thomas and libretto by Joseph Masteroff, was released on CD by Broadway Records. Her acclaimed production of Grigori Frid's opera, *The Diary of Anne Frank*, was nominated for an *Artistic Achievement Award* and played to over 4,000 people on its tour to Cleveland Opera.

At Encompass, she launched *Paradigm Shifts, Music and Film Festival*, to celebrate courageous people world-wide who are preserving our planet, oceans, wildlife, and sacred lands.

She served on the faculty of Manhattan School of Music for twelve years and taught master classes at the University of the Theatre of Nations; she served as Vice President/USA Delegate to the International Theatre Institute. She holds a Master of Fine Arts degree from New York University.

www.ingramcontent.com/pod-product-compliance
Lightning Source LLC
Chambersburg PA
CBHW011955150426
43200CB00016B/2914